Out of the Middle East

Out of the Middle East

The Emergence of an Arab Global Business

Kamal A. Shair

With respect and best wishes.

Kamal Shair

I.B. TAURIS

LONDON · NEW YORK

Published in 2006 by I.B. Tauris & Co Ltd
6 Salem Road, London W2 4BU
175 Fifth Avenue, New York NY 10010
www.ibtauris.com

In the United States and Canada distributed by Palgrave Macmillan,
a division of St. Martin's Press, 175 Fifth Avenue, New York NY 10010

ISBN 10   1 84511 271 7
ISBN 13   978 1 84511 271 4

A full CIP record for this book is available from the British Library
A full CIP record for this book is available from the Library of Congress
Library of Congress catalog card: available

Typeset in Caslon by Dexter Haven Associates Ltd, London
Printed and bound in Great Britain by TJ International Ltd, Padstow

To my wife Laura

and the past, present and future principals and
staff of all members of the Dar Group family

Contents

PREFACE

When I rented a small flat in Beirut in 1956 and started Dar Al-Handasah, a small engineering consultancy with just $3500 capital and one full-time member of staff, I had no idea that 50 years later it would have grown out of the Middle East and into a global business with $500m annual revenues and 8000 employees in around 40 countries.

Nor did I realise – although, given the turbulent history of the Middle East, perhaps I should have done – that sometimes violent challenges lay ahead. I had expected to deal with all the usual problems that any business faces – raising finance, hiring the right people, winning profitable contracts.

I hadn't bargained for some of the more bizarre and, sometimes, downright dangerous threats we'd have to tackle. So I didn't know that I'd have to rescue two employees who'd been kidnapped and held to ransom. Or that we'd have our entire transport fleet in one Middle Eastern country requisitioned for use in a successful coup d'etat. I certainly didn't imagine we'd have to evacuate 700 employees from offices in war-torn Beirut. Or that I'd be held at gunpoint by militiamen as I tried to go about my business in the same city.

But, more positively, neither did I imagine that my work would take me from the small one-roomed house in Jordan in which I'd been born into the palaces of kings and the residences of presidents. Nor that I would become a confidant and adviser to some of them and that I would be appointed to serve as a senator in Jordan's parliament.

The adventures I've had building a development consultancy in the Middle East, then expanding it across the world, form the central story of this book. But it is not a story that can be told in isolation, simply because the growth of Dar Al-Handasah has been entwined with the history of the Arab world. Events such as the Six Day War, the destruction of Beirut or violent revolution in Iraq have all played their part in our story.

But there is also a more hopeful side. I started a development consultancy because I believed projects such as irrigation schemes, schools, hospitals and new roads could make life better for people. Managing thousands of projects during the past half century has certainly been a profitable business, but it has also been, for me, a personally satisfying one. And that's because it's been a way of living out my personal credo – the belief that people should have the right of self-determination in free and open societies.

Sadly, for much of the past 50 years, free and open societies have been in retreat in the Middle East. But now I sense that slowly the people of the region are learning that democracies based on open discussion and debate – rather than dictatorships based on secret police and censorship – are the foundation of better governments that can improve the lives of all.

In 1956, when I founded Dar Al-Handasah, I was young. Now I am much older. But it is the young who must build the future. If there is one message that I would like to pass on to them in these pages, it is this: nothing is so difficult that it can't be accomplished given sufficient imagination, commitment and determination.

Kamal A. Shair
February 2006

CHAPTER 1

Kidnap at the house of engineers

Beirut 1986. Not exactly a business-friendly city. Its streets bore the scars of a civil war that had raged intermittently since 1975. Its downtown area, the famous Place des Martyrs, once the bustling heart of the metropolis, was ringed with the skeletons of gutted buildings. Rival armed militias roamed the streets. A random shooting could escalate into a gun-fight with predictable consequences for unfortunates caught in the cross-fire. The offices of Dar Al-Handasah, the development consultancy I'd founded in 1956, bore the scars. Its façade was pock-marked where shell shrapnel had chipped masonry before ricocheting into the street.

Management textbooks and business school academics, I'd discovered, didn't have much advice for those of us running a company whose offices were under fire. Yet although we were operating from a virtual war zone, we'd remained open for business.

At least we did until the day I had to make the toughest decision of my life.

I was in my own office in Amman, the capital of Jordan, pondering the unhappy state of affairs in Lebanon and wondering whether our situation there could get any worse when the telephone rang.

Omar Zein, head of Dar Al-Handasah's legal department, came on the line. Zein was normally an urbane character, unruffled as he went about his lawerly business. But this time he sounded agitated. As I listened to what he had to say, I realised matters just had got worse.

Much worse.

Saba Abdo, the managing director and head of the Beirut office had been kidnapped and was being held for ransom.

What, asked Zein, should we do?

*   *   *

This wasn't the kind of management decision I'd expected to be taking when I'd set up Dar Al-Handasah – the literal English translation is 'the house of engineers' – with four colleagues.

Like most young entrepreneurs, I had embarked on my first business venture with high hopes and unbounded enthusiasm. The plan had been forming in my mind for some time. I was working as an assistant professor of engineering at the American University of Beirut, but I'd first had the idea for an Arab engineering consultancy while I'd been studying for a PhD in chemical engineering at Yale University in the United States. Despite my confidence, I was aware that my plan was ambitious. At the time, there were no Arab consultancies capable of competing with the great engineering companies from Europe and the United States. They won all the big contracts in the Middle East simply because there were no local companies with a wide enough mix of skills, international standards, management capability and, perhaps, sheer audacity to take them on. But with the brash confidence of youth – I was only 26 at the time – I was convinced it could be done.

And in the three decades since, the growth of the company told its own story. Initially, we'd won large contracts for power stations, roads, irrigation projects and plenty more. We'd built up teams of consultants and engineers working throughout the region. We had established businesses in Kuwait, Saudi Arabia, Jordan and elsewhere. We'd expanded out of the Middle East into Africa, winning millions of dollars' worth of contracts in countries such as Nigeria, Algeria and

Angola. We'd opened offices in Europe and the United States. And, of course, we still had extensive interests in Lebanon.

When I and my colleagues had each put up $700 to start Dar Al-Handasah, Beirut had been the Middle East's city of light. It seemed like a perfect location for the new company that I was determined would make a mark throughout the Arab world and, perhaps, beyond. Beirut was dubbed the Paris of the Middle East, and with good reason. It was vibrant, full of life, brimming with enterprise. And Lebanon, of which Beirut was the capital, was one of the few surviving democracies in the region – a bastion of free thinking and the open exchange of ideas among an ever-encroaching circle of totalitarian states run by unpleasant dictators such as Egypt's Gamal Abdel Nasser.

But tensions between Lebanon's Christian and Muslim communities – and between factions within those communities – lurked never far beneath the surface. They had flared briefly in riots in 1958, burst into vicious civil war in 1975, been stirred by the Israeli invasion of southern Lebanon in 1981 and inflamed by the massacres in the Sabra and Chatila refugee camps in 1982 and other atrocities.

Against this unpromising backcloth, Dar Al-Handasah went about its business. Our Beirut office had grown from half a dozen to more than 700 employees. We provided jobs for people from all of Lebanon's communities without fear or favour. And although we employed thousands of people around the world, no matter how far afield the company spread, Lebanon remained the homeland of our founding. It was special to me. Even in the darkest days in the mid-1970s, when the streets of Beirut had become wastelands of lawlessness, we kept our offices open for business.

Yet in the past few years, as foreign troops from Israel and Syria had invaded Lebanon, and other countries meddled in its affairs (sometimes with well-meaning motives), the people of Lebanon had steadily ceased to be the masters of their own fate. Slowly the country's sovereignty had seeped away. So, I felt, had this proud nation's self-respect. In 1984 I decided to exile myself until the day – which I was sure would eventually come – when foreign troops left its soil for ever and Lebanon regained full power over its own destiny.

Hence it was that I was sitting in our Amman offices stunned by Zein's call and feeling that everything I'd worked for – indeed, the most precious of my cherished beliefs – were being challenged by sinister and powerful forces beyond my control.

*   *   *

After I'd overcome my initial shock at Zein's news, I asked him if he had any further details.

He said it appeared that thugs had grabbed Abdo as he was leaving our offices. They'd manhandled him into the back of a car and sped off. He was now being held captive, probably in a basement somewhere in the back-street slums on the outskirts of West Beirut.

Zein had established through his excellent contacts that the kidnappers were little more than criminals operating on the fringe of one of the militant groups which had been set up to resist the Israeli invasion of 1981. They wanted $500,000 for Abdo's safe return.

It was a ransom demand, pure and simple. And it placed me in a quandary. I knew that if I were to pay them, sooner or later the kidnappers would be back for more. That is how kidnappers operate. Yet I also owed a duty to Abdo. He would be in great distress, and so was his family, who had had no word from him. I had to balance the opportunity to win his release against the danger that paying the ransom would mean others would be kidnapped in the future.

Zein had asked me what we should do. As I replaced the telephone handset, I frankly had no idea.

*   *   *

By 1986, kidnapping had become a growth industry in Beirut.

It had started years earlier. In 1982, David S. Dodge, acting president of the American University of Beirut, had been kidnapped and held for a year in Iran. Although Dodge later went on to become president of the University in his own right, the experience had proved traumatic for him and his family.

In April 1986, Brian Keenan, a Northern-Irish-born English lecturer at the American University of Beirut, had been seized by four Shi'ite militiamen outside his home. Nobody knew where he was being held hostage. Then English journalist John McCarthy had been grabbed by the same group and was – we later learnt after he was released in 1991 – being held naked in a cockroach- and rat-infested basement in total darkness. The following year, Terry Waite, the special envoy of Britain's Archbishop of Canterbury, suffered a similar fate. He disappeared in West Beirut while trying to negotiate the release of other hostages. And these were only the high-profile cases. There were countless other examples of lesser-known individuals who were seized and suffered out of the gaze of public concern.

Worryingly, Abdo's abduction was not the first experience I'd had of the kidnapping of Dar Al-Handasah staff. A few weeks earlier, Raymond Beliki, an administrative manager in our Beirut office, had been grabbed as he was leaving the offices and bundled into a car. On this occasion, Zein, who had an encyclopaedic knowledge of the multifarious political factions in Lebanon, had been able to establish that Beliki was being held by representatives of one of the groups of the Syrian Socialist Nationalist Party. Beliki was, Zein had managed to find out, being well treated – if you count being snatched in broad daylight and thrown into a dank basement without light or the normal amenities of civilised life as good treatment. At least he wasn't being actively harmed, which was a horror reserved for some captives.

On this occasion, the motive seemed to be politics rather than money. At the time, I was in Beirut and I decided it was my responsibility to take an active part in negotiating Beliki's release. I asked Issam Mahayri, the leader of the faction of the Syrian Socialist Nationalist party which seemed to be behind the kidnapping – and, incidentally, the individual in charge of the district where our office was located – to come and see me. He duly arrived and seemed keen to reach a settlement. He told me a tale of rival hostage-taking in which Beliki had become unwittingly tangled.

It appeared that some of Mahayri's associates had been kidnapped by a gang from the largely Christian East Beirut. Beliki's brother was a Maronite priest, and Mahayri apparently thought a man of the cloth would be able to exert influence over the Christians to have his people released. The purpose of kidnapping Beliki had been to give the priest a powerful incentive to intervene in the way Mahayri wanted. Beliki would be released as soon as Mahayri's men had been freed by their Christian captors. It was a sorry story of hostage- and counter-hostage-taking to which Beirut had sunk at that time.

I gave Mahayri my views in no uncertain terms. I told him that kidnapping innocent civilians was no way to act for a political party that wanted to be taken seriously. I said that picking on Beliki in this way was grossly unfair. He'd had nothing to do with the capture of Mahayri's people. I pointed out that, being a fair-minded man, Beliki almost certainly abhorred the act, as I did.

Mahayri nodded and looked me in the eye: 'I have much respect for what you've achieved and what you've done for Lebanon,' he said. 'If you ask me to release Beliki today, I will do so. But, please, on humanitarian grounds, I want my own people back. Would you give me two days to try and achieve that? I guarantee that Beliki will not be harmed. He'll be released at the end of that time.'

What was I to do? It was wrong to keep Beliki, yet I couldn't help seeing Mahayri's point of view. All kidnapping was wrong and he wanted his people back as much as I wanted Beliki returned. So, not without some misgivings, I agreed to his request. My decision didn't make me popular with our company's lawyers, but I believed I could trust Mahayri to stick to his word – and he did. Under pressure from Beliki's priest brother, the Christians released their captors and Beliki returned to the office chastened but unharmed by his adventure.

But Abdo's case was more serious. His captors wanted money, and I feared they would stop at nothing to get it.

*   *   *

For some time I sat staring at the telephone on which I'd been speaking to Omar Zein and thinking about my options. There was, I decided, no easy way to get Abdo's release. I had to take some tough decisions. The first step was to close our Beirut offices and send the staff home. I was taking a calculated risk. I knew that our staff – loyal Dar men and women – would react angrily to the closure. But the worst of their anger would be directed at the kidnappers who had created this state of affairs. They and their families would protest to the Beirut authorities. And perhaps – just perhaps – they could create a big enough head of steam to push the authorities into taking the action necessary to rescue Abdo.

But there were also other worries on my mind. My first fear was that if we stayed open other staff would also be targeted as hostage victims on their way to and from work. Our offices were in a largely residential neighbourhood, and staff coming and going from work would be easy prey for copycat kidnappers. I had to make every effort to ensure that future hostage-taking was thwarted.

When the offices closed, I had been certain that our staff and their families would protest. What I hadn't anticipated was how swift and effective their action would be. They began to organise. They contacted one another and planned a campaign to put pressure on government leaders to act on the hostage-taking problem. The bottom line was this: they weren't going to have groups of lawless criminals depriving them of their livelihoods. They wanted the offices back open and they wanted to work. As many pointed out, they were the principal breadwinners in their families. Many more would suffer if the crisis continued.

They took their complaints to the top – to the Lebanese prime minister, Rashid Karame. They lobbied their elected representatives. They insisted the government should take firmer action against gangs of kidnappers. There would have been many in the government who shared their concerns and been willing to act. But, by 1986, Lebanon's security forces had been weakened by years of civil war and by the Israeli invasion. It was because the central powers of law and order were not in complete command of the city that hostage-takers were able to act with impunity.

Even so, the government wasn't entirely powerless. It still had security forces under its control and it started to apply pressure. The gangs began to feel the heat. But there was still no sign of Abdo.

*   *   *

What troubled me deeply as the search for Abdo widened was that the kind of people who'd kidnapped him had a broader agenda which challenged everything I believed in and stood for. No doubt they regarded themselves, as I did myself, as Arab nationalists and activists. But their beliefs and mine were at extreme ends of the spectrum.

I should explain that nationalism had been a driving force of gathering strength in the Arab world for much of the twentieth century. But unlike Europe, where nationalism in the twentieth century was usually associated with insular and chauvinist attitudes – and sometimes with downright fascism – Arab nationalism had focused initially on winning independence from colonial rule. At first, Arab nationalism had been all about the rights of nations to govern themselves, just as it had been in Europe in the eighteenth and nineteenth centuries. As such, it was a positive and generally liberal force with a commitment to democracy. But once Arabs had won their nationhoods, mostly by the 1950s, ideas about where the nationalist spirit should take them diverged widely.

I, and like-minded individuals, had taken the path where nationalism championed the shared culture of free and open societies. Our activism featured democratic debate and, where necessary, peaceful protest that changed societies for the better. But for some, nationalism was merely a disguise for dictatorship and their activism, like that of bullies throughout history, came out of the barrel of a gun. I'd devoted my life to opposing everything that people like Abdo's kidnappers stood for, and I didn't intend to give up. Getting Abdo back safely would be a victory – albeit a small one in the context of history – on the road to thwarting their ambitions and building a better Middle East.

And why did I hold these views so strongly? I suppose my starting point was (and still is) that I love the Arab world. I love its culture, its traditions, its history and its rich philosophy. I love the eclectic mix of its people – at once open and enigmatic, rich and poor, wise and foolish. I love their native ingenuity, their deep-felt compassion, their zest for life. Their spirit is my spirit and I identify wholly and without reservation with the very best that Arab learning and culture has given the world down the ages.

And that is something else I believe – that those of us in the Arab world should not only celebrate the achievements of our history but use them as a platform to regain our greatness in the future. As a young man, I would sit enthralled, my nose in a book, soaking up the stories of the Arab polymaths of the middle ages who gave the world a literature, science, medicine and engineering which had been unsurpassed since the heights of classical Greece and Rome. I also knew, from my reading, from talking to my family and friends, and from personal observation as a child and young man, how much of that Arab greatness has been lost over the centuries and later subsumed in the nineteenth and twentieth centuries by European colonial occupation.

I wanted to see the Arab world rise again and take its rightful place among the other great regions of the world. Those were the roots of my Arab nationalism, and that is the reason I had returned to the Middle East from America and founded my company. I believed it was the best way I could contribute to the development of the region, which at the time was trying hard to build representative democracies amidst the wreckage of the Second World War and the departure of colonial powers.

I settled in Lebanon in 1956 because it remained one of the few beacons of true open society in the region. But by 1986, that was all under threat from the armed militias that murdered with impunity and criminal gangs that kidnapped heartlessly, not even (albeit mistakenly) to defend a political point but to line their own squalid pockets. No people should have to live under conditions like those. But we did, and we had to to something about them. Starting with getting Abdo back safely.

*   *   *

On the third day of Abdo's captivity, matters took a sinister new turn.

Omar Zein called with disturbing news. Abdo's captors had made a particularly odious threat to him. They had said that they'd recruited a number of men who were going to abuse his family unless their demands were met. According to Zein's informers, Abdo had been holding up reasonably well until this news. Now he was on the point of collapse. He couldn't handle the thought of what might happen, and he was going to pieces. I was immediately worried that Abdo might have a mental breakdown that could do him long-term damage. I was also concerned that the kidnappers might make good on their threat to Abdo's family.

There was now only one course of action. We had to get Abdo released – and we had to do it quickly. The negotiations with the kidnappers through intermediaries were distasteful and not easy. But public opinion was turning strongly against them, especially as a result of the action taken by Dar Al-Handasah's magnificent staff in lobbying politicians for tougher official action against hostage-takers. There were fewer places for criminals to hide, even in usually sympathetic communities.

So we won our victory – and Abdo returned safely. Mercifully, he was physically unharmed, but he'd suffered much trauma during his incarceration. He needed a holiday, and I arranged for him and his family to come immediately to Jordan, where I could see him and he could relax and recuperate in a safe and comfortable environment. Later, we gave Abdo a job of equal status in our Cairo office, where he could work free of the threat of kidnapping which, not surprisingly, haunted him for some time. He resumed his working life and continued to contribute much of value to the company.

Abdo's was not, sadly, the last kidnapping in Lebanon. But it may have marked the turning of the tide in public opinion against hostage-takers. In the next few years, the country regained some political stability and started to rebuild its damaged towns and cities, a job in which Dar Al-Handasah played no small part.

*   *   *

Did I think, when I founded my company, that I would have to negotiate with kidnappers?

No more, perhaps, than that I would meet with presidents and prime ministers, emirs and sheikhs – the great and the good and, just sometimes, the not so good. I did not realise that creating Dar Al-Handasah would take me to every corner of the Middle East and then around the world – again and again – as I established the company as a global player in consultancy and engineering.

But then I was young, fired with enthusiasm and eager to succeed. I saw an opportunity and I was determined to seize it. It was the way I was, the way I'd been brought up in my home town in Jordan. So, perhaps, the story really started years before in Salt, where I was born.

CHAPTER 2

Gold in the mind

When I was five years old, my father took a decision that
changed my life for ever.

He sent me to school.

For children in the modern world, that is hardly an earth-
shattering event. Nor would it have been remarkable for those living
in developed countries in 1935, when I set off for school for the first
time. And it is not unusual in the modern Middle East, which has
rediscovered the value of education. It is taken as read that all children
go to school.

But in 1930s Transjordan, going to school was a truly life-
changing move. I suppose no more than one in ten boys attended
elementary schools at the time, maybe as few as one in 30 girls. Only
a fraction of all children would go on to secondary education. None
would have attended universities in Transjordan. There weren't any.
Most children – those without formal schooling – picked up what
education they could through a study of the Koran at their mosque
and on the street in the 'university of life'.

So when I say that my father's decision to send me to school changed
my life, I do not exaggerate. Without school, my life would certainly
have taken a very different path. Where it would have led, I cannot

say. But there would have been no universities, no keen young engineer, no Dar Al-Handasah. My father's decision remains the pivotal event of my life.

What made his decision the more remarkable was that he'd had only five or six years of elementary schooling himself. (That wasn't through want of ability. He had a brilliant mind. He could solve a maths problem before a student of the subject had even had time to get out his slide rule.) My father's great strength was that he possessed the two essential qualities of successful people – a progressive mind and an ambition to get on in life. He had travelled widely in the Middle East, eagerly absorbing new ideas from growing cities like Jerusalem, Damascus, Beirut and Cairo. And he read the newspapers voraciously – I have a mind's-eye picture of him clutching those recent newspapers he could afford under his arm. His close study of current affairs led him to one inescapable conclusion: it is the people with education that get on in life. And he was determined that his children would do so.

He summed up his philosophy when a friend chided him about spending so much money on educating his children: 'Abdo, why do you waste your money on school fees? You could make a lot of money by investing it in property.'

'Why would I want to leave my children property or money?' my father answered. 'If I educate them well, they will make their own money. I advise you, my friend, not to hoard money, but to invest your gold in the minds of your children.'

As I set off for my first day's school, I wouldn't have been aware that I was taking the first steps in a journey that would result in not a little gold being invested in my own mind. More likely, I would have been thinking about whether my teacher would be strict, whether I would like my fellow pupils, and what I would have to tell my mother and father about my first day when I returned home.

Understanding the wisdom of my father's philosophy came later.

*　　　*　　　*

I feel sure my father would have already developed his idea about investing gold in the mind by the time I was born on 10 August 1930 in our house at Salt, in north-west Transjordan. The reason I believe this is that I was the third child – sister Fahdeh and brother Jamal were ahead of me – and my father would have already been thinking about how he was going to meet the cost of their education. Later, he had to think about investing gold in the minds of my sisters Leila, May and Sahab as well as younger brothers Khaled and Waheeb.

And, at first, there was little gold to invest, but more came later. My father was a textile trader and had met my mother, Najla, whose parents came from Ramallah and Jerusalem, on his travels. His father, Afnan, had had ambitions to become a Greek Orthodox priest which, sadly for him, weren't fulfilled. Instead, he worked for the British mission that had been established in the area in the mid-nineteenth century. I'm told that we could trace our family's connections with Salt back three hundred years, to the time when Salt was a district seat of government for the Ottoman empire. But the Ottoman empire, ruled from Turkey, had become the 'sick man of Europe' long before I was born, and it finally expired after the First World War.

Our house, like almost all the others in Salt, was a simple one-storey construction made of mud bricks. The inside consisted of a single large room with a raised area at one end where all the members of the family would eat and sleep. In winter, the family's goats occupied the other, lower end of the room. In summer, all the family were relieved when the animals were packed off to pasture. The basic house was supplemented by a kitchen outside, as well as a lavatory, and a detached stone-built room where my father would receive his male guests and sometimes discuss his business. Our house was modest by any standard, but then so were most of the others in town. None of the houses in Salt had either electricity or running water. Light came from candles or oil lamps, and we collected our water in tins from public taps which had been installed nobody was quite sure how many years ago by the Ottomans. If you could afford it, you hired a donkey to haul your water home. A donkey could carry up to four 20-litre tins of water and saved a lot of back-breaking toil up and down Salt's steep streets.

In 1930 Salt was a crowded, raucous town, the largest in Transjordan with a population of 30,000, eclipsing Amman, which was at that time a fraction of Salt's size. The streets were dusty as there were no asphalted roads, except at the entrance to the city. As a young child, I recall only two automobiles. Both acted as taxis, one carrying people to Amman, the other to Jerusalem.

Today, Salt has grown into a thriving city of more than 80,000. It was, and is, perched spectacularly on the side of two hills, part of the edge of the Great Rift Valley which starts in Mozambique and carves a deep scar in the earth north for 8000 kilometres, ending north of Lake Tiberias, the Sea of Galilee of biblical fame.

From Salt's highest vantage points, 840 metres above sea level, on a clear day you can look west and see the Dome of the Rock in Jerusalem glinting and watch the River Jordan snaking lazily towards the Dead Sea. North are the brown hills of the Al-Balqa highlands and beyond them Syria. And 30 kilometres to the east – more south-east, in fact – lies Amman, now a cosmopolitan international city full of business and bustle. In short, Salt is a city that is dramatic, beautiful – and in a strategic location.

So it is no surprise that invaders throughout history have looked on the town as a useful stronghold. (The name Salt, incidentally, has nothing to do with the condiment sprinkled on food. Depending on which version you choose to believe, it comes either from the Greek *saltus*, meaning forest, although the only sign of forestation today is away to the north in the Zai National Park, or from sultana, a reference to the grapes grown in the region.) In any event, the city was called Saltus by the Byzantines who brought Christianity to the region and gave the city a bishop. Salt had a strong Christian population, with Anglican, Roman Catholic, Greek Catholic and Greek Orthodox congregations.

Salt was ransacked by the Mongols in the thirteenth century and subsequently rebuilt by the Mamluk sultan Bybars I. The Egyptian viceroy Ibrahim Pasha blew up parts of the city in the 1830s as part of his campaign against Palestine. Again, the inhabitants patiently rebuilt it in the years that followed.

The city I knew as a child was divided into two main districts – Al-Hara (meaning 'neighbourhood') and Wadi Krad ('valley of the

Kurdish'). People were fiercely loyal to their own district – perhaps not quite as fiercely as the street gangs who mark out their territory in south Los Angeles or Catholics and Protestants in Belfast – but you certainly knew which side of the line you lived. So the fact that our house was right on the edge of the Al-Hara district put us in the front line and made for an interesting life.

But in general Salt was not a violent town – except when it came to the annual payment of bills. The main agricultural product in the region was raisins made from the grapes which grew abundantly (until they were wiped out by phylloxera in 1943) in vineyards in the sur-rounding countryside. At the end of every summer, the owners of the vineyards met in the town centre to settle their accounts with customers who had bought their grapes. They also used the occasion to settle scores. Fights were commonplace and vineyard keepers carried vicious-looking sticks with bulbous ends, rather like an Irish shillelagh or South African knobkerrie, as their weapon of choice. To a child, the fights looked dangerous, but nobody ever seemed to suffer any serious injury.

Four years after I was born, we moved from the mud-brick house on the front line between Al-Hara and Wadi Krad. Evidently, my father's business was becoming more prosperous, because he had built a stone and cement house adjacent to the old house. By today's standards, it certainly wasn't a villa, but at the time there couldn't have been more than a hundred houses in Salt like it. In constructing it, my father had used his considerable ingenuity to make it more comfort-able for us. He had built a large cistern on the roof to hold water, and there was a further cistern on an intermediate floor. These cisterns still had to be filled by water hauled by the donkeys but, for the first time, we could have water piped to the bathroom, lavatory and kitchen. For a four-year-old running water was more than a luxury – it was a miracle. I cannot say for sure, but I wonder whether watching this miracle happen could have stirred in me the first thoughts about how engineering – even simple engineering – can change people's lives for the better.

Whether that was the case or not, it was from this house that I set out on that first trip to school.

*   *   *

The school I was making for on that morning in 1935 was run by the British. How the British came to be running a school in Salt – indeed why they were in Transjordan at all – needs some explanation in its own right.

I suppose it started on 28 June 1914 in Sarajevo, Bosnia, when Gavrilo Princip, a member of the Slav terrorist group the Black Hand, shot Archduke Ferdinand, assassinating the heir to the Habsburg throne and triggering the events which spiralled into the hell of the First World War. At the time, Transjordan was still part of the fast-crumbling Ottoman empire. As Europe divided into two warring camps, the Turks made their final disastrous strategic error. They allied themselves with Germany. In the Arab world, opposition to Ottoman hegemony had been growing since the nineteenth century. Now, with the Ottoman empire in the last stages of its decline – the 'sick man of Europe' was sinking fast – and preoccupied with a European war, Arabs saw an opportunity to throw off Turkish rule once and for all.

The British encouraged Arab nationalism as a means of fomenting the instability that would finish off the remnants of Turkish power in the region. In following this policy, the British plainly had their own motives. They were keen to protect their oil interests in Iraq as well as the Suez Canal trade route to India – the 'jewel in the crown' of the British empire. Undermining Turkey, Germany's key ally in the Middle East, was the obvious way to achieve these policy objectives.

The route they took to achieving this objective has become the stuff of legend. In 1916, a group of civilians and Arab former officers in the Ottoman army launched what became known as the Arab revolt. For the next two years, an irregular force of Arab nationalists – advised by, among others, T.E. Lawrence of Lawrence of Arabia fame – took on the Ottoman military in a series of guerrilla raids. By the end of the war, Feisal Ibn Hussein, a Hashemite prince who had led the Arab forces, had built enough prestige in the region to set up an Arab government in Damascus, which included Transjordan within its territory. Feisal made Salt, our family's home town, administrative centre of the Al-Balqa region in north-western Transjordan.

But, with the war over, the victorious Allies became less enthusiastic about promoting Arab nationalism. The French, in particular, wanted Feisal out of Damascus. At the San Remo conference in 1920, the Allies decided to create two mandates in the Middle East. (The mandates were confirmed by the League of Nations two years later.) The French would have control over Lebanon and Syria, the British over Palestine (which included Transjordan) and Iraq. Feisal was forced to quit Damascus, leaving the future of Transjordan firmly in British hands, despite military backing from a 2000-strong force raised by his brother Prince Abdullah.

Later in the same year (1920), however, Sir Herbert Samuel, the British high commissioner for Palestine and Transjordan, summoned sheikhs and leading figures to Salt and announced that Britain favoured giving self-government to the country. The following year, the British took the first tentative steps by inviting Abdullah to become ruler of Transjordan, recognising the country's 'independence' formally in 1923 and codifying the terms of the independence in a constitution in 1928, just two years before I was born. But a treaty that accompanied the 1928 constitution made it clear that while Abdullah was in charge of domestic affairs, matters of finance, military and foreign policy were firmly in the hands of a British 'resident'. There was little doubt about who held the ultimate power.

So in the years immediately before and after my birth Transjordan was making its first tentative steps to the full independence it finally achieved in 1946. Not that there would have been much sign of that as I was walking to school on that morning in 1935. True, Salt was the administrative centre of the Al-Balqa region of Transjordan, as it had been under the Ottomans. In some cases, officials who had been appointed during Feisal's brief rule in Damascus were still at their posts. But the signs of British influence were also very prominent – the missionary hospital and the school towards which I was making my way.

*   *   *

I still remember those walks to and from school up and down the steep streets of Salt. I had to trudge to school in the morning, home for lunch, back for afternoon school and then home in the evening. I suppose it was healthy exercise – which was good for me, for I soon found that I had little aptitude for sport – but it was a walk that had to be completed in all weathers. And in a pair of shoes that my father made clear had to last for a year.

Our teacher was called Miss Lester. At least I now know that she was called Miss Lester. At the time, we children thought her name was Mislester. You could hardly blame us. How were we to know the proper way to address an English maiden lady? Especially as we only learnt English as a second language, all the other lessons being delivered in Arabic.

Anyway, Miss Lester taught me more than she realised. While I was at the school, sadly her mother died and Miss Lester returned to England to attend her funeral. She was gone from the school for a good two months, and when she was due to return one of the other teachers decided she would be greeted with a song performed by all the children in the school. It was at this point I discovered something that I've had to live with for the rest of my life – I have no ear for a tune and certainly no singing voice. We rehearsed the song each day, but it was soon clear that whatever it was I was singing, it wasn't the same as the rest of the school. I was spoiling the performance. The teacher in charge told me I would have to be left out.

I stormed home to my father in a fury. This was a terrible affront and a humiliation for a child. I must admit I was surprised when my father didn't become as angry as I was. He thought about it for a moment and then said: 'I think I have a solution.' The next day, he came to the school with me and spoke to the teacher in charge. I was back in the choir on one condition. I could open my mouth in time with the music – as long as no sound came out.

It is an interesting question how early in life children begin to pick up habits about how they deal with the world around them. I suspect it may be earlier than many people think. I wouldn't have been conscious of it at the time, but I feel sure, looking back, that I was learning an important lesson – that lateral thinking plus a non-confrontational approach is a very effective way to solve intractable problems. As I've subsequently found, it's not a bad approach to use in business life.

I was at the British school for four years, then I transferred to a Roman Catholic school, run by two Italian priests. The reason for this was that the British school only covered the first four years of elementary education and I needed to complete seven before I could move on to the high school. I reached the Catholic school in 1939, and before long the priests were gone – taken away by the British and interned somewhere in Palestine as wartime enemy aliens. Despite their absence, education went on.

In both the British school and the Catholic school religion, not surprisingly, played a part. It was also a feature of our home life. My father was a devout Christian, and every Sunday the family would go to church. By the time I was 12, my attitude to these church services started to change. I was already developing an interest in broader Arab ideas. By contrast, I was finding little to interest me in the lengthy sermons the minister delivered each Sunday at church. In this respect, my father was, perhaps, not the best of role models. As the sermon began, he would discreetly close his eyes and take a nap, awakening in time to stand up with the rest of the congregation and join in the prayers that ended the service.

In any event, one Sunday I told my father I wasn't going to attend church any more. 'Have you become a Bolshevik?' he asked in surprise. I assured him that I had not, but that I simply didn't find anything to interest me in the service. I suspect my father was disappointed by my decision, but he accepted it. To this day, I believe that religion is a very personal and private matter on which everybody should be allowed to take their own decisions.

*   *   *

In due course, I moved on from the elementary school to the high school. The high school was free, but you had to pass an examination to gain entrance and the standards were high. That was hardly surprising, as the school was the only one offering secondary education in Transjordan, and attracted students from all over the country. But my father had always been strict about us achieving good marks in our examinations – he wanted some return for that gold he was investing in our minds – and I made it through the entrance exam without any undue alarm.

It was at the high school that I really began to gain a passion for certain subjects. Among the humanities, I developed a keen interest in Middle Eastern history and Arab philosophy. But my greatest love was for mathematics. I was taught by Khalil Salem, a brilliant teacher who subsequently became a governor of Jordan's central bank. Mathematics is about solving problems – and that is something that has always fascinated me, whether those problems be in engineering, business or public administration. The logic and rational thinking that mathematics demands can usefully be applied to all three areas. I was not to know, as I listened to Salem's fluent explanations of the principles of algebra and geometry, that later in my life I would join others in encouraging the American University of Beirut to establish a Centre for Advanced Mathematical Studies.

The high-school years were a time for learning and developing ideas about the world around me. But not all of those lessons came from my teachers. Events in the wider world were taking a cataclysmic turn.

*   *   *

Hitler invaded Poland in 1939 and war came to Transjordan.

Once again, my father's foresight ensured that we were well pre-pared. Apart from the cisterns he'd had constructed in our new house, he had also planned a large food-storage area. When news of hostilities came through in September, he started to stock the room with basics – rice, sugar and so on. Whenever there were shortages of supplies, we dipped into our store. He sensed dangerous times might be coming, and determined to hide the family's savings. He found some hand-kerchiefs, wrapped such gold as we had in them, and told me to give them to my mother with instructions that she should hide them in various cupboards. This was done, and the family's nest-egg survived the hostilities.

At first, nothing much seemed to change. I continued my four walks each day to and from school, but as 1939 turned to 1940 and Britain was defeated at Dunkirk, it was possible to sense a new atmosphere on the streets. Transjordan, as a British mandate territory, became part of the allied coalition, but many local people had sympathies for the Germans. You could hear the talk in the streets. There were arguments if you expressed support for the British. Most people had already decided that Britain had lost the war – that it was only a matter of time before the Germans arrived. In Amman, only 30 kilometres from us, there were anti-British riots. Salt was a more docile town, but there was a tension in the air which hadn't been present before.

Perhaps it wasn't surprising that pro-German sympathies were widespread. Hitler had built his power-base in Germany at least partly by demonising the Jews. This was appealing to much Arab opinion concerned about the growing strength of Jewish immigration to Palestine during the 1920s and 1930s in the wake of the 1917 Balfour Declaration. The Declaration had been made at a time when the political future of much of the Middle East after the First World War was still to be decided, and Britain, at a low point in the war, had been eager to appease Zionist opinion.

The Declaration took the form of a letter to prominent financier and Zionist Lord Rothschild from British foreign secretary Sir Arthur Balfour. It set out his government's support for the idea of a 'national home' for the Jews in Palestine. The phrase had been used deliberately in preference to 'state', and the British government reiterated the principle in a white paper in 1922, and on other occasions, that a state was not intended. At the same time, the Declaration made it clear that 'nothing shall be done which may prejudice the civil and religious rights of existing non-Jewish communities in Palestine'. But that vital caveat was largely ignored by a large proportion of both legal and illegal Jewish immigrants to Palestine. As a result, the years between the First and Second World Wars saw Palestine steadily become more unstable. The population balance changed, land ownership shifted, and tensions between the two communities became inflamed.

The pro-German flames were fanned by Amin Al-Husseiny, sometimes called Hajj Amin, the Grand Mufti of Jerusalem. A mufti is a scholar qualified to rule on matters of Islamic law and, thus, influential in the Muslim community. Al-Husseiny carried the most weight of all because he came from a family of 'sayyids', who traced their descent from the Prophet Mohammed. He held views that were radical, strongly anti-Jewish and popular with a large section of Palestinian as well as broader Arab opinion. And as one of the most important muftis in the Islamic world – the position of Grand Mufti of Jerusalem had been in his family for more than two hundred years – he was hugely influential. Although British forces tried to arrest him, he fled first to Lebanon, then Iraq, then Iran, and finally Germany, where he carried on his vilification of both the Jews and British rule in Palestine under the benign gaze of the Nazis.

What made Britain's position in Transjordan more insecure was the fact that both neighbouring Lebanon and Syria, which were under French mandate, supported the pro-Nazi Vichy government set up after the Germans invaded France. That made the French troops on the doorstep enemies rather than allies. But the British did what they could to placate local opinion in Transjordan and keep the lid battened down on dissent. One of their tactics was to ensure that the local economy remained prosperous despite the privations that traditionally accompany war. They invested in local amenities and promoted more trade. This was a policy, they hoped, that would prevent grievances building to a point where they could no longer be contained. One of their moves was to open up trade with Palestine, which helped my father's own import and export business.

But as 1940 turned to 1941, and Britain suffered more reverses, the mood in Transjordan became grimmer. We didn't know it at the time, but even Prince Abdullah was in a state of despair, according to Alec Kirkbride, the British resident in Amman. When pro-German officers launched a coup in neighbouring Iraq in 1941, many thought that it would herald the end of British rule in the whole Middle East. Iraq was also under British mandate, and if it tumbled, most people thought that Britain could not maintain its position in Transjordan and Palestine for much longer. But the British sent the Arab Legion – 2000 Arab officers and men commanded by a British officer John Bagot Glubb, known popularly as Glubb Pasha – to Baghdad to put down the coup.

It was a decisive victory, and it changed the mood on the streets. It gave British forces the confidence to clear the Vichy-supporting French troops out of Syria and Lebanon. That removed an Axis threat to Britain's Eighth Army, based in Egypt. It gave the army's commander, General Bernard Montgomery, the confidence to launch his successful assault on the German occupation of North Africa at El-Alamein in October 1942, which turned the tide of the war in North Africa.

It might have been no coincidence that in 1943, with the mood in the Middle East turning more positively in Britain's favour, our family took the first of five annual summer holidays to Ramallah in Palestine. My mother had many relatives in the town, and we stayed with various uncles and aunts. We spent our time socialising with a wide circle of friends. During those summers, the war seemed a million miles away as my brother Jamal and I took a bus into Jaffa or Jerusalem, sometimes to lounge in cafés, sometimes to visit the cinema.

As the war drew to a close in 1945, it was clear that the Arab world was changing fast. The desire for self-government, which had been suppressed during the period of British mandate, was finding its voice in Transjordan as well as elsewhere in the Middle East. The nationalist spirit raised people's hopes that they could take more control over their own countries and, ultimately, their own lives. As foreign troops shouldered their rifles and embarked for home, a vigorous debate started in the Arab world about how it should shape its destiny – about the kind of societies self-government ought to create. It was a debate, I sensed, that would have far-reaching consequences. And I wanted to be part of it.

CHAPTER 3

Of books and Beirut

The long journey from a mud-brick house in Salt to the chairmanship of a global company with 84 offices in 37 countries started in my earliest years as I watched and learnt while my father built his own import/export business. To me, it seemed natural to trade, to find customers with needs and to turn a profit by providing what they wanted. But as I grew older, into my teens, and war finally gave way to a peace of sorts, I started to realise that business took place in a wider context than I'd realised when I first watched my father go about his work in Salt's dusty streets.

I made an important discovery. Beyond the world of business was the world of books.

By the time I was 14, I had started the lifetime habit of being a serious reader. On top of my school work, I would devour at least three books a month. History and philosophy were top of my reading list, particularly the history of Arab civilisations and the philosophies of great Arab thinkers of the past. Both provided an adventure in intellectual exploration that was exciting to a young mind.

As I read, I discovered what I'd instinctively known, that the Arab heritage was one to be proud of. While much of Europe still languished in the dark ages and native American tribes roamed the prairies hunting buffalo, the Arab world was developing new ideas in philosophy, science and medicine. Its scholars were both open-minded and free-thinking. Al-Kindi, one of the earliest of all – he lived from about 801 to 860 – wrote: 'We should not be ashamed to acknowledge truth from whatever source it comes to us, even if it is brought to us by former generations and foreign people'. Certainly, the Arab thinkers of the age were not afraid to absorb new ideas. Translators such as Hunyan Ibn Ishaq, working about the same time as Al-Kindi, were translating the works of Plato, Aristotle and other Greek philosophers (and, incidentally, saving for later Western civilisation as well many ideas and works which would otherwise have been lost in the maelstrom of European history). Mathematicians, such as Al-Khwarazmi (about 800–847), were learning about the Indian approach to numerals and passing their knowledge on to the world, so that now the familiar numbers we use every day are called 'Arabic' numerals. Thinkers in medicine, such as Ibn Abi Usaybi'a, who translated the Hippocratic Oath into Arabic, were making the first tentative steps in turning medicine from a branch of magic into a robust new science. Historians, such as Al-Mas'udi, were developing the concept of 'isnad' – making judgements on the reliability of information based on the credibility of the chain of witnesses who provide it – upon which true historical knowledge (rather than mere myth) is based.

It wasn't just that these scholars were absorbing others' knowledge. It was fascinating to discover that, even in these far-off centuries, ideas were being swapped back and forth between the Arab and Western worlds. Ibn Khaldun, in his *Muqaddima* (or *Prolegomena* as it is sometimes called in the West), was developing an all-encompassing theory of the rise of civilisations that later provided the foundation for the thinking of Western historians. The great philosopher Ibn Rushd (known in the West as Averroes) worked out a way to reconcile the teachings of God as revealed in the Koran with the conclusions that philosophers reached by applying human reason. Ibn Rushd's solutions – such as arguing that some of the verses of the Koran should be interpreted metaphorically rather than literally – were later adopted by some Western medieval thinkers seeking to reconcile their own philosophies with Christianity.

I suppose you could call this trade in ideas an early form of globalisation. It certainly began to shape my thinking in a way that has endured during my life. The notion that good ideas can come from any source and that a person with an open mind is best placed to find them is central to my personal philosophy. I feel sure, looking back, that those long hours of reading helped me to realise that if you approach life in an outward-looking way you are more likely to succeed. So when I came to found Dar Al-Handasah, it seemed perfectly normal to start the company not in the country of my birth, but in Lebanon, one of the most open societies in the world and, eventually, to expand it to other countries with radically different cultures.

But it wasn't only the ancients that provided my reading matter. I also devoured the books of modern thinkers, especially those who seemed to have liberal and practical solutions to the problems we then faced in the 1940s Middle East. One book that made a particular impression on me was *The Arab Awakening* by George Antonius, which I read some years after its publication in 1938. Antonius had been born in Lebanon in 1891, gone to school in Alexandria, and then on to King's College, Cambridge. During the 1920s, he'd worked in various posts for the British mandate authorities in Palestine – some of the time as acting director of education. In the 1930s, Antonius became increasingly disillusioned with Britain's and France's failure to honour a promise he believed was implicit in the Treaty of Versailles – to establish an independent Palestine. He also became concerned about the growth of a militant Zionism and large-scale Jewish immigration to Palestine. So he embarked on a series of frenetic travels around the Middle East, as well as lecture tours overseas, researching *The Arab Awakening*. Reading it for the first time, it seemed like a powerful narrative of Arab heritage and the growth of liberal nationalism. The quality and vigour of earlier Arab civilisations, Antonius argued, remained latent, awaiting a vehicle to release, once again, the power of the Arab mind.

Reading, I soon realised, gives you lots of ideas. And when you're young, finding a brilliant idea is as exciting as discovering a sparkling gem. But reading, by itself, doesn't necessarily help you to evolve your own set of values and beliefs. When you're young and reading the works of great thinkers of the past and present, you soon find that there are many views of the world to choose from. It's like being confronted with a thousand sets of giants' footprints all heading off in different directions. You have to decide which set of footprints to follow. Of course your family, your teachers and your friends all play different roles in helping you discover your own beliefs by demonstrating their own values in the way they live their lives. So do the events of daily life taking place around you. By a process of osmosis – of which, in my case, reading was an important part – you start to soak up the values that will shape the beliefs you will use to guide your life.

So, there I was, sitting for hours reading, enthralled by the arguments of thinkers and philosophers. But I also had to take decisions about what I was going to do with the rest of my life. I seriously considered studying philosophy at university. Perhaps the house of engineers might have been the ivory tower of the philosopher. What stopped me was my father's insistence that his children should all have a profession. It meant I needed to choose a more vocational subject – engineering – for my studies. (Four of my brothers and sisters also entered the professions – Jamal as a doctor, Waheeb as an accountant and Khaled and Sahab as economists.)

As the war ended in 1945, I also began to think about where I should pursue my studies. A year earlier, my brother Jamal had won a place at the American University of Beirut to study medicine. The idea of studying in Beirut was extremely attractive to me – and I was determined to try and win my own place.

*   *   *

The idea of going to college in my home country was never going to be an option, because Jordan's first university did not open until 1963. Besides, the American University of Beirut was the beacon in the Middle East to which most bright high-school pupils aspired.

In theory, it would have been possible to win a government scholarship to attend AUB. Each year, the government awarded just one scholarship to Jordan's best and brightest student. But that was something I didn't aspire to. Apart from the fact that I was not certain that I could have beaten the tough competition, the scholarship came with conditions attached. After graduating, you had to return and work in the Jordanian government service for a period equal to the time you'd spent at the university. With my focus now on becoming an engineer, that wasn't on my personal agenda. Which meant that my father would have to invest some more gold in my mind – as he had done for Jamal and was to do for my other brothers and sisters.

But money wasn't enough. I also had to pass AUB's testing entrance examination. And this raised a real concern in my mind: whether my English would be good enough. Teaching in all subjects at AUB is in English (except, obviously, language courses). I had learnt English at the high school in Salt, but it was as a second language. To be successful at AUB, I now realised that I needed to become effectively bilingual. With some foreboding, I sat the entrance examination early in the summer of 1945 in Amman. My forebodings were only too real. I failed the English exam.

It was depressing. More than depressing, in fact, for if I could not pass the resit that candidates were allowed at the end of the summer, I should not be able to follow in my brother's footsteps – and would, incidentally, puncture my father's dream, to see his children enter good professions. In the summer of 1945 we went, as usual, for our holiday to Ramallah. It was the holiday during which I made far fewer excursions than usual to the sidewalk cafés of Jaffa or the cinemas of Jerusalem. It was hot and I was hunched over my books. At the end of the summer, I did visit Jerusalem: nervously, for the resit.

And I passed.

Little more than a month later, I stepped through the main entrance of AUB's enchanting campus in Ras Beirut. It was a proud moment walking onto that campus for the first time, knowing that I'd made it to what was unquestionably the premier university in the Arab world. Since then, many more universities have sprung up in the Middle East – there are now five in Beirut alone – as they have elsewhere in the world, and others may seek to challenge AUB's claim. But back in 1945 there was no contest. Certainly not in my eyes. As if to prove it, the founding session of the nascent United Nations, which had just taken place in San Francisco, had included 19 delegates who were alumni of AUB, more than any other university in the world had provided. So I had a powerful sense of joining an academic institution that was a real force not only in the world of learning but of world affairs.

But my delight was soon tempered by the realisation that I faced some exceedingly hard work. My lack of fluency in English dogged my first year at AUB. In the freshman year, you had to study six subjects – English, Arabic, mathematics, general science, sociology and history. Arabic was plainly no problem. And I loved mathematics, which, in any event, is a kind of international language in its own right. Science I took to naturally. But the sociology and history, like other subjects, were taught (and examined) in English. I found them very hard. Quite simply, the kind of English I had learnt at the high school hadn't prepared me for the study of these subjects at university level. They had their own vocabularies, which I'd never before encountered. The lecturers would use, in the natural way of spoken English, complex grammar and syntax, which I found hard to follow. Often, I sat in lectures desperately trying to follow what they were talking about. It was a painful, sometimes miserable, introduction to my university studies.

And then there was the English…I had learnt the language comfortably at the high school. But that had been at a relatively elementary level. Now I had to study and understand William Shakespeare's *As You Like It*. Great play it may be, but I didn't like it. At least not as I sat for hour after hour in the library trying to decipher its meaning. I can still see myself trying to puzzle out the twists and turns of the byzantine plot: Rosalind is banished to the Forest of Arden and pursued by her lover Orlando – who doesn't recognise her because she's disguised herself as a shepherd boy Ganymede and is now pursued by a shepherdess Phebe, who is really in love with Silvius, while Ganymede's – I mean Rosalind's – cousin, Celia, who has disguised herself as a country girl, Aliena, falls in love with Oliver, Orlando's brother, and a servant, Touchstone, who knew Ganymede and Aliena when they were Rosalind and Celia, falls for rustic wench Audrey…This was English

– seventeenth-century English with strange words and obscure syntax – that I'd never read before. I spent hours with a dictionary looking up word after word and sometimes still not really understanding what they meant. And some words – coz, carlot, jointure – certainly weren't in any dictionary I possessed. It was so painful.

I recall that at the end of my first quarter, when we were examined in all subjects, I failed in English and sociology, although I was doing better in the other subjects. But by the end of the freshman year, my English was improving and I passed in all subjects, with A grades in Arabic and mathematics.

That painful experience has given me a lifelong view about the teaching of languages. It is not enough to teach a language as a second language. To grasp the language like a native speaker, you have to learn other subjects in it as well. Effectively, you have to put the language to work. It's only then that you actually start to live the language and use it with confidence and fluency. Years later, when I was a senator in Jordan's parliament, I proposed to the government that English teaching in schools should start in the first grade (rather than the fourth) and continue for the 12 years pupils were at school. I am happy to say that my proposal was accepted. But now, I believe, it is time for schools to move even further than that and start teaching some subjects in the second language. I hope a future Jordanian government may introduce such a measure. The fewer students who can avoid my university baptism of fire the better!

But the painful process of learning tough subjects in a language in which I was not yet fully fluent couldn't disguise the joy I felt at being in Beirut and, particularly, at AUB. I had entered a world different to any I had previously experienced.

*   *   *

Where to start?

> This college is for all conditions and classes of men without regard to colour, nationality, race or religion. A man, white, black or yellow, Christian, Jew, Mohammedan or heathen, may enter and enjoy all

the advantages of this institution for three, four or eight years; and go out believing in one God, in many gods, or in no God. But it will be impossible for anyone to continue with us long without knowing what we believe to be the truth and our reasons for that belief.

With these words Dr Daniel Bliss, the university's first president, laid the cornerstone of College Hall, the oldest building on the AUB campus, on 7 December 1871.

Bliss was a former Protestant missionary in Lebanon who had been asked by the American Board of Commissioners for Foreign Missions to give up his evangelical work in order to found a university. He started a fund-raising drive in the United States in 1862, but when the American Civil War began turned his attentions to Great Britain, where he raised £4000 (more than £250,000 at today's prices). The state of New York granted a charter for the university, to be called the Syrian Protestant College, in 1862, and it opened its doors to its first 16 students in 1866. It changed its name to the American University of Beirut in 1922.

When I arrived, the university was more than fulfilling Bliss's original ambition. Indeed, I found the student body did consist of 'all conditions and classes of men' from around the Middle East and beyond. Around 40 per cent of the students came from Lebanon, with the remainder from a host of other countries. Many races, nationalities and religions were represented. This, I believe, helped to give AUB a uniquely tolerant atmosphere and an outward-looking approach.

The university occupied (and still does) one of the finest sites in Beirut – a 73-acre campus, shaded with palm and eucalyptus trees overlooking the Mediterranean. I lived in a dormitory on the campus, and the rules were strict. As freshmen, we had to be back on the campus by seven in the evening and in our dormitory by ten o'clock. There were penalties if you transgressed either of these curfews, but I'm not sure what the punishment was as, happily, it was never applied to me. Each dormitory was presided over by a professor who lived in. The professor in charge of our dormitory was the distinguished philosopher Charles Malek, who I later (when I had left AUB) came to know as a friend and mentor.

The fact that my brother Jamal had already been at AUB for a year made it easier for me as a newcomer to find out what to do and where to go. That was important, because punctual attendance at lectures and seminars was also a strict rule, and there could be significant distances to cover on the large campus. Jamal was already advancing fast up the university, as a junior (equal to a third-year student) as he had come to the university from high school with a full matriculation. That meant he could enter as a sophomore (second-year) student. I came a year early, aged 15, and had not matriculated, which meant I had to enter as a freshman. The rules for freshmen and sophomores were stricter than for juniors and seniors, so Jamal was living a somewhat less restricted lifestyle than I was.

In any event, in my first year I had to work so hard that I spent most of my time on campus. But there were still some opportunities to go out into the city, perhaps to see a film or visit a sidewalk café or just to marvel at the intensity and variety of big-city life. What a city – and what a time to be living in it.

Today, the image of Beirut has been scarred by the civil war of 1975–1989 and the Israeli invasion of 1982. But in 1945 it was a city tasting the first drops of freedom after decades of colonial rule. Just two years before I came, Lebanon had won its independence. After the pro-Nazi Vichy forces had been expelled by the British in 1941, the Free French, led by General de Gaulle, had been manoeuvring to retain Lebanon as a French colony. But that wasn't what the Lebanese (or Winston Churchill) wanted. When a newly elected national assembly met in 1943, it redrafted the constitution handed to it by the French, leaving out all reference to France. Boldly, it wrote its colonial masters out of the script. This outraged the French authorities, who imprisoned the new president, Bishara Al-Khoury, and his prime minister, Riad As-Solh. The population was incensed. The country teetered towards chaos. The uproar infuriated Churchill, who had enough problems without the distraction of a revolution in a small Middle Eastern country. He put pressure on de Gaulle's Free French to give Lebanon independence. Al-Khoury and As-Solh were released from prison and resumed their posts. They had become heroes in the eyes of the Lebanese, and their political future was assured.

During 1945, the French were in the final stages of pulling out the last of their forces from the country. They had all left by the time I arrived in Beirut. But you could see the French legacy all around the city – not least in some of the street names. When I stepped out of AUB's main gates, I had a choice of walking south down the rue Jeanne d'Arc or east along the rue Clemenceau towards the downtown area. If I chose the latter, I passed the magnificent French embassy and other fine mansions erected during the colonial years. But the heart of the city was the bustling Places des Martyrs, a fine square lined with elegant buildings, where you could linger in the shade of palm trees. Its name recalled a group of patriots campaigning for Arab independence who were hanged in the square by the Ottomans during 1915 and 1916. As I wandered the Places des Martyrs in those post-war years, I little realised it was to become a battlefield for gunmen in the civil war and the Israeli invasion and, eventually, with the exception of the martyrs memorial, be levelled by bulldozers.

Yet in 1945 Beirut, there was no sign of the violent struggle to come. Certainly not on the AUB campus, where 'all conditions and classes of men' debated the future of the Middle East with vigour – but in peace.

CHAPTER 4

Becoming an activist

In the spring holiday of 1946, during my first year at the American University of Beirut, my father proposed that we should take a short holiday in Cairo. The invitation arrived in a letter to my brother Jamal and myself.

At first, the letter made us angry because it didn't seem that our mother was included in the vacation plans. We decided to do something about that. Between us, we drafted a letter of protest to father demanding to know why our mother wasn't coming with us. 'Because your mother is going to have a baby,' came the reply. (My youngest sister, Sahab.) Somewhat shamefacedly, Jamal and I withdrew our protest and happily accompanied our father, as well as our other brothers and sisters, to Cairo.

Cairo made an immediate impact on me. At university in Beirut, I had already briefly experienced the cosmopolitan culture of a city with strong European influences, especially French. Cairo was similar, with British, French and other European influences, and was unquestionably the leading city in the region. It wasn't just that the city operated on a scale different from many others in the region at the time. Or that it was a city of dramatic contrasts. It had broad boulevards, such as Fouad I (now renamed July 26th Street) – which had been laid out in the 1860s by Baron Haussmann, who was responsible for much of the renovation of Paris – close by the narrow congested streets of the Islamic quarter that had been there since the Fatimid times in the tenth century.

But it was more than the city's streets and buildings that had such an influence on me. Cairo had an atmosphere – a 'buzz' – that came from being at the centre of the struggle for Arab self-determination. It was something that I'd begun to feel back home in Salt, but not as strongly as I did in Cairo. Looking back, I suppose that might not have been too surprising. In Transjordan, I had lived under the British mandate since I'd been born. It was only in that spring that Prince Abdullah and the British foreign secretary, Ernest Bevin, had signed a treaty that led to the creation of the independent Hashemite Kingdom of Jordan. Prince Abdullah finally declared himself king in May.

It wasn't that people in Transjordan hadn't been fighting to build a national identity and win their independence. We had struggled long and hard and, at last, we were achieving the success we felt we deserved. There were also Jordanians who had played a part in the broader fight for Arab freedom – for example in Palestine. As a family in Salt, we knew of those who had paid the ultimate price. I can remember attending wedding ceremonies in the late 1930s where emotional songs would be sung for fighters who had died in the Palestine revolt between 1936 and 1939. So the struggle for Arab nationalism had been both real and poignant in Transjordan.

It was just that, in Cairo, the struggle for a national identity had been going on longer, more passionately and, possibly, against greater odds than in many other places in the region. Most important, Cairo had been the city in which the Arab enlightenment – that vibrant renaissance in Arab philosophy, political ideas, literature and art – had first taken root at the beginning of the nineteenth century, and where it had bloomed most strongly. It was in nineteenth-century Cairo that Lebanese scholars and thinkers influenced intellectuals of the enlightenment as writers and journalists, establishing newspapers such as *Al-Ahram*, *Al-Hilal* and other publishing houses. Indeed, the Lebanese in Cairo pioneered the establishment of a free press.

This Arab enlightenment promised a liberal nationalism founded on democratic governments, free markets and respect for human rights – of the kind that I'd read about in George Antonius's book. It provided hope. But already there were signs that not all Arabs saw the future in the same way. The headquarters of the Arab League, founded in 1945, had opened in Cairo the year before I arrived for my visit to the city. The League, a confederation of independent member states, agreed about some issues – its opposition to the creation of a state of Israel, for instance – but it was already clear that some members had different views about how the nationalist dream should be realised in practice. There were signs that in some countries the kind of liberal nationalism I longed to see would in later years be overshadowed by a harsher kind, where national identities would be enforced on populations in command-and-control economies by dictators who denied their populations basic democratic and human rights. That spring, it seemed the great debate was coming to a head. And that Cairo was where the clash of ideologies would start and be the most profound.

*   *   *

Cairo has changed much since 1946. It is not just that some of the street names have been changed (to reflect shifts in political power), but some of the landmarks I remember from 1940s Cairo have also gone – the baroque opera house that used to stand on Midan Opera and the old Shepheard's Hotel, a symbol of Britain's presence in the country, sacked by rioters in 1952. Today, Cairo has swollen into a sprawling city of 18 million people.

But, back in 1946, I knew that a morning's walk around the centre of the city would take me to places that had a special part in the story of the growth of enlightened nationalism. In my reading, I had made an intellectual journey in the footprints of giants who had shaped the Arab mind. Now it was time to make my own footsteps around the streets of Cairo in search of the liberal nationalist dream.

A good place to start was the site of the palace of Alfi Bey, close by the Ezbekiya Gardens, then an oasis of lush green, now much reduced by new roads and commercial development. It is still strange to think that this palace, originally built in the fifteenth century, could be regarded as a starting-point for the profound changes that reshaped Egypt in the nineteenth century. But when Napoleon invaded Egypt in 1798, he requisitioned the building for his personal use. And it was Napoleon's time in Egypt that triggered the enlightenment.

The little Corsican certainly had no such thoughts in his mind when he brought his armies up the Nile. But among his retinue came professionals, scholars and craftsmen bringing with them new ideas and the paraphernalia of European civilisation – printing presses, windmills, even a hot-air balloon – never before seen in an Arab country. An Arab historian called Al-Jabarti was living in Cairo at the time and recorded how he visited the Westerners who travelled with Napoleon: 'and they would bring out all kinds of pictures and maps, and animals and birds and plants, and histories of the ancients and of nations and tales of the prophets'. Although the French stayed in Egypt for only three years, the impact they made was profound.

Among those they impressed was Muhammad Ali, a young officer of Albanian descent serving in the Ottoman army, born in Macedonia. Using a combination of military skill and political prowess, he had become Pasha (or ruler) of Egypt by 1805. It was to prove a turning-point in the country's history. Although the Ottomans had conquered Egypt as long ago as 1517, by the eighteenth century their grip was weakening, and after a revolt in 1796 the country became semi-independent. Nominally, Ali owed allegiance to the Sublime Porte. In practice, he was intent on carving out as much independence as possible and building Egypt into a modern Western-style state.

Ali's eyes had been opened by what he'd seen with the French. And he had the kind of vision that creates great countries (and, in the modern world, great companies). He began to transform Egypt. He did what a shrewd modern business does – he invested in 'human capital'. He sent 300 bright young Egyptians to Europe to study Western science, arts and literature. He brought European engineers, doctors and military officers to Egypt to train thousands more of the emerging professional class. By the time he died in 1848,

Egypt's economy had been transformed and was growing strongly. Importantly, the country was well on its way to developing the kind of middle class that had been the bedrock of liberal nationalist progress in Europe.

But if the story of Napoleon's visit and Ali's reforms were an encouraging start to enlightened nationalism, the next episode was less hopeful. I headed south through Midan Opera and along Sharia El-Gumhorriya to the Abdin Palace, built in the 1860s by Khedive Ismail, Muhammad's grandson. At the time, the new palace was a bold assertion of economic strength and of the changes he wanted to make in Egypt. Ismail was eager to build on Ali's legacy. He encouraged literature, the arts and newspapers, which fed the hunger of the growing middle class for news about the outside world. But much of Ismail's success rested on the prosperity of Egypt's cotton trade. And when the price of cotton collapsed at the end of the American Civil War, the country began to run up huge debts. By the time Ismail died in 1879, Egypt was close to bankruptcy.

His son, Khedive Tawfik, struggled to placate overseas creditors, but growing foreign influence within Egypt fanned nationalist feelings in the country. In 1881, Tawfik set up a chamber of deputies to placate nationalist feelings. But when the chamber met and rejected a tax bill designed to raise funds to repay creditors, foreign governments became alarmed. Tawfik tried to sack the deputies. They refused to go and, for a time, the country balanced uncomfortably on the edge of revolution. The British and French, concerned about the future of the Suez Canal, moved to support Tawfik – and in 1882 British soldiers marched into Egypt to begin a lengthy occupation.

The question was whether enlightened nationalism could continue to flourish under British rule. Part of the answer lay west of the Abdin Palace, in what is now Midan Tahrir (Liberation Square). Today it is arguably the centre of Cairo, a traffic-choked crossing-point where seven major thoroughfares meet. Back in 1946, it was the site of the Qasr El-Nil barracks, the heart of Britain's military occupation of Egypt. In the years after the British moved into Egypt, they encouraged reforms that gave the country free trade and a market economy. These strengthened the middle class and encouraged the growth of liberal nationalism.

But as the early years of the twentieth century rolled by, Egyptian attempts to win more self-determination – to turn the nationalist aspiration into the reality of a truly independent country free of foreign influence – were successively frustrated by British colonial ambitions and its concern for the Suez Canal. Some elements of the liberal Egyptian political establishment alienated public opinion by becoming too closely associated with British rule. So, by the 1930s the focus of Arab nationalism in the country was changing.

The middle class had become larger and more diverse. And there were plenty within it who had become progressively angrier at Britain's heavy-handed attempts to deny the country a measure of real self-determination. Moreover, the tensions over growing Jewish migration into Palestine sharpened regional concerns. By the time of my visit, the enlightened Arab nationalism, whose history I had traced in its streets and buildings, was under challenge from those who spoke about taking a more militant and radical approach.

I was not to know it at the time, as I strolled north from the Qasr El-Nil barracks along Suleyman Pasha Street that spring, but the beginning of the end-game of Egypt's liberal nationalism was to be played out close by. In those days, the walk was a pleasant one – under shady trees, past elegant buildings with pavement cafés that looked as though they could have been lifted from any Parisian boulevard. Among the cafés I passed as I walked (or perhaps I stopped for coffee – it was many years ago and I can't remember) was Café Riche. Just six years later, the so-called 'free officers' were said to have plotted the overthrow of King Farouk in one of its back rooms. Today, Suleyman Pasha Street has been renamed Sharia Talaat Harb (after a nationalist lawyer who founded the national bank). It has lost much of its elegance, but not its commercial vitality and zest for life. But the dream of enlightened nationalism in Egypt was lost with the free officers' coup, which eventually brought Colonel Gamal Abdel Nasser to power in Egypt and (as I shall relate further in chapter 11) changed the face of the Middle East for a generation.

Yet in 1946, all this was in the future. There was still hope in the air. Everything was to play for. And my visit to Cairo had convinced me that our future lay in following the path of liberal nationalism that I had read about and whose history I had charted in its streets. But it was also clear that the cause would be lost unless those who believed in it stood up to be counted.

I had come to Cairo as a student. I returned to my university in Beirut as a convinced Arab nationalist.

*   *   *

Arab nationalism came of age in the years immediately following the Second World War. They were great years for becoming an activist. Unfortunately, as it turned out, they were also the years when nationalism started to take a wrong turning. But in the spring of 1946, as Jamal and I returned to AUB after our vacation, that was in the future.

Universities, of course, have traditionally been centres of political activism. And students make natural activists. It is certainly true of AUB, which has long held a reputation as a centre of Arab nationalist thinking and other political traditions.

It was at AUB that I first realised that having opinions was not enough unless you made them count in the world. The debates we had there were endless and, in some ways, I find it depressing that sixty years later the subjects still haven't changed – what kind of Arab nationalism, what future for Palestine?

There was a lot of debate about priorities – should we struggle to improve people's freedom or fight for independence from colonial powers first? To me, it seemed (and still does) a false distinction. There is no reason why the search for individual freedom and the campaign for independence cannot advance hand in hand. I remember there was an organisation at AUB that provided a focus for the debate around Arab nationalism. It was called Alurwa Alwothqa (the Binding Tie), but it was exclusive and restricted its membership to those who were in the junior and senior (third and fourth) years. But many of us in the earlier years supported its broad objectives.

Then there was Palestine. Always Palestine. It was not until 1947 (my last year at AUB) that the United Nations finally reached its decision on a plan to create two states, one Jewish and one Arab. Although Jewish leaders declared their opposition to the plan as an inadequate basis to achieve their ambitions for the Israeli state, they accepted it as a tactical convenience. The Palestinians and Arabs rejected the plan. But it had been clear for years that a crunch was coming. The future of Palestine was a subject which, I remember, animated the student body more than any other. To give voice to our concern, we demonstrated against the Balfour Declaration every year on the second of November, the anniversary of its announcement in 1917. Arthur Balfour, Britain's foreign secretary, had declared that the British government favoured

> the establishment in Palestine of a national home for the Jewish people, and will use its best endeavours to facilitate the achievement of this object, it being clearly understood that nothing shall be done which may prejudice the civil and religious rights of existing non-Jewish communities in Palestine...

But, by my time at AUB, it was clear that unlimited Jewish immigration to Palestine was changing the balance of population and undermining the rights of native Palestinians, many of whom were dispossessed of their homes and land during and after the 1948 conflict.

Our demonstration was tame by modern-day standards. It consisted of a march round the university's campus (with the president's permission). I don't remember us venturing out into the streets of Beirut, certainly not the main body of the demonstration. A few of the more adventurous may have done so, where they would have encountered the Beirut police, who took a fairly dim view of student demonstrations. The police station was conveniently (from the police's point of view) situated next door to the campus. So it was a simple matter for them to scoop up any wayward demonstrators and treat them to a couple of hours in the cells. But, as far as I know, nothing worse happened. The demonstration always ended with speeches decrying the iniquities of the Balfour Declaration and the damage it was doing to the native population of Palestine.

The march and speeches were a heady introduction to activism. But I think that even as student I was beginning to realise that you don't solve problems simply by talking about them. I was also coming round to the view that it is practical activism – often direct, but peaceful, activism – that is the way to change people's lives for the better.

One issue that I and a group of friends thought was especially important was the problem of the high levels of illiteracy that still existed in Jordan in the immediate post-war years. Schooling of any kind had not advanced very far under the British mandate, despite the well-meaning efforts of some missionary groups to bring teaching to the country. This was compounded by a culture in which it was simply not thought necessary to send children to school. Even in those families that did understand the benefits of education, it was by no means unusual to find some children sent to school while others were put to work as soon as they were able. It was no wonder that as many as 90 per cent of men and 98 per cent of women were functionally illiterate.

In the summer vacation of 1946, a group of us decided that we should try to do something about this. We knew one another through a club that met in Salt to discuss cultural subjects. Most of us were attending universities at various places in the Middle East – some in Damascus, others in Cairo, others in Beirut. I don't think we had any big ideas about changing the new government's policy on education.

Instead, we thought we could make some difference on the ground in our home town of Salt. We contacted the local schools – the English school that I'd attended myself and the Catholic school – to ask if we could use their facilities while they were closed during the summer holidays. They were delighted to help. Then we announced our classes and invited pupils to come to them. During that summer, we must have taught around two hundred pupils, mostly aged between fifteen and forty. We were able to teach them to read the newspapers and to write a few lines. It wouldn't have made a huge impact on Jordan's illiteracy problem – even on Salt's – but it was a start. And it was a practical manifestation of our new-found activism.

But it led me into an awkward situation at home. Naturally, my mother knew what I was doing, and decided that she would like to read and write. I could hardly demand that she attend the classes like everyone else. And, even if she did, it would be very embarrassing to be teaching my mother in front of the other members of the class, so I decided to give her private lessons at home. She was an attentive pupil, but as you get older, learning to read and write – or learning anything – doesn't get any easier.

At the school, we had given our pupils a test to see how much progress they had made. I don't know what possessed me – over-zealous enthusiasm for my task, perhaps – but I decided my mother should take the test at home. She tried hard, but when I came to mark the paper I was disappointed to find that, by the standards we had set for the other students, she had failed. When she found out, she started to cry. I shall never forget the image of her distraught face. It was so sad. It was a lesson for me: there are times when the activist can be too active.

*   *   *

As I advanced from freshman to sophomore, I realised that I was facing the most important decision of my life so far. I wanted to become an engineer, but AUB offered no specialist engineering course that would lead to the professional qualification I wanted. In the sophomore year, there was an engineering module in the science course, but it was not enough. Besides, I found that much of it involved technical drawing. And I made another discovery: I hate technical drawing.

So if I was to gain an engineering degree, it would have to be elsewhere. But where? I was not attracted to the idea of finding another university in the Middle East. Besides, my experience at AUB had given me a taste for the American style of university education. It seemed that if I was to qualify as an engineer, I would have to look much farther afield – to the United States.

CHAPTER 5

Slow boat to Michigan

I knew I'd made a mistake after the first day at sea. The apples ran out. We'd been promised there'd be fresh fruit on the voyage. The fresh fruit proved to be apples. And at the end of the first day they'd all gone.

It was August 1947 and I was on my way to America for the first time. The first time also that I'd ventured outside the Middle East. I was off on my biggest adventure so far – an adventure that proved to change the direction of my life decisively. I was enrolling at an American university.

And my mistake? My father had offered me the choice of travelling to America by plane or ship. Today, there would be no difficulty in taking that decision. You'd travel by plane and cover the distance from Lebanon to the United States in little more than ten hours. Back in 1947, mass intercontinental air travel was in its infancy. Travelling by plane from anywhere to anywhere took time. The trip to the United States would take more than a day, with stop-overs along the route.

So I chose the ship. I think I would have relished the idea of a long sea voyage anyway. I had heard of the great liners that ploughed the Atlantic and the opulent passengers who travelled in comfort, even luxury. There was the prospect of healthy days at sea, quoits on the promenade deck, civilised dinners with my fellow passengers. Perhaps there would even be the chance of a shipboard romance. After all, I was only 17.

Then I saw the *Marine Carp* moored in the port at Haifa, on the coast of what is now Israel but was then still British mandate Palestine, and my dreams of romance on the high seas died. The *Marine Carp* was an ageing rust-bucket that had seen active service during the war transporting troops into battle zones. It still bore the scars. The accommodation below decks was designed for rough soldiery on active service rather than elegant travellers on the transatlantic run. There were no signs of luxury, or even comfort. We slept in dormitories of seventy or eighty. We used open showers and lavatories. After the apples ran out on the first day, we dined on greasy hamburgers washed down with warm sodas.

As I recall, there were no deck quoits or any other form of onboard entertainment. The ship wallowed in smooth seas and pitched when the ocean swelled. I spent most of the 18-day crossing – we lingered through the Mediterranean, stopping at various ports to pick up other unfortunates – whiling away the long hours by playing cards and debating with my fellow passengers. Debating until the arguments were running round in circles in my mind and I could talk no more. The experience has given me a life-long aversion to sea travel.

It was perhaps as well that I had at least something to keep my mind active during the voyage. For I had a secret, and if it was discovered I might not be admitted to the United States. In the dark watches of the night, as I lay awake listening to the snores of my fellow passengers – I was in a middle bunk with one above and one below – the secret worried at my mind. If it was discovered by the strict immigration authorities when I arrived in New York, I would be refused entry. I would not be able to take up my place at university. Worse still, I would be imprisoned on Staten Island, before being returned unceremoniously to my country of origin on the first available ship that could be persuaded to take me. My dream of studying in the United States would be in ruins. And my life plan with it.

The secret was that I suffered from glaucoma. Now glaucoma can be a serious condition leading to blindness or, at least, seriously impaired vision – which is why the US immigration authorities were keen to reject immigrants suffering from it. In my case, the glaucoma was dormant. I have never been in any danger from it and even today, apart from using spectacles for reading, my eyesight is as good as it ever was. I had been told that when I landed in the United States my eyes would be tested as part of the physical examination required in those days. The signs of even dormant glaucoma would show up under examination. And it would be enough to put me on the next boat home.

During the summer before I left for America I had visited a doctor in Jerusalem. He said the condition couldn't be cured but that he could give me some drops that would disguise the symptoms of it for a few hours. I had to put the drops in shortly before my eyes were examined. Back in Jerusalem the doctor had seemed confident this would work, and I thought little more about it. Now as we approached the shores of America, I wasn't so sure.

So as the *Marine Carp* edged its way into the Hudson River and made its painful progress towards its berth on Ellis Island, I wasn't up on deck with the other passengers gaining my first excited glimpse of the New York skyline. I was below, in my grim quarters, contemplating a bottle of eye-drops and wondering when – and how – I should put them in. And whether they would work.

As the *Marine Carp* nudged up against the quayside, I found a quiet spot away from my fellow passengers and administered the drops. There was no particular sensation and it was impossible for me to tell whether they were working or not. With a certain sense of fatalism, I gathered my belongings together and made my way up on deck.

I'm not quite sure what I thought the medical examination would be. I suppose I must have thought we'd be taken to a clinic somewhere and examined. So when I saw doctors standing at the top of the gangways examining passengers before they let them off the boat, my heart almost stopped. I hadn't expected the examination to take place quite so soon – or so publicly. Had I given the drops enough time to work? And if they didn't would I be sent back down below – humiliated in front of my fellow passengers?

I had no choice but to join the line and shuffle forward. I watched what the doctors were doing. The examination involved just looking in the eyes. It was pretty cursory and seemed to take no more than a few seconds. I was wondering whether there was anything else I could do when: 'Next.'

I hadn't realised I'd reached the front of the queue. I stepped forward. The doctor leant forward and peered into my eyes. I could feel his breath on my cheek. Surely, he was taking longer over my eyes than those who'd gone before. Time stopped.

*   *   *

I had never felt more relieved as I stepped out of the immigration station. The good doctor had waved me through without even a question. I made for the Battery Park ferry to take me to Manhattan. It was another voyage but, mercifully, a brief one. On the way, the ferry passed the Statue of Liberty and I looked up at her with my mind poised half way between relief and apprehension. 'Give me your tired, your poor / Your huddled masses yearning to breathe free / The wretched refuse of your teeming shore / Send these, the homeless tempest tossed to me / I lift my lamp beside the golden door,' reads the inscription on the Statue. I couldn't honestly have claimed that all of it applied to me, but after 18 days on the *Marine Carp* and a heart-stopping couple of hours in the immigration station, I knew what she meant.

Once finally ashore at Battery Park – and vowing never to set foot on a ship again – I called a yellow cab and set out to find somewhere to stay. I feel sure the cabby would have been the usually garrulous Brooklyn type, but my mind wasn't on his chatter. As the cab crept up-town, I was progressively stunned by the city. It was like nothing I'd ever seen before. Even though I'd seen both Beirut and Cairo, the two most sophisticated cities in the Middle East, nothing had prepared me for New York. The sheer scale of the city, its buildings and its zest for life took my breath away. It was, as I was to find in my brief stay, a city that buzzed around the clock.

I put up in an undistinguished hotel in a not particularly noteworthy neighbourhood – but anything was better than life on board the *Marine*

Carp – and hurried out to see the city. I could stay in New York for no more than a couple of nights and I wanted to see as much as possible.

In 1947, New York was one of the largest cities in the world, with a population of more than eight million. From an engineer's point of view – or, perhaps, I should say a prospective one – the city was like a primer in engineering greats. I hurried to marvel at the world's tallest building, all 1454 feet of the Empire State, and the Brooklyn Bridge, the world's first steel suspension bridge with an awe-inspiring and graceful 1596-feet span. Then it was on to the Flatiron building at the junction of Broadway, Fifth Avenue and 23rd Street – the world's first iron-framed building and the tallest until 1909. Could there be more engineering marvels crammed into one city? There were.

But it wasn't just the engineering and architectural wonders that amazed me – although they seemed to be almost everywhere you looked. It was that the hustle and bustle of New York life was like nothing I'd ever experienced before, certainly not in Salt, nor even in Beirut or Cairo. New York seemed geared to live life in the fast lane. As I tramped exhausted back to my hotel, I wondered whether this was true of the whole of America and, if it was, whether I could maintain the pace. But there was little time to worry about that.

Two days later, I humped my luggage round to Grand Central Station – another engineering marvel with a vast vaulted concourse – and took the train on the hour-long journey west to what I then thought, wrongly as it turned out, would be my ultimate destination.

Philadelphia, on the Delaware and Schuylkill Rivers, was one of the most historic of America's cities. Founded in 1682 as 'the city of brotherly love', it had been the US capital from 1790 until 1800. There was a link, too, with my native Jordan. Philadelphia, actually a Greek word meaning 'love of two brothers', had been the Romans' name for Amman. America's Philadelphia could not trace its history so far, but it had had a distinguished past nonetheless. The Declaration of Independence was signed there in 1776, and I could see a copy of it, hand-written by Thomas Jefferson, in Library Hall.

My destination was the University of Pennsylvania, which I found occupied a spacious campus close to the Schuylkill River. My tutor at

AUB had advised me to apply to two universities in the United States – the other was the University of Texas in Austin. At the time, the University of Texas didn't have the reputation which it has subsequently built. I wanted the best, and the University of Pennsylvania – or Penn as the students called it – fitted the bill.

It was a genuine Ivy League American university. Benjamin Franklin, himself, one of the distinguished Americans who'd worked on the drafting of the Declaration of Independence, had helped to found it way back in 1751, when Pennsilvania (as Franklin spelt it) was still a British colony. The university had a strong engineering faculty and was at the cutting edge of that new and exciting technology – computers. The year before my arrival, engineers at the university had built Eniac, the world's first electronic, large-scale, general-purpose computer.

So I arrived in Philadelphia looking forward to my study. I was greeted warmly by the dean of students. I was given my own room in a hall of residence on the campus. I was thrilled to be a member of the student body at an Ivy League university and I settled down to concentrate on my courses. But whether I was missing my homeland or whether I was finding it too difficult to come to grips with a new culture, I found it hard to settle.

As a city, Philadelphia was smaller-scale than New York, and life seemed to be lived at a less frenetic pace. But in every way of life – from the way Pennsylvanians talked to the food they ate and the new television sets most of them watched – they represented a culture that was completely new to me. It wasn't that I lacked the desire to come to grips with the culture. But when you're 17 and living away from any family members for the first time – I had my brother Jamal for company at AUB – you welcome some comforting links with the familiar. And there were none.

What I found particularly difficult was the fact that there were no other Arab students at the university. There was nobody with whom I could share a private joke or converse in my native tongue. I was at an age when most young people today will still be at high school and living at home. I was four thousand miles from mine. And I was feeling lonely.

After a few weeks of this, I discussed my feelings with the ever-helpful dean of students. He understood my plight and sympathised. I had heard that there were some Arab students at the University of Texas. Perhaps I would feel more at home there. He agreed that I should try it. The university was prepared to accept me even though the semester had already started. Sadly, I said goodbye to the University of Pennsylvania and took the 1500-mile train journey south-west to Austin.

It was a tiring journey, and perhaps I wasn't in the most receptive of moods when I arrived in Austin on a hot and sultry day. Austin, the state capital of Texas, was in 1947 a much quieter city than Philadelphia. There was less traffic and noise, and life was lived at a slower pace. As my taxi took me from the railway station to the University of Texas campus, it seemed that much of the city revolved round the impressive capitol building.

The campus was just off Guadalupe Street, which locals seemed to call The Drag for reasons I was never able to work out. As at Pennsylvania, I was warmly received and shown to accommodation on the campus. Within a few days, I had started the engineering course and I had met some of my fellow Arab students. But, again, I couldn't settle. For one thing, the climate didn't agree with me and I found it difficult to concentrate on my studies.

But most of all, I didn't feel the standard of the courses and the standing of the university as a whole came close to what I'd briefly experienced at Ivy League Penn. (To be fair, I should add that the modern-day University of Texas has advanced from the more modest establishment I knew in my brief stay in the late 1940s.) My problem was that I wanted a better-quality university. In fact, the best quality. It is true that I was aiming high – but I have never seen much point in aiming anywhere else.

One evening, I was sitting in a small restaurant eating my evening meal and feeling rather sorry for myself when I fell into conversation with another student at an adjacent table. He was a fellow Jordanian and, for a time, we swapped stories about our experiences of America, as you do when you meet a countryman for the first time abroad. He joined me at my table and we talked more about the difficulties of studying in the United States. I discovered he was a graduate student at the University of Michigan. What brought him to Austin, I'm not sure. Perhaps he was touring the United States between semesters.

In any event, I was looking for a sympathetic ear to share my troubles, and he was it. I told him about my difficulties. He said I should try the University of Michigan. It had not been on my original application list. But in the next few days I looked into what Michigan might have to offer, and it seemed as though it could provide what I wanted. It was one of the older universities in the United States, had a good reputation – indeed it was nicknamed 'the Harvard of the mid-West' – and it was strong in engineering.

It took time to make contact with the admission authorities at Michigan, but eventually I completed the formalities and was accepted as a student, even though the academic year was now well advanced, I had missed the first two semesters, and 1947 had become 1948. So my brief stay in Austin came to an end, and it was time to make the long rail journey north-east, this time to Ann Arbor in Michigan state.

I knew I would like Ann Arbor and the University of Michigan as soon as I arrived. The city is in the south-east corner of Michigan, about 40 miles from Detroit, on the Huron River. The university dominated a city full of modest but homely houses in tree-lined roads. But I guess you'd expect a town with Arbor in its name to have plenty of trees. (Ann, I discovered, happened to be the name shared by the wives of the town's two founders.)

The fact that the university was the largest single institution in the city meant that Ann Arbor was a young place geared to meeting the needs of students. And it was clear as soon as I arrived that the University of Michigan – not to be confused with Michigan State University – was the kind of first-class, progressive place that I was looking for. It had been among the first universities in America to admit both black (1868) and women (1870) students.

The university had a long history of welcoming outsiders and, although I was still getting used to life in America, I felt that Ann

Arbor was a place that I could be at home. In fact, I found the adjustment to America's way of life and culture relatively simple. I had been introduced to the way the US university system worked at AUB. I had also managed to gain some glimpses of the American culture and lifestyles there. So I was well prepared, and adapted quickly.

Even so, it was not easy getting used to the mid-West climate. In Ann Arbor, the temperature would soar above 100 degrees Fahrenheit in the summer but sometimes dip below zero – 32 degrees Fahrenheit – in winter. There were times when it became cold in Salt, but in that first winter the cold in Michigan seemed to be on an arctic scale. Initially my body – and my wardrobe – was not equipped to deal with it. I still remember one occasion when the temperature sunk to minus-28 degrees Fahrenheit. I made the mistake of walking a short distance to the university union for lunch. When I arrived, I'd lost all feeling in my nose, and it was some time before sensation returned and I could sit down and enjoy my meal.

But the privations of the mid-West's climate were a small price to pay for the benefit of the University of Michigan's renowned engineering teaching. Professor John S. Worley, who had done much to build the Engineering College's reputation, had retired the previous year, but he had left his remarkable collection of books, reports, pictures and documents behind him. And future leading members of the engineering faculty, including John C. Kohl and Wilbur Nelson, had either joined or were shortly to do so. Happily, I paid the $300 annual tuition fee and settled down to my courses.

I had already decided that I was going to specialise in chemical engineering. This was partly because it was an excellent way to avoid the horrors of technical drawing, but mainly because it included a strong focus on physics and chemistry, both of which I thoroughly enjoyed. Having effectively wasted two semesters at Pennsylvania and Texas, I had a lot of ground to make up, so I decided to set myself a hot pace.

Studying for a first degree at an American university involved accumulating a specific number of credit hours of study. This was one of the reasons why I'd chosen to attend a university in the United States, because the credit hours I'd accumulated at AUB counted towards my degree. At Michigan, you had to take at least six credit hours. Initially, I took nine or ten hours. When, during my first semester, I found I could cope with that, I increased the pressure. In subsequent semesters, I wound my credit hours up to the maximum of 18 and for a time, with special permission, 20.

During the summer of 1948, while my fellow students were out trekking or boating or, in the case of my Middle Eastern friends, travelling back to their homes, I was hitting the books studying hard. My aim was to graduate with a bachelor's degree by the time I was 19 – and that meant I had to complete my studies by the end of the following year. It was tough and it didn't leave much time for recreation. It meant studying into the summer of 1949, too, but by August I had finished.

Did I my miss my family during these long months hunched over my books? Of course I did. Did I yearn to go back to Jordan and revisit Lebanon? Yes, again. But I was also aware that I had a unique life opportunity that would only come once, and that if I failed to grab it and make a success of it, that opportunity would be lost for ever. By the late summer of 1949, I had completed – successfully I believed – two years of solid work. I was as certain as I could be that I had obtained my bachelor's at a good level. And I badly needed a holiday.

*   *   *

Although I haven't a musical bone in my body, one of the culture shocks I'd discovered in America was that there was music everywhere. Everybody had radio sets in their homes. Some even had them in their cars. Coffee shops and diners – of which there were many in Ann Arbor serving the large student population – had juke boxes which, for a nickel or dime, would play the record of your choice. I wasn't a great player of music, but you couldn't help hearing it – and I suppose some of it must have sunk into the subconscious.

One of the songs we would have heard a lot of during those years was 'Get your kicks on Route 66', which the black American crooner Nat King Cole had made a hit in 1946, the year before I arrived. It was taken up by other singers and played endlessly. The song glamorised what was becoming a new phenomenon in America – touring the country by car. It told of the thrills to be had driving down Route 66, which winds across America from Chicago to Los Angeles.

During the two years in Michigan, with head bowed over books, I'd promised myself that I'd see more of the country when the opportunity came. With my bachelor's complete, this was the opportunity. I don't think 'Route 66' played any conscious part in my decision to make the trip by car, but it certainly provided a topical backdrop.

I knew of three friends who were also attracted by the idea of touring. We hired a car – not difficult in a state which, with Henry Ford's Dearborn nearby, was virtually the world capital of the automobile industry – and set off. Today, there are more than two hundred million registered vehicles on America's roads. In 1949, there were fewer than thirty million – but there were fewer roads, too. It would be another seven years before the interstate highway system was started, leading to the building of more than 42,500 miles of roads with federal funds.

But there were still plenty of roads traversing the country along interesting routes. Our route took us across the north of the United States, following broadly the line of what is now US2, the Great Northern, across Wisconsin, Minnesota, North Dakota, Montana and Idaho into Washington state. It was late summer, the best time to see these states, after the raw heat of the high summer but before the blizzards and intense cold of the winter. I was stunned by the variety of the scenery – the northern woods of Wisconsin, the lake country of Minnesota, where the headwaters of the Mississippi rise, and the endless plains of North Dakota and eastern Montana, where you drive for miles wondering when you'll next see a hill or even a tree.

Then it was on through the majesty of the Rockies in western Montana with Glacier National Park, down through the valleys of Idaho and into Washington state. We had an opportunity to make a detour and see one of the engineering wonders of the world of the time, the Grand Coulee Dam, finished just seven years earlier in 1942 and still, I believe, the largest concrete structure in the world.

When we reached Washington state, we turned south and made our way through Oregon and into California. The weather became progressively hotter as we motored south, passing through San Francisco and Los Angeles, even in 1949 the undisputed centre of the movie world but not yet the sprawling, car-choked, monster of a city it has subsequently become. Our destination was San Diego, just north of the Mexican border.

San Diego changed for ever from a sleepy village with a perfect natural harbour where boats went out to fish for tuna when the United States Navy's Pacific Fleet was stationed there after Pearl Harbor in 1941. But in 1949 it was not too late to experience the character of the village it had been before the rapid development that has now turned it into a huge city with two-and-a-half million inhabitants. San Diego marked the turning-point of our journey. About as far as we could go without leaving the United States.

We turned the car round and headed back for Michigan, travelling east through California and Arizona, with the breathtaking Grand Canyon, then swinging north to pass through the Rockies in Colorado and on to the cowboy country of Wyoming and South Dakota. It had been a memorable trip, and one that had impressed on me how great and diverse the United States is in its geography. Although we'd driven more than 5000 miles – and I don't think we'd touched Route 66 – we'd seen more wonders than the song promised.

The trip had been a much-needed period of relaxation before returning to lectures and library. For I had more work to do. I was determined to add a master's degree in engineering to my bachelor's, and I wanted to start work straight away. Again, I set a hot pace. I completed the studying for my master's in two semesters, ending in the summer of 1950. I suppose that could have marked the closing of a chapter on my education, but I was determined to go further and take a doctorate.

It was tempting that summer to fly back to Jordan and be reunited with my family, whom I had not seen for three years. It was a temptation I resisted. Apart from the fact that I wanted to prepare the ground for a doctorate, there was another task that I had started while at Michigan – an important task which I wanted to see through.

* * *

My experience of travelling thousands of miles from my homeland to be educated in a foreign country with a culture that was like nothing I had ever encountered before, had proved a deeply formative event in my life. Those early months, as I tried to settle, first at the University of Pennsylvania then in Texas, brought home to me in a very personal way what it is to be alone in a land where few understand or care about your worries and concerns. At the University of Michigan, I had met other students from the Arab world, and I realised that many of them shared the same sense of isolation as myself.

So it wasn't surprising that during my first two years at Michigan I regularly met informally with other Arab students. By 1949, the last year of my undergraduate studies, I thought it would be a good idea to form a club for Arab students. The idea was looked on favourably by the university authorities, who encouraged students from different countries to establish their own societies. The Iranians already had their own club, run by a friend, Mahmoud Reza Pahlavi, the half-brother of the then Shah, Mohammad Reza Pahlavi. (At least, I thought he was a friend until I called on him some years later when he visited Beirut. He received me formally, uttered a few stilted words, then dismissed me in a haughty manner that I suspected was a family trait.)

In any event, whatever the Iranians could do at the University of Michigan I was sure the Arabs could more than emulate. We called our club the Arab Students Club at the University of Michigan, and we soon attracted around forty or fifty members, a very high proportion of the Arab students on the campus.

One of my motives in setting up a club was certainly to provide a focus for those Arabs who wanted to meet with other students from their own region to talk about the issues that concerned us all. Submersed, as we were, for years at a stretch in a society that was foreign to us, I felt it would be all too easy to lose touch with those cultural imperatives that had been important in our lives. So the number one objective of the club was to help preserve those cultural and national identities.

But there was more to it than that. In my two years in the United States, events in the Middle East had been moving on the world stage in an alarming way. The presentation of those events in the US media was shaping Americans' views of the Arab world – and not always for the good. We wanted to play at least a small part in redressing that balance by promoting Arab culture and ideas in a positive light within the communities in which we lived. So we actively sought invitations to address local clubs and societies to talk about the Arab view of the world. I had been elected president, so it wasn't surprising that I was expected to take on a good part of the burden of speaking at these meetings.

It was my first experience of public speaking in any significant way. I found that I enjoyed it. There was an intoxicating challenge in marshalling an argument and putting it across in a manner designed to convince an audience of my case. In my studies, I had been concerned with the laws of physics and chemistry and the structure of objects. Now I had to master the laws of logic and rhetoric and the structure of argument. They are skills that seem to have served me well both in my career in business and in my service in public affairs, and I commend them to others who are setting out on their paths in either or both directions.

As we toured the church halls and school rooms of Ann Arbor and district in 1949, there was one issue that was raised time and time again – the future of the recently born state of Israel and the Arabs' attitudes towards it. I little realised as I stood before a small audience putting the case for an independent state of Palestine that this was to be an issue that would cross and recross my life as I advanced through my career. Or that, even today, the question would still seem as far from resolution as ever.

*   *   *

When I sailed for the United States in August 1947, it was from a Palestine which had been ruled under Britain's mandate since 1922. As I crossed the Atlantic, the idea that within months an independent state of Israel would be created never crossed my mind. I was at the University of Pennsylvania in November when the United Nations passed resolution 181 which paved the way for the creation of Israel on the expiry of the British mandate on 15 May 1948.

In the months that followed, as I unhappily decamped from Philadelphia for Austin, and then back north to Ann Arbor, I was so absorbed with my own travels and troubles that I had only limited time to give any attention to the issue. But I was deeply concerned by what was happening on the very doorstep of my homeland in Jordan while I was far away. In those days, it wasn't even easy to get news by telephone. I had to rely on the newspapers and the occasional letter from home to find out what was happening.

The news was certainly disquieting. The United Nations had drawn up a plan to apportion the land of Palestine in order to create two sovereign states – Israel and Palestine. The plan had created fury in the Arab world. Because I was not living in the Middle East at the time, I can only imagine the foment it created in the cities and villages from what people who were there have told me and what I have read. I can imagine that it would have aroused deep anger and fuelled passions. Perhaps that was a source of the problems that followed. When passions are inflamed, reason flies out of the window. Four thousand miles away, I also experienced those passions, but later came to understand the need for a rationalist approach to what was, at root, unquestionably a deeply emotional issue for all who were living it.

*   *   *

It made no sense at any level to go to war in 1948 – not least because the Jewish forces were larger in number than those of the Arab states that opposed them. The Jewish military numbered around 74,000 compared with the Arab League's Jaysh Al-Inqadh (Army of Deliverance), a hastily assembled body of 5000 volunteers from different countries, which proved ineffective. To this small force should be added the armies of individual Arab states. Probably the best of these militarily was Jordan's Arab Legion, which consisted of 7500 officers and men organised into three mechanised regiments and 16 infantry companies. Some other Arab countries also committed forces, but in most cases held back significant reserves to deal with contingencies in their own territories. Whatever the exact numbers, it is clear that the Arab states started the war at a disadvantage – whether measured in numbers, training or equipment.

Indeed, many among the Jewish forces were battle-hardened, having seen active service in the British or American armies during the Second

World War. And, with the exception of the Arab Legion, they were better led. Had passions not been so inflamed and had reason been allowed in, Arab opinion should have seen these self-evident truths and called for different action.

But, with the exception of a small minority of enlightened Arab opinion, it did not. I believe that the Palestinians should have taken the opportunity of the first truce that started on 11 June 1948, and of sympathetic opinion in the United States and Britain, to start negotiating for a just peace and an overall solution to the issue. I knew at first hand that there were plenty of people who were sympathetic to the Arab case within the United States. But the leaders of the Arab world did not seek to appraise their situation rationally or proceed in a constructive way.

The Israelis made good use of the period of truce to obtain further military equipment and supplies, and ensure that the Arabs were not re-equipped and re-supplied. It became clear at a meeting of Arab prime ministers in Cairo that the truce would not be extended and negotiations would not proceed. The truce was broken on 9 July. The Israelis took the initiative, and in ten days of fighting they made substantial additional territorial gains. By the second truce, which started on 18 July, less than half the territory allocated to the Arabs in the UN Partition Plan remained in their hands.

Winston Churchill once described Russia as a 'riddle wrapped in a mystery inside an enigma'. The history of Palestine and Israel has become a tragedy wrapped in a disaster inside an injustice. The tragedy is the failure to establish two states that can live peacefully side by side. The disaster was the Jewish Holocaust, which created the climate in which the United Nations moved so swiftly to sanction the creation of Israel without thinking through the consequences for the other peoples of Palestine. The injustice was the Balfour Declaration, which promised a homeland for the Jews without defining precisely those safeguards for the native Palestinians that should have accompanied its generous promise.

Growing up in Transjordan in the 1930s and 1940s, we had discussed the unease which our relatives in Palestine felt as Jewish immigration shifted the balance of population and, critically, land ownership. When we went on our summer holidays to Ramallah – and travelled to other towns such as Jerusalem and Jaffa – we met and spoke to people who could see what was happening at first hand and were deeply troubled about the future.

I believe that what fuelled the anger was the failure of the British authorities to consult with the local Palestinian population about the implications of the Balfour Declaration. True, the Palestinians (and indeed the whole Arab world) were opposed in principle to the idea of the Jewish homeland in Palestine enshrined in the Declaration. But if there had been more consultation, I feel certain that the British would have come to see some of the practical consequences of increased Jewish immigration. That could have encouraged the authorities to give more practical weight to the important qualification that Balfour had added to the original draft of his Declaration – '…it being clearly understood that nothing shall be done which may prejudice the civil and religious rights of existing non-Jewish communities in Palestine…'

As it was, the civil and religious rights of native Palestinians were steadily eroded. It is difficult to understand now why the Palestinians and their allies in the Arab world rejected the notion of a state based on the land allocated by the United Nations. It was, they argued, their land, so why should they give up any of it? So it was not surprising that while the Jewish leadership had accepted the plan in principle (although arguing about some of the detail of the land apportion-ment), the Arabs rejected the idea in its entirety.

But was it wise to go to war? By the time hostilities started formally on 15 May 1948, the day after the British mandate ended – there had been isolated skirmishes in the weeks leading up to the withdrawal – I was safely registered as a student at the University of Michigan. There were other Arab students with whom I could share my hopes and fears. And, as the war progressed, there were more fears than hopes. From what I could gather from the newspapers and the letters we received from family and friends, the war went badly for Arab forces from the beginning.

Egyptian, Syrian, Iraqi, Lebanese and Jordanian forces had entered Palestine. But it was only the Jordanian forces, the Arab Legion, commanded by John Bagot Glubb, who distinguished themselves.

Glubb concentrated his forces in what became known as the West Bank, and managed to expel Jewish forces from East Jerusalem, the Old City. The result was that when the Jordan–Israel armistice was signed on 3 April 1949, more than 2000 square miles and 400,000 Palestinians were incorporated into Jordanian territory.

As we debated among ourselves in the Arab Club at Michigan, we tried to find answers to what had gone wrong. I believe that the first mistake made by the Arab world was to underestimate the impact on Jewish feeling, and on world opinion, of the Holocaust. Back in the 1940s, I know there were those in the Arab world who questioned whether it had been as bad as we now know it was. In effect, the Holocaust changed the psychology of the Jewish people, made them think in a different way, added a sense of urgency – even of desperation – to their search for a homeland. Arab opinion simply didn't understand the deep visceral emotions that the experience had unleashed in the Jewish psyche.

The point that the Arab world should have been making – indeed, the point those of us in the Arab Club did make whenever we got the opportunity to address a local organisation in Ann Arbor – was that you don't right an injustice by creating a second injustice. It was an injustice for one group of people to move into a country and take away the homes, land and livelihoods of another group of people. Arabs had lived in and occupied Palestine, in one guise or another, for more than 1500 years. Historical longevity, let alone the rule of international law, made this their land.

But, if under the force of international opinion, there was to be a compromise, it had to be agreed on the basis of reason. Perhaps that was expecting too much of an Arab world that was greatly provoked, and many of whose legitimate concerns had been brushed aside. But an Arab world that in earlier centuries had produced great thinkers such as Al-Kindi – 'We should not be ashamed to acknowledge truth from whatever source it comes to us…' – should have tried harder to rise to the challenge of finding a reasoned solution.

For those of us in the Arab Club who wanted our governments to take a more enlightened approach, it was infuriating. And it made it more difficult to put the case for the kind of fair deal for Palestine that reasonable-minded people were willing to listen to. Instead, the issue was allowed to drift into successive rounds of bitterness and violence, further polarising opinion on both sides.

And, for me, the biggest tragedy is that the Arab world lost twice over. We lost the war and we lost our democratic societies. Those of us who combined a liberal view with hard-headed realism recognised that the Arab nations had lost the war because of the balance of military power that existed between Arabs and Jews. We needed to learn that lesson and move forward by building free democratic Arab societies that would live peacefully alongside the infant Israel.

But that's not what happened in the years ahead. The majority in the Arab world thought their armies had lost because the leaders of their governments were incompetent and corrupt. It only needed more committed and staunchly patriotic governments to succeed. It was a twisted view of the notion of patriotism, but in country after country in the Middle East it prevailed. In the next few years, dictators who repressed the Arab enlightenment and crushed democratic institutions swept to power in Syria, Egypt and Iraq, among other countries. But that was a problem for the future.

As the war ended in 1949, I tried to put the tragedy from my mind and concentrate on my studies. I was successfully completing my bachelor's degree and moving on to my master's. I little realised that the Palestinian issue was to surface and resurface throughout my life, like an old piece of wreckage bobbing in a stormy sea.

CHAPTER 6

The key to Yale

I f I'd fallen asleep on the train I guess I'd never have got into Yale. It had been a long day, a frustrating day. I was tired. The train was rocking gently. And I felt so sleepy...

It was 1951 and I was determined to study for a doctorate in engineering at one of the Ivy League universities on the east coast. After completing my master's at Michigan, I had spent several months doing some preparatory work for a doctorate. My original thoughts had been to pursue that at Michigan, where I'd already been successful and had lived happily.

Then, in the summer of 1951, I returned to the Middle East for the first time in four years and saw my family again. It was a moving and emotional experience. People change in four years. And while you may not notice the tiny day-by-day changes when you live closely with them, I returned to see four years of changes in one instant. My family may have looked older, but they were still the people that I'd grown up with and loved, and within minutes it was as though I'd never been away.

The main reason for my return was to attend the graduation of my older brother, Jamal, from the medical school at AUB, having finally completed the lengthy course with great success. He had achieved his own ambition as well as my father's, of seeing a doctor in the family.

Returning to AUB was also quite a life-changing experience for me. I met many students who had been studying in the United States or who planned to do so. Some of them intended to live and work outside the region when they completed their courses. But the activist, not to mention the Arab nationalist in me, convinced me that this approach wasn't in the best interests of the Arab world. It was certainly right that we, as young Arabs, should go abroad to study, because that meant we could attend the world's best universities and acquire world-class knowledge and skills. But I also believed deeply that if the Middle East was to develop and prosper into a set of democratic and liberal independent societies, it was incumbent on those who had been privileged to receive the best education abroad to return and use their knowledge and skills in their own region.

So by the end of my all-too-short stay in Jordan and Lebanon in that summer of 1951, I had become convinced of two things. The first was that I definitely wanted to study at one of the best universities in America, but that when I had completed my doctorate I would return and work in the Middle East. The second was that I wanted to form a new association for Arab students in the United States with the aim of providing a forum that would encourage some of the brightest Arab brains not only to consider how we could build a better Middle East but to encourage those who were studying in the States to return to the region afterwards and contribute their skills to its professions, business and public affairs.

Which brings me to that sleepy train journey. I had flown back to New York with a promise from my father to pay me $2000 a year while I completed a doctorate. I decided I would enrol at an Ivy League university. So, after landing in New York, I took the train to Boston and asked the first cab driver I could find to take me to Harvard. It was my intention to go straight to the school of engineering on the campus and seek to enrol.

Looking back, I suppose it was a bold, even daring, ploy to fly four thousand miles, walk in off the street, and expect one of the best universities in the world to accept me with open arms and enrol me for a doctorate. And, of course, my plan failed.

I suppose I should have checked first that Harvard had a school of engineering. I'd assumed that such a great university would. But in 1951 it didn't. My journey had been wasted, and now I faced the prospect of the tiring trek back to New York, where I would have to check into a cheap hotel and decide on my next move. So it wasn't surprising that my head started to nod forward as I was lulled into sleep by the rocking of the train as it made its endless journey across New England.

We seemed to be stopping at every town on the route. Just as I started to nod off, I'd be woken by the conductor shouting out the name of the next stop. Providence, Westerly, New London, New Haven…

New Haven? Suddenly, I was wide awake. Wasn't Yale in New Haven? It was. And I hadn't realised the train would be stopping there. Hastily, I gathered my luggage together, threw open the door and leapt out of the carriage. Within seconds, I was standing on the platform of New Haven Union Station, watching the rear-lights of the New York train disappear into the distance – and wondering, anxiously, whether Yale had an engineering faculty either.

Outside the station, I climbed into the first taxi on the rank and asked to be taken to the engineering faculty at Yale. The driver didn't look blank or throw up his hands and laugh or roll his eyes and exclaim: 'You must be kidding!' A good sign. We took off through the streets of New Haven.

And, yes, Yale had a school of engineering (although it has one no longer). At the reception desk, a kind lady directed me to the dean's office. I don't suppose the dean had many potential doctoral candidates arriving on his doorstep unannounced but, yes, he would see me. He heard me out, looked at my academic achievements – I had all the relevant certificates and letters of recommendation with me – and then gave me the bad news: Yale accepted only five doctoral chemical engineering candidates each year, and all the places had been offered.

But there was a glimmer of good news. One of the potential candidates hadn't yet accepted his offer. He had another two days in which to do so. But if I called up three days later – and if the other candidate hadn't accepted – I would be on the course. It seemed a big 'if', but it was better than nothing.

The dean advised me to return to Ann Arbor, where I did have a place in the postgraduate school. It was a long, tense, thoughtful journey. It's not in my nature to want to stand in the way of other people achieving their ambitions. After all, we all deserve a fair chance to grab life's prizes. But I was hoping against hope that the late candidate, for one reason or another, would not be taking up his place. The following days were torture. I was so preoccupied with whether or not I was going to be offered the place.

On the third day, I picked up the telephone and nervously called up the dean. His secretary answered the phone, and there was a delay before she put me through, perhaps only a few seconds. It seemed like a year. Then I heard his voice: 'Mr Shair?'

'Yes.'

'I'm glad you called. As it happens, we do have a place free. Will you accept it?'

*   *   *

The journey back to New Haven, via New York, was in stark contrast to my journey from the university town a few days earlier. I made it with great relish and joy. The dean had provided me with the opportunity I craved, and I was determined to pursue it with vigour.

Within days of my arrival at Yale I'd completed the registration formalities and found myself some excellent lodgings in Whitney Avenue, the main street that runs north through New Haven towards the adjacent city of Hamden. Stepping into Yale – especially into Old Campus through Phelps Gate – was like stepping back into part of history. The university had been founded in 1701, and moved to New Haven (from Killingworth, Connecticut) 15 years later. Down the centuries, it had turned out a host of prominent alumni in the world of politics, literature, science and, most important for me, engineering.

This last category included Eli Whitney, who had invented the 'cotton gin', the machine that first mechanised the production of cotton fibre, and thus became one of the cornerstones of the industrial revolution. Whitney also established a gun factory in New Haven, where Samuel Colt invented the first automatic revolver. Whitney had given his name to the street in which I'd found lodgings. So I was thrilled to be living in this city as a member of its most famous academic institution. And, after my abortive experience at Harvard, not a little relieved.

Yale, I discovered, was like an academic island in the bustling, industrial city of New Haven which, by 1951, had settled into a long period of slow decline. Today, its population is 40,000 lower than the 160,000 when I was a student. And I wouldn't recognise much of the city's downtown area, which was demolished in the late 1950s and early 1960s in one of the first major urban renewal projects in America.

The core of a doctorate in any subject is a piece of original research submitted as a thesis. But at Yale, before you were allowed to embark upon your research you had to spend a year on advanced engineering courses designed to take you beyond what you'd learnt for both your bachelor's and master's degrees. So, at the end of the first year I faced more exams on the courses I'd studied during the year.

But worse, I found, was in store. Apart from passing the exams on the courses, you also had to sit a daunting set of papers called the 'comprehensive'. I had been so busy with my courses and, as I shall relate, setting up another Arab student organisation that it was barely two weeks before the comprehensive that I fully turned my attention to it. I suppose I'd regarded it as a mere extension of the exams we were having on the year's course. But when I questioned my tutor about it, I was horrified to learn that it was more. Much more. I was to be examined on everything I had learnt – or was supposed to have learnt – at AUB and the University of Michigan as an undergraduate student.

I'd hardly digested this unwelcome news when my tutor then informed me that the comprehensive would be spread over a whole week. Starting on Monday, there would be a gruelling eight-hour written paper every day except Wednesday. (They graciously gave you a half hour-break at lunchtime for a sandwich.) The first day was what was known as a 'closed-book' day. That meant you had to rely solely on the information in your head. On the other days, you could visit the library to look up information, and do pretty much what you wanted – as long as you delivered the paper by the eight-hour deadline.

I left my tutor's study in a daze. How could I revise nearly five years' work in two weeks? Was it possible? Could I even try? What really worried me were my tutor's parting words. The comprehensive was marked on a simple pass-or-fail basis. And I had to pass in order to embark on my research. If I failed, I was out. Unlike many graduate schools at other universities, at Yale there was no second chance.

So it wasn't surprising that, two weeks later, I entered the examination room for the first day of the comprehensive with a sense of foreboding. It was the closed-book day. All day I laboured painfully on the paper, and by the end of the afternoon I left the examination hall close to despair. I was certain I had failed. I felt I had done somewhat better the next day, but was it good enough to avoid a second failure? Wednesday, the day off, was miserable as I waited for Thursday and, no doubt, the paper that would seal my fate. I could not possibly fail three of the four papers and expect to pass overall. But by Thursday evening, I was moderately happier. I felt that I had just achieved a pass on the paper. And I ended the week with a flourish, completing a paper I was certain was at A+ grade.

But that weekend, as I looked back on the whole week, my spirits sank again. Could one good paper outweigh one failure and two marginal passes to deliver a pass overall? I had my doubts. The university authorities seemed rather vague about when the results would be provided. Perhaps in about three weeks, they said.

That was a terrible three weeks for me. I went over the papers again and again in my mind trying to work out whether I'd passed or failed. I hardly slept, and when I did fall into a fitful doze my rest was troubled by bad dreams. I had been told that if you passed, your name was pinned up on the engineering faculty noticeboard. As a doctoral student, I had a key to the building. And as the time for the results to be published arrived, I would sneak into the building at night to look at the board. I used to light a match – I smoked cigarettes heavily in those days – and peer at the board looking for the announcement. Nothing.

Strange behaviour? Possibly. I suppose I didn't want anybody to see my reaction, especially if I had failed and my name wasn't posted.

I knew I wouldn't be able to hide my devastation, and I didn't want to inflict it on my fellow students. I was scared of myself and what I would do. I was really in a state of fear. And when a fear like this has taken you over, you don't think rationally.

But I could see the consequences of failure lying ahead. I would have to leave America and return to Jordan to face my family. The latest gold my father had invested in my mind would have been wasted. I would creep back in disgrace. What would make it worse was the fact that I had turned down a senior job in the Jordanian government in order to come to America. Now I would be returning with my tail between my legs, hunting for such work as anybody would be willing to give me.

As I lay awake during the long watches of the night, I formulated a plan. I had to know what to do if I failed. When I failed...I had almost convinced myself. I would kill myself. I would commit suicide. It would be better than the total humiliation of returning in disgrace to face my father, my family and my friends.

The following night, a Friday, I made my last nocturnal visit to the engineering faculty noticeboard. My name was not on the board. I returned to my lodgings in a grim mood wondering whether I could face my friends the following morning.

A group of us used to meet every Saturday for a martini followed by lunch. We would take it in turns to visit each others' houses and mix the cocktails. It was a pleasant way to spend the first day of the weekend. But on this occasion, I wondered whether I could endure it. On the other hand, I was certain that the results would be published during the following week. And if I'd failed, and carried out my suicide pact with myself, this would be the last time I would see them. With a heavy heart, I tramped over to Prospect Street, on the other side of the university, where they lived.

I was the last to arrive, and tried to put on a cheerful face as I entered. 'Congratulations.' The word echoed from all corners of the room.

'You mean me?' I looked around confused. Stunned might be a better word.

'Of course we mean you. Haven't you been to the engineering faculty this morning? The results were posted on the bulletin board. You've passed.'

The martini that followed was a large one. And the best I've ever tasted.

*   *   *

I looked forward eagerly to embarking on my research. And I did so from an enviable position of financial strength. When I had been accepted at Yale, I'd been offered a fellowship if I was willing to conduct my research in the area of the peaceful use of nuclear power. Six years earlier, the world had witnessed its destructive capacity at Hiroshima and Nagasaki. Now, in 1951, there was a drive to discover its commercial uses, and much of the research was in the very early stages. (As an indication of how early, the world's first electricity-producing fast-breeder nuclear reactor at Dounreay, in the north of Scotland, didn't achieve 'criticality' until May 1958.) In any event, the bottom line was that they were willing to award me a fellowship worth $2000 a year for the duration of my studies.

By the way, they said, would you also be interested in taking on a post of teaching assistant? Tell me more, I said. It turned out that they would pay me a further $1000 a year and exempt me from tuition fees − another $700 a year in those days − if I'd take the post, which simply involved a few hours a week, mostly helping undergraduates with their work in the laboratories. And this was on top of the $2000 a year my father had generously offered me. (I decided it might not be a shrewd financial move from my point of view to share my good news with him.)

The result was that in my first year at Yale I had an income of $5000 (and no fees), with $4000 a year for the subsequent years, after I gave up the teaching-assistant role to spend more time on my research and setting up the Arab student organisation. In those days, it was perfectly possible for a young single man to live comfortably on $2000 a year. So, for a student, I had attained a condition of modest prosperity.

As the new academic year of 1952 started, I buckled down to my research. It concerned the polymerisation of acetylene by gamma rays.

This is not the place to go into it in any detail. (I wrote a 600-page thesis on the subject if you're desperate to know more.) But the research involved many long hours in a well-equipped laboratory, firing gamma rays at material and measuring the impact made, then going back to the theory to see whether the measurements reinforced or made a nonsense of it.

It was exacting work, and also involved me in making a detailed literature search of other relevant research. In order to do this, I had to study two of three languages from French, German and Russian to a level that would enable me to read technical literature. I chose French – which I sailed through in the exam – and German, which I failed at the first attempt but subsequently passed.

As the deadline for handing in my thesis approached, I stepped up the number of hours I spent in the lab. I needed a 24-hour session to write the abstract – a summary that fronted the main document. I remember surviving through the long hours on a diet of Italian cheese (Italian immigrants had flocked to New Haven in earlier years) and bread. I kept awake by drinking coffee brewed up on a Bunsen burner.

How far my work advanced the peaceful use of nuclear energy is difficult for me to say. I can't recall any direct practical use of it, but new knowledge is not necessarily useless because it has no immediate application. All knowledge goes into an intellectual bank that future generations can draw on, and I would like to think subsequent students have used my own work as a building-block in their own research.

It is a sadness to me that although I have obtained three degrees I have never been able to attend any of the graduation ceremonies to collect them. So when the envelope bearing the certificate proclaiming that I was now Doctor Kamal A. Shair arrived, when I was back in Beirut in 1956, it should have been a proud moment. But it felt like something of an anticlimax.

*   *   *

Apart from studying for a doctorate, the other main factor that had drawn me back to the United States was my passionate desire to form a country-wide organisation of Arab students. The previous club had been limited to the University of Michigan. As soon as I'd settled in at Yale and got my work underway, I made a start.

I'd developed plenty of useful contacts in my years at Michigan. Other contacts I knew from my time at AUB or from my life in Jordan. I started telephoning around, sounding out people with the idea. Many, I was delighted to learn, were as enthusiastic as I was.

But we needed help to get what we called the Organisation of Arab Students in the United States off the ground. It came from a most welcome source. Dorothy Thompson, the journalist whose thrice-weekly column in the *New York Herald Tribune* was syndicated to two hundred other papers across the States, was a household name. As a foreign correspondent, she had been the first journalist kicked out of Nazi Germany by Hitler. In 1939, *Time* magazine had named her one of the two most influential women in America (the other being the then president's wife, Eleanor Roosevelt). Thompson had inspired Katherine Hepburn's character in the 1942 film *Woman of the Year*. In her earlier years, Thompson had supported the Zionist cause. But as she saw the damage it had inflicted on Palestine, she changed her views and, in 1951, helped found the American Friends of the Middle East. (The organisation thrives today as Amideast, headquartered in Washington DC.)

The Friends, as I shall call them (and as they became to us in more ways than one), were willing to help both with funds and in enabling us to acquire office accommodation to work from. We opened a small office in Madison Avenue, New York and set about recruiting members. I started by travelling to Michigan, where I had most contacts. We had an encouraging founding meeting, which attracted about thirty members. It elected a working committee of three, with me as president. We decided to organise a convention, which would bring together Arab students from all over the United States to discuss issues of concern in the Middle East. In the months that followed I clocked up thousands of miles as I travelled the country – to Austin, Chicago, Boston and other cities where universities had high numbers of Arab students.

I also spent time cultivating prominent Arab emissaries to the United States. Those that helped us included the distinguished Professor

Charles Malek, who had gained a doctorate in philosophy at Harvard and who'd been one of a committee – it included the ever-present Eleanor Roosevelt and French Nobel Prize winner René Cassin – who had drafted the United Nations 1948 Universal Declaration of Human Rights. Others who helped us included Fayez Sayegh, Malek's senior adviser, Abdallah Bakr, the Iraqi ambassador to the United States, and Abdul Khaleq Hassouneh, the secretary-general of the Arab League. Some provided useful financial assistance, and we raised several thousand dollars to fund the organisation.

By the summer of 1952, we were ready to hold our first week-long convention. The University of Michigan offered free board and lodging for delegates attending and accommodation in which to hold our meetings. In the weeks before the convention, we had been busy in our Madison Avenue office recruiting people to present papers on the different topical issues – political, economic, cultural, social and so on – facing the Middle East. It meant that when the 350 delegates convened, we were able to break into working groups and discuss the topics on the back of some useful original research. Looking back on those discussions, I find it fascinating that many of the issues that we were discussing more than fifty years ago are still live subjects for debate in the Middle East – the creation of an integrated Arab economy, the need for social and political justice and, of course, the future of Palestine.

At the end of the week, the working groups reported back. The leader of each group wrote a summary of its findings, and we collected them together in a book published as *The Young Arab Speaks* with the aid of the ever-helpful American Friends of the Middle East. I wrote an introduction in which I summarised the main findings of the convention and argued that in the 'cold-war' world that was developing – with sharp ideological splits between the West and the Soviet bloc – Arab countries should adopt a position of 'active neutrality'. The principle behind active neutrality was that Arab nations should not align themselves formally with either the West or the Soviet bloc but should take an active position on the issues that concerned them. As I said in my speech to the convention (and in the book), 'From an ideological viewpoint, it is the only unprejudiced approach which judges each case only in as much as it increases or decreases the prospects of world peace'. Active neutrality, I argued, 'is the only attitude that enables the Arab to judge whether or not a certain issue is favourable to the process of achieving the goals of the Arab countries themselves'. I added that

> whenever the world is in a state of tension due to a conflict between the two major powers, a tremendous vacuum is created, and this vacuum has to be filled by a nation or group of nations that will stabilise the precarious balance of power. The countries of the Middle East, together with some countries in Africa and south-east Asia, are the only countries which geographically, historically and culturally qualify to fill this vacuum.

The convention elected a new committee to carry the work of the organisation forward. It contained people who were to go on to distinguish themselves throughout the Middle East. They included Saeb Jaroudi, who became a finance minister in Lebanon and president of the Arab Fund for Economic and Social Development, Muhsin Mehdi, who became a professor of Middle East studies at Harvard, and Ziad Shawaf, who became a Saudi Arabian ambassador. There was also Bahgat Al-Tawil from Egypt and Naima Shamma from Iraq. I remained president, and was re-elected again at our second convention, held at Earlham College in Richmond, Indiana in the summer of 1953. But a few weeks later, the pressure of work for my PhD was mounting, and I decided I had to bow out.

Looking back on it, I believe we largely succeeded in one of our key objectives – to persuade well-educated Arabs to return and use their knowledge and skills in the Middle East. In the years that followed, as I was building Dar Al-Handasah, I frequently ran into people I had first got to know while I was helping to build the Organisation of Arab Students. It was heartening that the work had been worthwhile.

And, as it turned out, not bad for business, either.

*   *   *

In 1955, I returned to the Middle East after spending most of the previous eight years in the United States. I did not return alone.

In 1952, I had met my future wife, Laura. It happened like this. One of our aims in the Organisation of Arab Students was to put American citizens of Arab origin in touch with their language and culture. To this end, we organised Arabic classes for those Arab Americans who'd never learnt the language. Laura was one of my students. Her parents had emigrated from Lebanon to the United States and Laura had been born there.

We were married on 3 January 1953 at Trinity Church on New Haven Green, the centre of the town's original settlement. My closest friend, Saeb Jaroudi, who I'd worked closely with in the Organisation of Arab Students, was best man. I'd been worried about the fact that he would be a Muslim in an Anglican church. But Saeb went to meet the minister and so charmed him that there was no difficulty.

Laura's sister, Rose, was her matron of honour, and she was supported at the ceremony by members of her family. Four thousand miles away, members of my family weren't able to attend. I had cabled them with the great news and received telegraphic congratulations in reply.

We held a wedding breakfast at the Sage Grill, New Haven's best restaurant, and then left on a honeymoon of sorts. I say 'of sorts' because we went to Washington DC, where I had a number of meetings connected with my work for the Organisation of Arab Students. I can't honestly claim that the new Mrs Shair was entirely happy with the romantic possibilities of our honeymoon destination. Nor with the news that, because he was involved in some of the meetings, Saeb would be coming along with us.

But in any event, there was only time for the briefest of honeymoons. After three days, we returned to New Haven, where Laura and I settled into married life. My bachelor apartment in Whitney Avenue wouldn't suit the two of us, so we moved somewhere larger. It was a pleasant enough apartment in a good district. I couldn't say the same for the landlady, who was plain nasty. When, 10 months later, our first daughter, Leila, was born, the landlady made it perfectly plain she didn't want any babies on the premises and threw us out.

Worse was to follow. Although we'd paid the rent with prompt regularity, we hadn't been quite as meticulous as we should have been about keeping the receipts. The landlady claimed we owed back rent. And I'd thrown away my bank statements which could have proved that we had. I had to get the bank to produce the cancelled cheques to settle the matter. It was a lesson I learnt – and never forgot – about being very careful in accounting for expenditure, and which stood me in good stead when I started my business.

Out on the streets, Laura and I discovered it wasn't easy to rent a good-quality apartment with a babe-in-arms. Eventually, we found somewhere suitable in a more down-market neighbourhood of New Haven. The apartment wasn't as classy, but the landlady, a Mrs Santiago, couldn't have been nicer. When our first son, Abdo, came along the following year, we stayed in Mrs Santiago's apartment. In fact, it was our base until we headed back to the Middle East.

*   *   *

The autumn of 1955 marked the end of eight years' living in the United States. It was sad to leave – America had given me so much – but I was looking forward to returning to the Middle East with my family.

We travelled back by air via Britain. I had never visited Britain before, and I wanted to see the country. It also provided a good opportunity to meet my brother Jamal who was, by now, pursuing further medical studies at Cambridge University. The visit provided me with a small and unexpected opportunity to make a contribution to British political debate.

Jamal had become a committed socialist, and had got to know a number of people in the British Labour Party. Every autumn, the main British political parties each hold a conference, usually in a seaside resort. It was October, and Jamal was planning to attend Labour's conference, which was being held in Margate on the Kent coast. I remember it was bitterly cold, but I'm told British seaside resorts often are at that time of year.

However, I was more concerned with what was taking place inside the conference hall than strolling along the wind-swept promenade. Jamal had arranged for me to address one of the conference's fringe meetings on the Palestine issue. I was surprised that there was a full hall, and I gave them an uncompromising account of my views. I told them that the Allies had won the war in order to stop minorities being persecuted by the Nazis. If the persecution of minorities continued – whether they be Jews or Palestinians – that wouldn't be consistent with the sacrifices many had made to win the war. I was given a generous round of applause and left pleased that I'd made at least a small mark on a party that aspired to form Britain's government (although they were not to do so for another nine years).

After a few days, we left Britain for the final leg of our journey back to Jordan. What a great homecoming that was going to be. My own family hadn't met Laura, let alone our two children. And I would be stepping off the plane as Dr Kamal Shair, having fulfilled all my academic ambitions. But our carefully choreographed arrival didn't go quite as I had hoped. The plane hit bad turbulence and one of the children was sick over my suit. I managed to scrub it clean in the washbasin of the plane's lavatory. But by the time we landed, it seemed to have shrunk several sizes.

So I found myself waddling down the steps of the aircraft wearing a pair of trousers so tight they wouldn't have disgraced Elvis Presley, the new sensation who was about to burst upon an unsuspecting world.

CHAPTER 7

Teaching with business in mind

T he Middle East to which I returned had seen much turmoil during the eight years I had been living in the United States. In country after country, one regime had followed another as a result of violent uprisings, assassinations or coups.

It had all started in Syria in 1949, when Colonel Husni Al-Zaim overthrew the constitutional government that had held power since the country had gained its independence from France three years earlier. Colonel Al-Zaim established the first of the many military dictatorships from which the country was to suffer in the decades that followed.

In July 1952, King Farouk of Egypt was ousted in the so-called 'free officers' coup, which turned the country into a republic under the presidency of General Muhammad Naguib. Any hopes that Egypt might develop itself into a beacon of liberal democracy for the Middle East died with that coup.

Lebanon, where I had spent two years at AUB, was the exception to the rule. Bishara Al-Khoury guided Lebanon to independence in 1943. At the end of his term as the Republic's first president, Al-Khoury sought and succeeded in gaining a second term, contrary to the constitution. In September 1952, midway through that unconstitutional term, a general strike paralysed the country and Al-Khoury's government fell. Although the new president, Camille Chamoun, retained an elected parliament, it was a reminder that in Middle Eastern countries respect for the constitution had not yet taken root. At least in Lebanon the 1952 strikes showed it was possible to correct unconstitutional acts through peaceful protest rather than armed force.

My native Jordan had seen no less dramatic changes during my absence. Jordan's parliamentary institutions were originally established in 1928. (These institutions, and my participation in them as a senator in the upper house, are the subject of chapter 17.) For the first time, a parliament representing both the East and West banks had been elected in 1950. Since Jordan and Israel signed their 1949 armistice, the West Bank – which had been part of the territory under the British Palestinian mandate – had been under Jordanian military administration. West Bank leaders held conventions in Jericho and Nablus that unanimously called for unification with Jordan. In response, Jordan's electoral law was modified to provide equal representation in the elected lower house for deputies from the West and East Banks.

Following the election, a joint session of both houses of the new parliament formalised the union of the East and West Banks. Significantly, the unanimously adopted resolution included a provision – inserted at the instigation of Anwar Nusseibeh, a Cambridge University law graduate who represented Jerusalem – that an objective of united Jordan would be to defend the rights of Palestinian Arabs and that the union should not prejudice the creation of an independent Palestine. The union resolution approved by the joint session was immediately carried to King Abdullah, who signed it at five in the afternoon of the same day and then ordered an immediate 21-gun salute to celebrate the occasion.

The influence of deputies from the West Bank in the Jordanian parliament proved to be significant, generally enhancing the quality of parliamentary proceedings and the trend towards more democracy. Only Britain, Iraq and Pakistan immediately recognised the union. Jordan's ambition to join the United Nations was delayed by this lack of international recognition. But, with time, other nations gave *de facto* recognition. The East and West Banks enjoyed a workable union in spite of some tensions for 17 years, when the West Bank was occupied by Israel during the 1967 war. Although large numbers of refugees were absorbed in the aftermath of the 1948–49 war, there is no question that Jordan benefited greatly from the generally well-educated West-Bankers and the diversity of skills available in the West Bank.

Few were to realise at the time just how much impact the fate of the Palestinians would have on the state of Jordan in the years that followed the union of the East and West Banks. Nor was I to realise, as I observed these events from the United States, how much the issue of Palestine was to enter my own life.

Jordanians were to find out sooner than they expected just what an unpredictable cause they had embraced. In July 1951, King Abdullah visited Jerusalem to pay homage at his father's tomb and attend Friday prayers at the mosque. As he was about to step into the mosque, a young Palestinian – angered at the King's perceived complicity in the events leading to the creation of the state of Israel and the loss of Palestinian territory – emerged from the crowd of worshippers and killed him with a single shot to the head.

Abdullah's son, Talal, succeeded to the throne. Nobody doubted his good intentions or his patriotism, but for years he had been receiving treatment in Switzerland for a serious psychological disorder. After he assumed the throne, his mental illness became worse. The government set up a medical committee that included Jordanian and other Arab physicians. They submitted a report on the King's health that confirmed that his condition was serious. In August 1952, the Jordanian parliament, meeting in secret session, debated the medical report and decided he should be deposed. He was replaced by his eldest son, the 17-year-old Hussein, who was still a student at Harrow, the top English school that numbers Winston Churchill among its former pupils. Hussein reigned as regent – attending a crash-course on military science at the Royal Military College, Sandhurst, the British army's officer-training school – until his eighteenth birthday, when he acceded to the throne.

Despite these abrupt changes, I felt optimistic about Jordan's future. In the months before his mental health deteriorated, Talal had instructed his government to introduce a new constitution that had been drafted before King Abdullah's assassination. It made the government as a whole, and ministers individually, accountable to the elected lower house of parliament. Members of parliament from the West Bank introduced a number of amendments to the constitution designed to make it even more democratic. I had welcomed the news of these reforms as a significant step in turning Jordan in the direction of a constitutional monarchy with a free parliament.

So the Middle East in which I found myself living in 1955 was one which had seen rapid and violent change, but where there were some signs of hope in Lebanon and my native Jordan. What troubled me, despite the progress in Jordan, was that the region as a whole was heading in the wrong direction – away from freedom and democracy. And that presented me with a serious dilemma.

*   *   *

The dilemma I faced was this: while at Yale I had decided that I wanted to start a business in the Middle East. But in order to thrive, a business needs a stable political environment in which free enterprise is prized for the contribution it makes to the prosperity of society. In 1955, the countries in the Middle East where that could be said to be true were fast disappearing. In any event, business such as it existed in the Middle East outside the oil industry was largely a parochial affair. There were few, if any, native companies that were serious players on the global stage.

The other problem I faced arose from the fact that I was hoping to set up a consultancy business that would advise on a wide range of engineering issues. There were plenty of companies already doing that work in the Middle East but, without exception, they were foreign. There were native Middle Eastern consultants in engineering, but they were usually self-employed individuals who focused on particular specialisms such as structures, mechanical engineering or hydraulics. The kind of business I hoped to create would bring together many engineering specialisms under one roof and compete directly with those Western companies already offering similar services.

So, in fact, my dilemma was a double one – in which country to start the business and how to set about attracting other quality engineers who might want to be my partners. I settled the country question instantly. After Egypt had turned its back on liberal democracy, there was only one Middle Eastern country that, at the time, provided both the political stability and the business climate in which to start my enterprise: Lebanon. In the mid-fifties, Beirut was a bustling business city that rivalled some of those in Europe. Of course, I knew that even Lebanon had had its political problems. But I assumed that lingering tensions between rival religious and political factions were in the process of being reduced and eliminated. I never imagined the course those tensions were to take in the years ahead.

Lebanon had established a balance in its society that guaranteed stability and prosperity. I felt sure this balance would become deeply rooted in Lebanon, providing the country wasn't subjected to external forces from the volatile surrounding region. The balance among the diverse communities in Lebanon was delicate, but the republic was a beacon of democracy. As it turned out, the delicate balance in Lebanon was to be destroyed when the country became the victim of political interference from neighbouring countries that had turned their backs on democracy. Just the external forces I had feared.

My second dilemma was how to attract the kind of quality engineers I needed as partners if I was to establish an enterprise that would look credible when compared by potential clients with existing Western competitors. There was one place where I knew I could find a significant number of well-qualified engineers – my former *alma mater*, the American University of Beirut. AUB had had excellent professors when I'd been a student, and since then it had, in 1952, established a fully fledged School of Engineering and Architecture. I decided the way to make contact with the kind of academics I was seeking – so as to interest those of like mind in my proposition – was to join them.

So, in early 1956 I applied for a post as an assistant professor of engineering at AUB. I was accepted. But when I took up my post in July, I was somewhat surprised to be told that, even though this was my first year of university teaching, I would be the acting senior professor.

The permanent senior, Professor Robert W. Sloane, a physicist who specialised in electrical engineering and who'd originally come from Glasgow University, was taking a year's sabbatical back in his native Britain.

I was given a larger office than I'd expected and a secretary, and told to manage the department in addition to my regular teaching duties. Those duties primarily consisted of lecturing first-year students on the basic principles of engineering science. All students, whether they were going to specialise in architecture or mechanical, electrical or civil engineering, took a foundation course that focused on the essentials.

There were about a hundred students on the course, and I had to deliver a lecture to them three times a week at the appallingly early hour of eight in the morning. As I was rapidly to discover, it was not a good time to listen to a lecture. It is an even worse time to deliver one, after a hurried breakfast and then a lengthy trek to the other end of the huge AUB campus to find the lecture theatre.

I suppose it is in the nature of students throughout the ages to be mischievous and to test their teachers' patience to see how far they can go. Especially so when that teacher is young and in his first job. Mine were no exception. The first two or three lectures I delivered turned into something of a bear garden. Every time I turned to write something on the blackboard – this was in the days before sophisticated teaching aids such as electronic whiteboards – a small riot would break out behind me. I decided I had to put a stop to the problem. We had to teach our students in English, but after one particularly raucous outburst I turned, threw down my chalk and spoke to them in Arabic. I was angry and I can remember that furious little speech even today. 'I'm here for one purpose,' I told them.

> And that's to offer you something that, I hope, you'll find of value in your studies. It's up to you whether you do or don't want to learn – I'm not going to force you. But this is your first year and you have four years ahead of you. If you want to graduate in five years time, my strong advice to you is to listen. So let's not have any more of this stupid buzzing and childish behaviour every time my back is turned. I won't stand for it.

That put an end to the problem, and I learnt the lesson that it's important for a teacher to make an impact and assert authority on students at an early stage. Respect without some degree of authority from teachers simply does not happen. For my part, I believe that I did earn my students' respect. For a start, many of them found it refreshing to be taught by a young Arab. At that time, most of the other professors and assistant professors came from the United States or Britain. Secondly, I made a point of practising a genuine 'open-door' policy. If any student had a problem and wanted to discuss it privately, I'd be there for them. That's not to say I made life easy for them. I set tough examination papers and I know that some of the students struggled painfully with the questions, but most succeeded.

I suppose I was trying to put into practice ideas about education that I'd already formed from my own experiences at schools and universities. Education, more than any other single factor outside the family, makes people what they are. And whether students receive good or poor education depends on what they learn and, more importantly, how they learn it. I put it that way deliberately. I firmly believe that education should be a process of *learning* rather than a process of *teaching*. By that, I mean that education should never be authoritarian – laying down how pupils should think. From the earliest ages – right from nursery schools – pupils should be helped to discover ideas and develop their minds. They should be encouraged to discuss, to debate and to learn how rational argument works. Sadly, the opposite approach currently prevails in the Arab countries. It is something that will have to change if Arab states are to progress successfully into the modern world.

Yet my emphasis on learning through discussion and debate doesn't mean I don't believe students shouldn't be encouraged to aim high. Education is largely about raising students' aspirations – helping them to see that they can achieve even more than they think they can – so I have never believed it is helpful when teachers set standards that are too rigid. Of course, any educational establishment, whether it's a school or university, will have pupils of different abilities. That is all part of human nature. But education should be about ensuring that every pupil develops his or her ability to the very fullest. Lowering standards –

what's sometimes called 'dumbing down' – may give less able students the impression they have done well, but it is just that, an impression not a reality. Real achievement is about jumping the highest bar you can manage.

Imitation, it is said, is the sincerest form of flattery, but I believe caricature may sometimes not be far behind. At the end of my first year as an assistant professor, *Outlook*, the AUB students' newspaper 'rewarded' me by publishing a full-page cartoon of the young Assistant Professor Shair. I wouldn't say it's the greatest honour I've received, but it was certainly one of the nicest.

At the beginning of my second year at AUB – the academic year 1957–58 – Professor Sloane returned from his sabbatical. As a result, I ceased to be the acting senior professor in the engineering studies department. I lost my big office and my secretary. I also lost responsibility for delivering the lectures. Instead, I took on some of the tutorial work. The body of engineering science students was divided into tutorial groups of between twenty and thirty, in which assistant professors led discussions on lecture topics. During my two years as an assistant professor, I tutored students in all five years of the engineering course. I must say I found the fourth- and fifth-year students easier to teach because they were more mature. First-year students were always a problem – and, I guess, always will be the world over.

I was not sorry to lose responsibility for managing the engineering science department as, by the summer of 1956, I was already thinking about setting up a company. And some tough decisions lay ahead.

With brother Jamal (left). Both went on to study at the American University of Beirut.

above Salt in the 1930s when it was a small, sleepy town in what was then Transjordan.

below K. Shair (second in back from left) returns to the Middle East to celebrate his older brother Jamal's graduation (MD) from the American University of Beirut with immediate family (mother and father seated in centre), 1951.

above A typical Salt home in the 1930s.

below Beirut in the 1950s. Before the troubles in Lebanon, Beirut was hailed as the Paris of the Middle East.

above K. Shair (third from left) with American University of Beirut President Bayard Dodge (fifth from left) at a graduation ceremony (intermediate section), 1947.

left With classmates (fifth from right, front row) at the American University of Beirut, 1946/47.

opposite, top K. Shair (right, standing) chairs a meeting of the 1952 convention of the Organisation of Arab Students in the United States, a conference that focused on contemporary issues in the Middle East.

opposite, bottom At the 1952 convention with (from second right) Inayet Chichakli, Syria, Baghat Al-Tawil, Egypt, and an Iraqi graduate student.

Dar's offices in Beirut, pictured in the 1970s. The building has since been completely renovated but still houses some of Dar's head-office staff.

Dar's first partners (from left to right, top to bottom): Kamal Shair, Managing Partner; Robert Wakim, Architect; Mounir I. Nassar, Civil Engineer; Ghassan Klink, Architect; Marwan Mazhar, Roads Engineer; Nabil Nassar, Civil Engineer; Wahdan Oweis, Civil Engineer; George Yannieh, Civil Engineer; Samir Abu Rahmeh, Mechanical Engineer; Vladimir Choulika, Electrical Engineer; Sami Khoury, Architect.

opposite, top With Takieddin Solh in 1966. Solh was twice Lebanon's prime minister.

opposite, bottom With former Lebanese prime minister Rafik Hariri in 1983, receiving Lebanon's highest civil award: the Cedar Medal.

above The destruction of Beirut, August 1982. Thick smoke rising from the shoreline of the city, a result of military shelling during the Arab–Israeli war. Dar kept its offices open despite the fighting. (Photo by Dirck Halstead/Time Life Pictures/Getty Images.)

this page and opposite Beirut Central District before and after
reconstruction efforts. Following the cessation of hostilities in
1990, Dar masterplanned the Beirut Central District, which
was designed to serve a population of 300,000. The main
objective was to re-establish the destroyed business centre and
provide a social gathering point; it included a new transport
network, the renovation of buildings, the preservation of
archeological sites, marine protection works and comprehensive
infrastructure systems.

opposite, top
Meeting the late
King Hussein
of Jordan.

opposite, bottom
Meeting King
Abdullah II of
Jordan.

right Meeting
French president
Jacques Chirac.

below Meeting
US senator
George Mitchell.

Within half a generation Dar has offices across the globe and consults on structures that range from harbours to airports, from hospitals to hotels, from tunnels to bridges.

opposite Los Angeles Federal Courthouse, California.

above Dubai International Airport Expansion, United Arab Emirates.

right Four Seasons Hotel George V, Paris.

K. Shair makes the commencement address, American
University of Beirut, 2003.

CHAPTER 8

First steps in a business

In the early summer of 1956, I invited four of my colleagues at AUB for coffee. It was more than a social invitation. Much more.

I had been quietly sounding them out about my idea of setting up an engineering consultancy. They'd been making encouraging noises, but so far I'd received no firm commitments. Now it was crunch time. If my dream was to become a reality, I had to move my colleagues from vague talk to positive action. So I had a lot riding on that meeting.

Sitting round the table on that warm morning were some of the finest scientific brains in the Middle East. Professor Khalil Malouf was a specialist in hydraulics who'd gained his doctorate at Imperial College, London. He was older than the rest of us, and I considered him the 'wise man' of the group. Samir Thabet was a highly respected professor of chemistry. Later he went on to become AUB's provost. Nazih Taleb was a capable mathematician and structural engineer – so capable, in fact, that he'd been allowed the rare distinction of completing his doctorate at Princeton University in the United States without experimental work. Victor Andraous was an industrial engineer who also served as director of the Institute of Industrial Research in the Lebanon. As my speciality was chemical engineering, I thought that, with the others sitting round the table, we had most bases covered.

As I remember it, all of us bought into the idea that the Middle East was ripe for a truly Arab multi-disciplinary consultancy that could compete on equal terms with those Western enterprises that currently won all the big contracts. Certainly the activist in me wanted to do something, and I was impatient for action. The oil industry was developing fast throughout the region, making it a rich source of potential business. More than that, the revenues that oil brought to Middle Eastern governments meant they were able to contemplate the kind of development projects – roads, harbours, irrigation schemes, hospitals, schools and more – that lack of finance had precluded in the past. All these projects would need big-scale engineering consultancy. And, much as I deplored the dictatorial turn some governments in the region were taking, I couldn't deny the fact that most of the others were keen to demonstrate their mettle by spending on big infra-structure projects that proved they could deliver economic benefits to their populations.

So, sitting around the table, we debated the arguments, nodded our heads and agreed that our moment had come. What we had to decide was how to realise the opportunity. In a sense, we had one big advantage. We were all working professors or assistant professors at AUB earning salaries quite sufficient to enable us to keep body and soul together. The university was happy to see us embark on this entrepreneurial endeavour, believing rightly that the experience we gained would make us better professors. Running a consultancy would provide a commercial dimension to our academic knowledge. So, providing we launched the company alongside our academic work, the downside for us in terms of lost income was minimal.

But we still needed to raise some capital to start the business – to rent some premises and engage administrative staff. After much discussion, we agreed that the initial capital should be 25,000 Lebanese pounds. At the time, the exchange rate was 3.5 Lebanese pounds to the US dollar, so we were looking to raise just over $7000. However, we decided that half the sum should see us through the first six months and, if we needed more money, we would put in the other half later. So we each wrote out our cheques for $700 to make up the initial

$3500 capital. (In fact, we never did have to write a second cheque because, within six months, we were generating sufficient revenue to avoid the second half of the capital drawdown.)

The next item on the agenda was what to call ourselves. This also provoked much discussion, partly because we couldn't initially agree on whether to use an Arabic or English name. There were arguments on both sides. On the one hand, we were making great play of the issue that we were an Arab consultancy, so it would look rather odd if we chose a non-Arabic name. On the other hand, buyers of engineering consultancy at the kind of level we were hoping to operate were used to dealing with firms with impressive-sounding English names in which words such as 'international', 'amalgamated' and 'consolidated' figured. We solved the problem with a compromise. We decided to have two names. We called ourselves Dar Al-Handasah in Arabic, Associated Consulting Engineers in English. As Dar Al-Handasah was written in Arabic script, there was little chance of the non-Arabic reader realising that the two names weren't the same. Those who did realise, we figured, would probably admire our innovative spirit. And that proved to be the case.

We left the coffee party in high spirits, but realising we had much hard work ahead of us if we were to make a success of our plans. The first step was to register the company with the relevant government department, a necessary piece of bureaucracy that we soon accomplished. Then we solved the problem of premises by renting a three-bedroomed apartment in Abdul Aziz street in the Hamra district of Beirut. It was an up-market area so it gave the right impression to potential clients. It was also handily close to the university, so that we could make the regular journeys back and forth between the two without wasting too much time. As we'd be building up a consultancy as well as holding down our jobs at the university, we expected to be busy in the months ahead.

As we hadn't yet won any contracts, we couldn't afford to build up a large staff – and we didn't need one – but we did require some basic help to enable us to run the office. Zaki Jishi, a Palestinian who lived in one of the refugee camps that had grown up on the outskirts of

Beirut following the 1948 Arab–Israeli war, became Dar Al-Handasah's first full-time paid employee. We hired a secretary who came two hours a day, and a part-time book-keeper, who came in two hours a week. And, in November 1956, we formally opened for business.

So we had everything we needed to call ourselves a proper consultancy, with one important exception – clients.

There was no doubt in my mind that we were in the right place to win clients. In the mid-1950s, the Lebanese economy was booming as regional capital flooded into the country, partly the result of the oil boom and partly a flight of capital from those other Middle Eastern countries slipping into business-unfriendly dictatorship or enterprise-sapping military government. Most Western companies in the oil, transportation and construction industries that wanted to do business in the Middle East had an office in Beirut. They were all our potential customers.

But first we had to become known to them. And that's where some good friends came to our aid. Emile Bustani was a self-made millionaire who had built his CAT construction company – the CAT stood for Construction And Trading – into a shining commercial success in the Middle East. CAT was headquartered in Beirut. I regarded it as a model of what an indigenous regional company should be. The superbly managed company reflected Bustani's own strong beliefs in democracy and open society. The month after we'd launched Dar Al-Handasah, Bustani threw a reception for us at his impressive CAT building. It was well attended by both Lebanese and overseas business people, and we made many useful contacts.

A second piece of good fortune came our way when Burhan Dajani, a former AUB professor who now ran the Lebanese Chamber of Commerce, wrote an approving article about us in the Chamber's regular magazine. The article made the specific point of welcoming the first Arab engineering consultancy in the region, a factor that was to be significant in our winning contracts in the early days.

As we moved into 1957, the first contracts started to trickle in. Aramco, the oil company that was owned by a consortium of US oil interests, was in expansionist mood. Its Dhahran oilfield in Saudi

Arabia was pumping millions of barrels of crude oil through the 1060-mile Trans-Arabian Pipeline – the Tapline – which terminated in Lebanon. The company had recently confirmed the huge scale of two new oilfields at Ghawar and Safaniya, the last being the world's largest offshore field at the time.

Aramco had an office in Beirut, and Shafic Qombarji, its manager, was a friend of mine. The company commissioned Dar Al-Handasah to carry out four feasibility studies at Dhahran in the oil-rich eastern province of Saudi Arabia. I flew to Dhahran, which seemed then more like an American than a Middle Eastern town. It was already displaying the comfort that oil revenues bring. Even though I'd lived in the United States for eight years, I remember being deeply impressed with the luxury of Steinecky Hall, the guesthouse that Aramco used for its visiting executives and guests. It was in marked contrast, with a few exceptions, to the then poor quality of hotels throughout most of the Middle East.

I stayed in Dhahran for about six weeks working on the feasibility studies. In those days, our fee for that kind of work was between $1000 and $1500 per study, so I earned the company about $5000 – more than the capital we'd put up to start the firm. But we gained more than vital revenue from the project. We demonstrated to an influential client that we could deliver work of the quality required on time and to budget – and we started to learn more about what the commercial world required of a professional consultancy firm.

Another project helped to establish our name in Lebanon, where we were later to win a large number of contracts. Maurice Gemayel came from the notable Lebanese family that went on to produce two presidents, one of whom, Bashir, was assassinated in 1982 before his inauguration. Maurice was a scholar, a philosopher and a thinker, with ideas ahead of his time. He believed that because Lebanon was such a small country its environment should be carefully preserved. He developed these ideas long before the 'green movement' became fashionable.

He commissioned Dar Al-Handasah to conduct a planning study of the Metn region, one of the most beautiful parts of the country centred on Mount Lebanon. It was further evidence that we were spreading our wings and winning more business. At the end of our first year, we had earned fees of nearly $30,000. It wasn't at all a bad start, but it was a fraction of what the larger Western consultancies were earning in the region. And I was eager to get on equal terms with them.

*   *   *

The opportunity to do so soon came knocking. A few years earlier, in 1951, when I'd attended my brother Jamal's graduation ceremony at AUB I'd met other graduates who became personal friends. One of them, Abdul Muhsin Al-Qettan, a Palestinian, introduced me in the summer of 1957 to a member of the ruling Sabah family of Kuwait. His name was Sheikh Jaber Al-Ali, and he was the head of the department responsible for electricity and water in Kuwait. Al-Qettan had the post of inspector general in the department. Sheikh Jaber was a magnificent man, and I liked him immediately. He had a sharp natural intelligence, although not much formal education, and a fine sense of humour.

Many Kuwaitis used to visit Lebanon during July and August to get away from the suffocating heat of their own country and enjoy the mild climate of the Lebanese mountains that overlook the beautiful Mediterranean sea. That year, Sheikh Jaber was among them, and I was invited to take tea with him. It was an enthralling experience. He wanted to know what educated Arab nationalists were thinking, and what their attitudes were to the issues of the day. I discussed my views on these subjects with him, but I also managed to slip into the conversation some information about the consultancy I and my colleagues had recently set up.

I obviously aroused his interest, because a few days later he visited me at our offices and we had a long and wide-ranging talk. He questioned me closely about our expertise, and I described the background of our partners and some of the projects we'd been working on. As our discussion progressed, it was clear that Al-Ali was interested in more than just the skills and services we might have to offer. We talked at length about the objectives of Arab nationalism and I got the firm impression he was delighted by the broader implications of what we were doing – establishing an Arab consultancy to challenge the existing hegemony of Western consultants in the region. At the end of the meeting, we shook hands and he invited me to visit him in Kuwait at the end of the summer.

So, a few weeks later, I took the plane to Kuwait City and held a further meeting with him at his home. He told me he wanted to give Dar Al-Handasah a project. I had expected my visit to result in some business, but I wasn't prepared for the size of the project he had in mind – a 90-megawatt power station.

Kuwait was growing fast as its oil flowed. It needed more and more electricity. Already the country had constructed a 20-megawatt power station, then a 40-megawatt station, but it was clear that demand was fast outstripping supply. The offices and apartment buildings that were springing up all around Kuwait City urgently needed air conditioning to combat the blistering 40-degree-centigrade temperatures of high summer. The 90-megawatt power station – three units of 30 megawatts each – was the largest by far yet to be built in the Arab world. It would have been a challenge to any consultancy, even one with a long track-record in the technologies involved. We had no experience in this area.

I sat there as Al-Ali set out what he wanted with a mixture of thoughts racing through my mind. There was little doubt that a project of this size would put us on the map in no uncertain terms. The fee alone would catapult us into a new league. More than that, the prestige of the project would attract widespread attention throughout the Middle East and beyond. It could be just what we needed in order to provide the credibility to take on the big players in the consultancy world. But we'd only get that credibility if we delivered successfully on the project. So this was not only our biggest decision yet, it was also our riskiest. If we delivered the project successfully, the sky would be the limit in the future – but failure could finish us.

I accepted the challenge without hesitation. On the flight back to Beirut, I started to think about how we could approach the project when we didn't yet have the full range of skills needed for it. I discussed the matter with my colleagues. There was only one answer – we had to recruit the experts we needed. And we weren't going to find all of them in Lebanon.

So I flew to Britain and looked up colleagues I'd known, some from university days, to tap into their experience. They gave me useful pointers on the kind of electrical and civil engineers we'd need and where we might find them. Major engineering companies, such as English Electric and GEC, had already picked up on the grapevine that we'd won the contract and were aware that we'd play a key role in specifying which contractors were used for the construction work. They were keen to help with contacts and information.

I widened my search to include the Middle East. I visited Cairo, because I knew the city's power authority employed some highly skilled and experienced electrical and mechanical engineers. Slowly, the team started to come together.

My big breakthrough came when – back in Britain – I was introduced to Knud Hanson. He was a Danish electrical engineer who spoke good English and, crucially, had had experience of managing major power-station construction projects. He turned out to be a key member of the team.

But, perhaps naively, I hadn't realised what impact our winning this contract would have on those companies that had also been bidding. The English consultancy Ewbank (that became part of the Ewbank Preece Consulting Group that was subsequently absorbed into the Mott MacDonald Group) had been lead consultant on the 20-megawatt and 40-megawatt projects, known as power stations A and B. They'd expected to be an automatic choice for the big one – power station C. And they weren't happy to be beaten by a group of parvenus who'd never run a project like this before.

First, they wrote to Ken Weidner, the dean of engineering at AUB, to complain. It wasn't fair competition, they claimed. The partners at Dar Al-Handasah, they maintained, were paid by the university, and therefore the firm could afford to undercut full-time consultants. That argument worried me, and I was not sure how much Ewbank had discovered about our agreement with the Kuwaiti authorities. The normal scale of fees at the time, laid down by the Association of Consulting Engineers in Britain, was that the consultants should receive 4 per cent of the total project cost. In order to be sure of winning the contract, I'd agreed to a 30 per cent reduction – 2.8 per cent of project cost. Even so, and to his credit, Weidner gave short shrift to Ewbank's undercutting argument. It was common practice in Britain and the United States, he pointed out, for academics to provide consultancy services.

Having found that avenue of complaint closed off to them, Ewbank's Middle Eastern managers next lobbied the British resident in Kuwait. Since 1899, Kuwait had been under British 'protection', first from the Ottomans, later from the Saudis and Iraq. The resident, a British Foreign Office career civil servant, advised the Emir of Kuwait, Sheikh Abdullah Al-Salem Al-Sabah, on the policies his country should follow. Since the Suez debacle the previous year, which had made Britain unpopular throughout the Middle East, Abdullah had been quietly pressing the British government for more control over the country's internal affairs. (Kuwait finally became completely independent in 1961.) So, while the resident still had considerable influence over security and foreign affairs, Abdullah was increasingly taking his own line on domestic matters. Even so, Abdullah was a shrewd enough politician to realise that he had to be seen to be responsive to the British resident's concerns.

That was why a week or two after being awarded the contract I received a summons to come for an audience with Sheikh Abdullah. In theory, the contract was firmly ours, but this was the first time I'd experienced international lobbying at this level, and I couldn't be certain about the outcome of the meeting. I decided to leave nothing to chance. I hurried to Kuwait City, taking Professor Sloane and Dean Weidner with me.

We arrived in Kuwait, and were put up in the government's comfortable guest house. The next day, not without some concern, we called at the palace to be received by Sheikh Abdullah. The very word 'palace' conjures up the idea of splendid chambers with luxurious furnishings, so I was astonished when we were shown into Abdullah's office. It was a modest room, with a small metal desk. My own office – in fact, all our partners' offices – were smarter and better equipped than this. As an Arab nationalist, I felt ashamed that this great man – he not only led Kuwait to independence but introduced reforms that laid the foundations of a successful modern state – should do his work from such humble accommodation. We were invited to take seats. Al-Ali, Abdullah's nephew, sat on the carpet, a traditional mark of respect accorded the Emir by other members of the family.

Abdullah wasted little time in getting down to business. He asked me what kind of engineers we had to work on the power-station project. I replied that we'd put together a team that included engineers from both the Middle East and Europe, and I outlined the specialists we had recruited. He asked how we would organise the project, and I described our plans.

The meeting was proceeding well, in a formal but relaxed way, but I had little doubt that he was quietly probing to see whether we knew our business. He'd heard, he told me, that some engineers used 110-volt cables while others preferred 220-volt. What was the reasoning behind that, he asked? I said the 110-volt was supposed to be safer. Why, he asked? Because if somebody accidentally touches it while its live, a lesser charge passed through them and they stood a greater chance of surviving death or serious injury. He nodded, considering my answer.

Then he leaned forward and looked me in the eye. 'Can you promise me that you will deliver this power-station project on time?' he asked. For a moment, a silence hung over the room as I held his gaze.

'Yes,' I replied. 'I can promise that.'

'I will hold you to that promise,' he said. I could tell from the way he looked at me that he meant to.

He turned to Professor Sloane and asked: 'What do you do?' Sloane replied that he was a physicist but he specialised in electrical engineering. 'So you know the capability of these people well?' Abdullah asked.

'Yes, of course,' replied Sloane. 'They are among the best in the world.'

Dean Weidner chipped in with his own testimonial. By this time, I had already given notice that I wanted to step down from my responsibilities at the university to concentrate on building Dar Al-Handasah. Weidner pointed out that, despite this, he'd recently promoted me to associate professor and he was so sorry that I'd be leaving the university he'd agreed to keep my post open for me for three years in case I changed my mind.

Abdullah seemed satisfied with that and called for coffee. Over coffee I explained how we were building an Arab engineering consultancy capability in the region. Abdullah commended us for our efforts and wished us luck. We sipped our coffee and left. I don't suppose the meeting had lasted more than fifteen minutes. Al-Ali accompanied us as we walked down the corridors on the way out of the palace. I asked him whether the Emir had been satisfied with our answers. He smiled: 'He's satisfied,' he said.

With the competition safely seen off, it was time to get serious about the detail of the project. We already had some of the team, which eventually rose to around 40 people, in place. We had agreed that our 'wise man', Professor Malouf, would be the project manager on the ground in Kuwait. But I was aware that this was the project that would make us – or break us – and I was determined to keep a close personal watch on every aspect of it.

And not without good reason. The chief engineer hired by the Kuwaitis to oversee the actual construction work was a Brit called Jim Addison. He was clearly uncomfortable with the fact he was working with a group of consultants who had no power-station experience. But he was a generous man and proved very helpful with advice. For example, he advised me to make it a condition of supply for the turbine manufacturer that it also provided the design for the footing and foundations on which the turbines rested. Turbines cause a lot of vibration and there was, he assured me, a black art in calculating the correct stresses and strains that would be imposed on turbine foundations.

Titbits of advice like that were more than welcome as we were gingerly feeling our way into the project. Our principal task was to draw up specifications for the many components of the power station and to issue invitations to tender to potential suppliers of the different equipment needed. Then we had to evaluate the tenders and select the most appropriate suppliers. We'd never done this before, so I decided to take a peek at the tenders drawn up by Ewbank on the previous two power stations. This, I hasten to add, was completely above board. The government tenders were public documents and anybody could look at them. It was useful to discover how Ewbank had parcelled out the work – for example, one contract for the turbines, another for the boilers. There were separate suppliers for the switching gear, the transformers, the water-cooling systems and so on. I realised that we'd be cooling the system by using sea water, so we'd need to construct a jetty so that water could be pumped ashore and into the power station.

All this work was proceeding, as I thought smoothly, when I received a jolt. I heard from one of my contacts within the Kuwait government that they were worried about the way the project was being managed at their end.

We discussed the problem at an urgently summoned partners' meeting in Beirut. It could have been bitter and confrontational, but I was determined that we needed to set aside personalities and find a constructive solution that everybody was happy with. I'd been told that Al-Ali wanted me to run the project personally. It was not what I'd originally planned, but if that's what the client wanted, it seemed I had little choice. My partners agreed with me and I took over.

We made the change, and I started a gruelling period in which I doubled up on my work – flying out to Kuwait City every Saturday and Sunday (working days in the country) in order to oversee the project's progress on the ground. The weekend commute was on top of the heavy burden I was already bearing in the Beirut office, but it paid off. By 1958, we had the project on course and on time, with a happy client.

It was while I was working on the power-station project in Kuwait that I had my first brush with Yasser Arafat, who was to become the leader of the Palestine Liberation Organisation. Arafat had been working at Kuwait's Ministry of Public Works as an engineer, and later he set up his own contracting firm. At the time, Kuwait, which was growing fast on the strength of its buoyant oil revenues, was a comfortable and welcoming host for Palestinian professionals.

Arafat was in the process of setting up the Fatah movement – the word is a reverse acronym of Hataf, which means Palestine Homeland Liberation Movement – and was looking for funding. Kuwait, like other Arab states, was courting nationalist ideals, and Fatah's stated aim for an independent state of Palestine fitted well with those principles. In any event, the new movement received support from the Kuwaiti authorities. Others, including myself, were invited to subscribe to its founding fund. I made a nominal contribution. I was not to know that Arafat's organisation would later cause me considerable trouble.

But, for the time being, the aims of young men with political ideas took up little of my time. I was completely focused on the power-station project that meant so much to Dar Al-Handasah. Then events completely outside our control threatened to blow everything we'd worked for out of the water.

CHAPTER 9

The business of coups

Five thousand US marines stormed ashore in Beirut on 15 July 1958.

Within days, the government of Camille Chamoun, Lebanon's president since 1952, had fallen. The army's chief, General Fouad Shehab, had become the new president, and all of us were living under a dusk-to-dawn curfew. In the streets of Beirut, and other cities, more than 2000 – perhaps as many 4000 – casualties were tending their wounds or lying dead as the result of fighting between rival factions.

It was not, to say the least, an ideal situation in which to be running a business. Especially a new business. Especially a business that had recently won its largest contract ever in the shape of Kuwait's power station C. We had a very worried client. And I was acutely aware of the personal promise I'd made to the Emir of Kuwait to deliver the power-station project on time.

The troubles of the summer of 1958 was the first – but by no means the last – time our business was disrupted by political events beyond our control. The genesis of the current turmoil lay in the fragile coalition which held the disparate elements of Lebanese society together. It is worth remembering that the country was younger than most people who lived in it. Lebanon had only gained its independence from the

French in 1943. Since the seventh century, the region had been a haven for persecuted religious minorities, both Muslim and Christian. So it was no wonder that Lebanon had a diverse population.

Since independence, politicians had observed an unwritten convention to ensure that the main groupings were represented in the political process. The president was a Maronite Christian, the prime minister a Sunni Muslim, the speaker of the national assembly a Shi'ite Muslim. The convention had kept the rivalries of the various groups below the surface, but hadn't made for particularly smooth politics. There had been a bloodless coup in 1952 – the 'rosewater revolution' – when Chamoun had overthrown the government of Bishara Al-Khoury. Yet despite the political undercurrents, Lebanon had a climate in which business could thrive. And thrive it did through most of the 1950s as the economy boomed.

But the political problems started to rise to the surface in 1957 when Chamoun decided he would like a second term as president. The constitution forbade second presidential terms, and the only way Chamoun could change it was through a two-thirds vote in the chamber of deputies. He called elections and won a big majority, but opponents claimed the vote had been rigged.

In any event, a spirit of pan-Arab feeling was sweeping the Middle East, driven by the speeches of Egypt's president Colonel Nasser. Chamoun was violently opposed to Nasser's policies, but a significant number of Lebanon's population supported them, including Nassib Matni, editor of the *At-Talagraph* newspaper. Shortly after the elections, Matni was assassinated. His death ignited the already febrile atmosphere among the country's dissidents. In February, news that Egypt and Syria had joined together to form the United Arab Republic further fanned the pan-Arab flames in Lebanon.

When, on 14 July, a revolution in nearby Iraq overthrew the monarchy, excitement in anti-Chamoun communities reached fever-pitch. With fighting in the streets of some towns and radio stations calling for the violent overthrow of the government, Chamoun turned to the Americans for help. The year before, Chamoun had signed up to the Eisenhower Doctrine – named after US president Dwight D.

Eisenhower. Under its terms, the Unites States promised to use armed force to help any country threatened by 'international communism'. Chamoun claimed those Lebanese Muslims who wanted to overthrow the government were being aided by Syria, which itself was in receipt of Soviet arms. It was a tenuous claim, but Eisenhower bought it and the marines arrived.

These events took place within a tense political climate in the region at a time when the Cold War had split the world into opposing camps. Iraq was, with Turkey, a founder member of the Baghdad Pact – they were later joined by Britain, Pakistan and Iran – that took a pro-Western stance against the Soviet Union. Nasser backed the Soviet camp, while Chamoun was identified with the pro-Western sympathies of the Baghdad Pact. Inevitably, this climate fanned the tensions within Lebanon.

Most of the fighting took place between rival Lebanese factions, and few of the marines saw action. At the same time, General Chehab prudently realised he couldn't commit the Lebanese army against insurgents without risking it fracturing into factions along religious lines. Gradually, common sense prevailed among the warring groups, the fighting died down, but the curfew remained for some weeks. So did the atmosphere of fragile truce. And pictures of American troops arriving *en masse* to quell a civil revolt in a foreign country had been beamed around the world.

No wonder our Kuwaiti client was worried. But the work I'd been doing during those tough weekend visits during the past year had paid off. The client now seemed happy and, as a company, we were communicating openly and regularly with them on all issues concerned with the power station's progress. They could see we were doing what we said we'd do and that we were on track. Nurturing the relationship had ensured that there was goodwill on both sides.

So much goodwill, as it turned out, that when the crisis hit the Kuwaitis were eager to help us to find a way to resolve the problem and keep the project moving forward. If there is a problem for staff working in Beirut, said the client, bring them to Kuwait City.

We swiftly took up their generous offer. We moved around forty staff – sometimes with their families – the 780 miles between the two cities. For a company of our size, it was a mammoth undertaking. We not only had to move the people, we also had to shift some of their equipment and all the working papers, which on a project of the power station's size were voluminous.

But the Kuwaitis couldn't have been more eager to help. They provided us with office accommodation, just like the contractors that were building the power station. They even paid for the costs of the move and the salaries of the staff who were now working in Kuwait. The project moved forward, hardly missing a beat.

By the autumn, the political situation in Lebanon stabilised. We were able to resume normal working in our own offices on other projects, but many of the power-station staff stayed in Kuwait. I can't deny that Dar Al-Handasah benefited from the arrangement. Even though we'd reduced our fee by 30 per cent, we ended up making a handsome profit on that project because the Kuwait government had picked up many of the extra costs. When the power station finally switched on in 1961, the government held a large reception attended by politicians and diplomats. I bowed my head modestly as Kuwaiti ministers lauded the efforts of the consultants in bringing the project to completion on time.

My only regret was that I never got an opportunity to remind Emir Abdullah personally that I had kept my promise.

*   *   *

Two days before the US marines landed in Beirut, I was in Cairo on business.

Egypt had some excellent engineers who we wanted to work on the Kuwait power station and other projects. But since Nasser had come to power it had been very difficult to get permission for them to work outside the country. One of the worst side-effects of the wrong kind of nationalism – the kind Nasser practised in a particularly virulent form – was that it was inward-looking. Despite his professed support for pan-Arabism, Nasser took the view that Egyptian engineers should be doing Egyptian work. It didn't occur to him that by working on overseas projects his home-grown engineers would gain broader knowledge and experience that would benefit Egypt when they returned home. Or, if it did occur to him, it wasn't something that he wanted to get in the way of his political prejudices.

So it wasn't easy to recruit Egyptian engineers, because any who wanted to work abroad had to get an annual permit to do so. And that wasn't a simple matter. Fortunately, I had a good contact, Fouad Galal, an adviser to the government on Arab relations, who was influential in the presidential palace. I had to go to Egypt periodically to meet him and get him to use his influence to win permits for the engineers we wanted to hire.

On some occasions on my trips to Egypt I met socially with General Ali Abu Nuwar, who had been the army's chief of staff in Jordan and who was now living in exile. Abu Nuwar, who came from my native Salt, had harboured leftist sympathies since the early 1950s. In April 1957, he was suspected of leading a coup against King Hussein. The attempted coup was foiled within hours, and he was allowed to leave the country, at first for Syria, then Egypt. Nasser had provided him with a house and an aide de camp. On one visit to Egypt, in July 1958, I invited Abu Nuwar to have dinner with me at my hotel, the Semiramis. He accepted, but asked if he could bring Rashid Ali Al-Kilani, a former Iraqi prime minister who'd led a pro-German revolt against the British authorities in Iraq in 1941.

It was always interesting to meet Abu Nuwar, but on this occasion not as much as Al-Kilani. Al-Kilani seemed edgy when he arrived, as though he was expecting important news, and as dinner progressed he seemed to become more and more excitable. He couldn't stop talking about the political situation in Iraq. He fulminated about the supposed injustices wrought by Prince Abdul Ilah, the uncle of the 23-year-old King Faisal II. The King had acceded to the throne five years earlier after a period of regency by his uncle, Abdul Ilah. According to Al-Kilani, Ilah continued to hold considerable power. As the evening wore on, Al-Kilani's talk became more intemperate. He spoke about a coup and about getting the head of Ilah and of those who supported him. I was uncomfortably aware that he wasn't speaking metaphorically.

I listened to this diatribe with no pleasure. King Faisal's regime was not perfect. On the other hand, it had adopted a pro-Western stance. Faisal had steered Iraq into the Baghdad Pact partly to provide a Middle Eastern buffer against Soviet ambitions in the region and partly to combat the aggressive nationalism of Egypt's Nasser. As such, I thought Iraq could be a force for stability in the Middle East, but Al-Kilani disagreed.

I was also generally supportive of the Iraq regime because, earlier that year, the country had entered into a federal arrangement with Jordan. It was called formally the Arab Union of Jordan and Iraq, or the Arab Federation for short, and the aim was both to strengthen the Hashemite monarchies of both kingdoms and to co-operate more on issues of common concern. As a mark of how seriously both countries regarded the union, they had chosen a common premier, the Iraqi Nuri As-Said, with the Jordanian Ibrahim Hashim as his deputy, and a federal cabinet. A coup would fracture this arrangement and probably put a block on future co-operation between the two countries. But Al-Kilani seemed positively delighted at the prospect.

I wasn't sorry when the evening ended. We parted formally and I went to bed. The following morning, I awoke to news that a coup executed by officers of the Iraqi Nineteenth Brigade led by Brigadier Abdul-Karim Qassem had taken place in Baghdad. King Faisal had been killed, along with Abdul Ilah and other members of the Hashemite royal family at the Al-Rihab Palace. Their bodies were put on show in the streets in a bloody and brutal display of revolution. I later learnt that prime minister Nuri As-Said had tried to escape disguised as a veiled woman but had also been captured and executed, a fate shared by Ibrahim Hashim.

Did Al-Kilani know what was about to take place when we had dinner? Did his forewarning stimulate his excitable table-talk? I shall never be able to answer those questions, because I never saw him again and he died in 1965. But I suspect he had a firm intimation that the revolution was coming, even if he was not certain about the timing.

What I do know – as does the world – is that the 1958 revolution in Iraq was not the last outbreak of violent political change in that unhappy country.

*   *   *

The events in Lebanon and Iraq in that summer of 1958 were a sharp and unpleasant reminder that I had set myself the task of building a company in a region that was politically unstable and becoming more so. Coups, revolutions, counter-coups and civil unrest became a part of the backdrop against which I developed the business during the next five decades. The problem we've faced is that for much of the time the region has been, politically speaking, moving backwards.

The recent history of Iraq is but one example of that. By and large, Iraq enjoyed an imperfect but blossoming democracy and a flourishing economy until 1958. The coup of that year set off a chain-reaction of political instability that ended in Saddam Hussein and two wars, both of which devastated Iraq and caused political turmoil throughout the world.

The key issue that many countries in the Middle East are still struggling to resolve is how to combine diversity with democracy. I firmly believe that diversity can enrich democracy, and there are many countries in the world – not least Britain and the United States – where this rule is proved. But totalitarian governments always use diversity for their own ends – playing off one group against another, or favouring their own group against the legitimate interests of others. In Iraq, the Sunni-dominated regime of Saddam Hussein consistently excluded both the Shi'ite Muslims and the Kurds from a fair share of political power. More than that, Hussein persecuted both groups mercilessly.

But in a country in which the seeds of democracy are not firmly planted, there is a dilemma in diversity. Politics can become an all-or-nothing game in which each ethnic or religious grouping is either in or out of power completely. And if one group is in, it has to persecute the outs in order to stay in because it knows that it will receive the same treatment at their hands. I know of only one key that can unlock this vicious cycle – and that is tolerance.

But learning tolerance in the face of half a century of exploitation – whether you've been the exploiter or the exploited – is not an easy task. It requires both trust and goodwill. Tolerance has to be promoted and nourished at every opportunity. Perhaps that is something that is difficult for politicians, with their certainties and their easy answers and their need to pander to their 'core constituencies'.

The value of tolerance is certainly something that those of us running international businesses have learnt to value in abundance. An international business, such as ours, could not possibly be successful if it did not seek both to understand and to respect the cultures and traditions of the countries in which it operates. Among our thousands of employees are people with many different religions or none and of many different ethnic origins.

We make it an absolute point of principle only to appoint and promote on merit. An individual's race, religion or politics are irrelevant to us. We focus only on what that individual can contribute to the company. Not only is any kind of discrimination anathema to me, I do not believe that we would have been able to build the kind of cosmopolitan company Dar Al-Handasah has become had there been even a hint of it in our recruitment and human-resources policies.

With tolerance as a watchword among all staff, they work harmoniously and successfully together. To use an engineering analogy, tolerance is the lubricant which lets us rub against one another without causing unnecessary heat or friction.

Of course any company has more limited aims – to meet the needs of its customers and make a profit for its shareholders – than those of a sovereign state, whose objectives may be driven by the competing claims of different groupings within its population. Despite this, I still believe that tolerance should be every country's guiding principle. But, as we built our business through the late 1950s and into the 1960s, there was little sign of political tolerance in the Middle East. As a result, we had to navigate our way around, and sometimes through, more violence and more coups.

*   *   *

In the long and unstable history of the Middle East, one of the most bizarre events – for me at least – took place in my own home in Beirut in 1963. I was entertaining two guests, Michel Aflaq and Salah Al-Din Bitar. The pair had already risen to prominence in Middle East politics by founding the Ba'ath party, which was based around a loosely defined socialist, nationalist and pan-Arab ideology. The word Ba'ath is variously translated as 'revivalist', 'resurrection' or, more commonly, 'renaissance'.

I had first met both after I had become an assistant professor at AUB in 1956. They had been keen to cultivate academics as potential members of their party. As I have mentioned, I shared liberal nationalist aspirations for the countries of the Middle East, but I was not enthralled by their socialism and doubted the practicalities of their pan-Arabism. Nevertheless, I became a friend of both and we met from time to time.

Aflaq was a Christian Syrian who had shown considerable academic promise and gone on to study at the Sorbonne. He had returned to Damascus and briefly worked as a teacher. But his heart was in his politics. In 1940 he joined with Bitar, a Sunni Muslim, to found a study group called the Movement for Arab Renaissance, which by 1947 had developed into the Ba'ath party.

Bitar had met Aflaq in Paris in the 1930s, where they had first developed their political ideas together. Aflaq was the theorist, but Bitar was more the man of affairs and had served briefly as a minister of state during the ill-fated merger of Egypt and Syria into the United Arab Republic between 1958 and 1961. Aflaq had been one of the main theorists behind the idea of the UAR, and I can remember discussing it with him during long walks we took together when I visited Damascus. As part of the arrangement, Nasser had insisted that Aflaq and Bitar dissolve the Ba'ath party. They had done so, but after the union of the two countries had taken place it was clear from what Aflaq said to me that he was working to recreate the party's organisation in Syria. I felt seriously uneasy with the concept of the UAR, especially as it allowed Nasser to gain a political grip on Syria. But the fact that Aflaq was reneging on the agreement with Nasser – admittedly a man whose own word was suspect – filled me with apprehension about the future of the two countries' union.

Even so, although we differed on a number of political issues – not least the UAR – my friendship with both Aflaq and Bitar continued. Which was why they were sitting in my home on 8 February 1963.

Both were elated because a coup was taking place that day in Iraq. The current regime was still led by Qassem, who had overthrown the monarchy in 1958, but had been under threat for some months. Qassem had claimed sovereignty over Kuwait, which had been given its independence by Britain in 1961. But Britain had sent troops to support the Emir of Kuwait, who had faced down Qassem's threat to the territory. Humiliated, Qassem had faced rising nationalist resentment and unrest in Iraq. Now, as I sat talking with Aflaq and Bitar, news was coming through that Qassem had been assassinated in the coup.

Aflaq and Bitar were witnessing the fulfilment of their political ambitions – to see their Ba'ath party gain real political power. And it was clear to me from the way they were talking that the revolution in Iraq would not be the last. They animatedly discussed a revolution they expected to take place next in Syria, which had been politically unstable since the collapse of the UAR. What struck me most forcibly was that Aflaq and Bitar seemed to be more concerned with talking about when the coup should take place than what it hoped to achieve.

I particularly remember Bitar asking Aflaq what his views were on the timing. Aflaq thought about it for some time. He liked to portray himself as the wise intellectual, thinking deep thoughts. On other occasions, I had watched him surrounded by faithful acolytes hanging on his every utterance. His manner was to let conversation flow around him and then interject a few words which would be eagerly seized on by his followers and dissected for their genuine or supposed profundity.

In any event, on this occasion Aflaq didn't need to give Bitar's question a great deal of thought. 'We will be celebrating the Iraqi revolution on the eighth of February,' he said. 'Let's celebrate the Syrian on the eighth of March.' I sat there astonished that the two could discuss the future of a sovereign state in such a cavalier manner. But, as I was to discover, Aflaq meant what he said. The Ba'ath Arab Socialist Party seized power on 8 March in what became known in Syria as the March Revolution.

Even as I listened to them plotting these revolutions, I had a foreboding about the ultimate outcome. They had three slogans – Arab unity, socialism, freedom. But beyond those, there seemed to be little in the way of practical policies or programmes about how the ideas encapsulated in the slogans were to be achieved. As far as Arab unity was concerned, even the recent history of Syria – with the collapse of the UAR – had demonstrated that was an illusion. How was it possible to unite countries as diverse as, for example, Morocco, Yemen, Saudi Arabia and Lebanon? Then their socialism was ill-defined. I think both Aflaq and Bitar veered towards a moderate and humane approach to socialism, similar to that practised in the democracies of Western Europe. But, as they were to discover to their cost, they attracted bedfellows who took a more militant stance that veered towards communism. And if they were to champion freedom, they should be promoting freedom of thought, opinion and speech. That meant they ought to be seeking to persuade people of their views and to win power through the ballot box rather than organising military coups.

In any case, within the month Bitar was prime minister of Syria, following the coup. Aflaq held no government post but remained the Ba'ath party's political theoretician. Both were to discover, perhaps sooner than they realised, that when it comes to politics there is much truth in the old saying that he who lives by the sword dies by the sword. By mid-November, Bitar was out of office, although he was to return for further brief stints as prime minster of Syria in 1964 and 1966.

But a coup within the Ba'ath party on 23 February 1966 forced Bitar from office and into exile. Aflaq was in Lebanon that day, and he knew that there was no hope of returning to Syria. He feared for his life. Fortunately, he had relatives in Brazil and sought my help in reaching the sanctuary which that vast country was able to provide. As

I saw him off on his long journey, I wondered whether that was the last time I would see my friend in the Middle East.

I had underestimated his capacity to bounce back. Following the 1963 Iraq revolution, the Ba'ath party had lost power in a further coup in 1966. But in 1968, after the Six Day War, the Ba'athists were strong enough – and nationalist sentiment within Iraq was sufficiently fired up – to enable them to retake control under the presidency of Ahmed Hasan Al-Bakr. Saddam Hussein was deputy secretary-general of Iraq's Ba'ath party at the time, but Aflaq remained by far its most distinguished theoretician and he was invited to return to Iraq to resume the party's leadership.

So, less that two years after fleeing to South America, he was back at the heart of Middle Eastern politics. But it didn't take long before Aflaq fell out again with other members of the regime over what he saw as their lack of support for the Palestinians in their fight against the Jordanian regime (which I describe in chapter 12), and he returned for a time to Lebanon. Aflaq went back to Iraq in 1974 to lead the national command of the Ba'ath party, which by now controlled an ever-more-brutal regime. By this time, we had drifted apart. I felt that he had made a terrible error in allying himself with a regime that showed no respect for human rights. I felt I could no longer regard him as a friend. I no longer contacted him, nor he me.

Aflaq, I believe, knew deep inside himself that he did not have what it takes – an amoral brand of ruthlessness – to serve in the kind of government that Saddam Hussein eventually controlled as president of Iraq from 1979 until his defeat after the invasion by coalition troops in 2003. I believe he had an image of himself as an idealist. The trouble was that he also had a thirst for power. But because he knew he would never hold the highest positions of state, he manoeuvred to make the most of his prestige as a thinker and co-founder of the Ba'ath movement. Much good it did him in the later years of the Saddam regime, where he was accorded all due honour, but effectively ignored when it came to policy-making and decision-taking.

His life even had a sad coda to it. After he had died in Baghdad in 1989, the Saddam regime announced that he had converted to

Islam on his deathbed and had received a Muslim funeral. Having known him well, I believe the claim of his conversion to be a nonsense. One thing I am certain about Aflaq is that he remained a devout Christian until he went to meet his maker. Others were also outraged that Aflaq's religious belief should be traduced in death. I recall taking a call from my friend, Ahmad Baheaddin, editor of the leading Cairo newspaper *Al-Ahram*. Baheaddin was furious that Saddam had sunk even lower than he could imagine. 'Why do they have to take his religion away from him in death?' he asked me.

*   *   *

Michel Aflaq was not the only refugee I helped after the 1966 Syrian coup.

A few weeks after it had taken place, I was working in my office in Beirut when I received an urgent telephone call from Laura, my wife. There was an edge to her voice and she seemed guarded in the way she spoke. 'A friend has arrived at home and you should come back immediately,' she told me. I sensed something was wrong, so I didn't argue or enquire further, but went straight home.

The friend was Kamal Nasser, a Christian Palestinian who'd been a voice of reason within Syria's ruling Ba'ath party, and within the PLO. He was sitting down looking tired, haggard and shocked. Slowly, his story came out.

The coup of which Kamal was a victim had been especially vicious and bloody. He was one of many who had been imprisoned. But he had managed to escape. He had succeeded in smuggling himself across the Syria–Lebanon border, and he still bore the scars – cuts and bruises to which Laura was ministering. Now he planned to live quietly in Lebanon, keeping a low profile in the hope that the Syrian authorities would forget about his existence and that no hit-squad would be sent to eliminate him. I thought it a wise course of action. I knew Kamal to be a man of peace and reason, a view of life he had inherited from his father, a Protestant minister. From his family's background, Kamal had good connections with the Christian hierarchy in Lebanon, and he was sure they would help him to settle somewhere, as proved to be the case.

About two months later, I had a further worried call from Laura. Another friend had turned up at the house seeking help. Could I come immediately? I went straight home and was shocked to see Mounif Razaz sitting at the table. He had succeeded Aflaq as secretary-general of the Ba'ath party. On a personal level, he had also been our family doctor in earlier years.

Like Kamal, Razaz had also been imprisoned. Although he had been released, he feared for his life if he remained in Syria. He had not only smuggled himself out of Syria, he had also smuggled himself into Lebanon. He was in the country illegally. As a director of a company based in Lebanon, this presented me with a difficult dilemma. I could not hide an illegal immigrant from the authorities, but at the same time I could not let down a friend whose life was in danger.

I contacted the politician Takieddine As-Solh, who later became prime minister, and explained my dilemma to him. He promised to mention the difficulty to President Charles Helou. I had made the point to Solh that, even leaving aside humanitarian considerations (which I, for one, was not prepared to do), it would do the Lebanese government no favours to have a high-profile assassination in the country. As-Solh and Helou accepted this argument and brought in the head of national security, Tawfic Jalbout, to devise a solution. In the meantime, Razaz remained as our house guest.

Diplomatic channels were set to work, seeking a country that would be prepared to accept Razaz discreetly – no questions asked, and certainly none answered. Greece was willing to do so. There remained the question of how we could spirit Razaz out of Lebanon without anybody discovering what had happened. There were certainly elements who would have been only too pleased to give – or possibly sell – the information to the Syrian security services.

Jalbout arranged for Razaz to fly out of Beirut Airport on an Olympic Airways scheduled flight to the Greek island of Rhodes. Plainly, however, Razaz couldn't queue up at the check-in desk with the other passengers. Instead, Jalbout planned to smuggle Razaz onto the plane at the last minute. My job was to drive my friend to a gas station near the airport, where Jalbout would meet us. I left my car parked at the gas station, and Razaz and I got into Jalbout's car. Jalbout drove us into the airport through a side entrance and across the tarmac to where the plane's propellers were already turning. Seconds before the plane's retractable steps were pulled up, Razaz jumped out of the car and, with a hasty goodbye, rushed onto the plane. Outside the airport, Jalbout and I watched the plane take off and head out over the Mediterranean. I have rarely been more relieved to see a flight leave on time.

But Razaz had been forced to flee his native land in fear of his life. Living in Beirut, Kamal thought he was the lucky one. Until some years later.

It was 1973, and my wife and I were driving back from a dinner engagement. It was during the years of continuous skirmishes between Palestinian militias and Israeli forces in southern Lebanon near the Israeli border. We became caught up in a military operation – as it turned out a diversion that was part of the planned assassination of three Palestinians targeted by Israel. There were suspicions that the killing was organised by Israeli military intelligence. One of the Palestinians killed that night, for reasons I have never been able to understand, was my friend Kamal Nasser. Laura and I joined a large crowd of mourners at his funeral, walking in procession to the church and onwards to the cemetery.

CHAPTER 10

Start small, think big

By 1959, Dar Al-Handasah had been trading for three years and our growth was accelerating. Despite the uncertain political prospects for much of the Middle East, our future looked bright. So I was surprised when three of my four partners – Khalil Malouf, Samir Thabet and Victor Andraous – came to see me with concerns about our strategy. They were worried that we were growing too fast. They wanted me to apply my foot to the brake rather than the accelerator.

When we had set up the consultancy, I had expressed the view that we should grow fast and seek to overtake other consultancies to become a leader in our region, and then – well, who knows? But, plainly, three of my colleagues – the fourth, Nazih Taleb, was happy with the progress we were making – were uncomfortable with the implications of the fast-growth strategy. This was an honest difference of opinion between three colleagues and myself, but clearly it had to be resolved.

Over a period of weeks, we discussed the difficulty in a friendly and constructive way. I could understand why they thought as they did. Like me, they had relished the idea of setting up Dar Al-Handasah. But, unlike me, they didn't see it as the only interest in their working lives. They had other interests they wished to maintain, and it was becoming clear that this would be ever more difficult if Dar Al-Handasah continued to grow at its present rate. Malouf and Thabet were respected professors at AUB, and wanted to continue in their roles. Andraous was making a success of his post at the Institute of Industrial Research in Lebanon, and didn't want to give it up.

Yet with the Kuwait power station C project at its height and more work on the horizon, it was clear that, if Dar Al-Handasah was to continue growing at its present pace, it would soon require the full-time commitment of all five of us. We talked round and round the dilemma, but there seemed no way to resolve it. The three didn't want to let go of their existing interests, and I didn't intend to slow the growth of the company. Our debate over the speed of growth revolved around the question of how we could achieve the original vision of the company.

Right from the beginning, we had set out to become a multi-disciplinary consultancy. This was what marked us out from other indigenous Middle Eastern consultants, many of whom worked as sole traders in their own specialism. If we were to take on the big Western consultancies at their own game, we had to offer a range of services, just as they did. That was one of the reasons I had assembled the diverse team in the first place. In the fullness of time, we needed to extend our existing expertise and bring a range of other skills under one roof – civil and structural engineering, architecture, electricals, expertise in dams, irrigation, bridges and much, much more. This was where the larger consultancies scored. They added value because they could take on the big projects using their own resources. They had individual consultants in different disciplines under one roof, and the whole was more than the sum of its parts.

To compete effectively with the multi-disciplinary houses, we had to achieve the same kind of critical mass they had already built. Moreover, we had to achieve that critical mass quickly if we were to be taken seriously by potential clients. That was why the speed of growth was such an issue between us.

After lengthy discussion, it was clear our differences on this question were irreconcilable. So, amicably, we agreed to part and go our separate ways. We reduced the number of partners from five to two – myself and Nazih Taleb – and turned our faces to the future. With Taleb's agreement, I became chief executive and we made plans to forge forward. But the change – the first of a number of key turning-points the company was to undergo – made me reflect more deeply on what it was we were seeking to do and why we wanted to do it.

*   *   *

There was never one blinding flash of light that revealed the vision – that caused the business philosophy I followed in building Dar Al-Handasah to jump fully formed into my mind. Rather, that philosophy had grown steadily as the result of my experiences and observations gathered from the earliest moments of watching my father go about his own business and through my university years. These experiences were allied to my own beliefs about how I could contribute most to the region in which I was born and in which I have lived much of my life.

But if I have to track back to one moment when the spark ignited, I suppose it was as I sat in my room at AUB reading about the history and philosophy of the medieval Arab world. What struck me most forcefully was that the great philosophers and scientists of the time – Al-Kindi, Ibn Khaldun, Ibn Rushd and the others – had led the world in their thinking and provided much of the intellectual platform from which European civilisation later advanced. They had taken the learning of the great men of classical Europe and reinterpreted it to provide a philosophy for their new age. Allied to their science and technology – in areas such as medicine – it made them what today we would call 'world class'.

What struck me particularly forcefully was that these Arab thinkers were not afraid of the power of ideas. They would absorb ideas from anyone and anywhere and reflect upon them with an open mind. The free and open exchange of ideas became the intellectual currency that built the philosophies and guided the ways they lived their lives and ordered the societies they created. As a student, I could see how intoxicating the notion of a free and open society, in which people determined their own form of government, would be for peoples in the Middle East. It had certainly proved so in the nineteenth century when the movement for Arab nationalism, to free the region from Ottoman domination, had first taken root.

But by the time I'd reached AUB, the dream of liberal nationalism as a political force was under siege, and during my university years in the late 1940s and early 1950s the flame of freedom was snuffed out in one Middle Eastern country after another. That made me even more determined than I had been before to return to the Middle East and play my part in fighting for the ideals in which I believed. As I have related, I had realised that the world is changed by activists – and building a world-class development consultancy business was going to be the principal way in which I would exercise my activism and try to influence my region for the good.

So when we set up Dar Al-Handasah, it was – for me, at least – more than just a way of using my professional qualifications or earning some money. It was, rather, a decision that was central to my own philosophy of life – that the people of the Middle East would live most fulfilling lives within open societies that engaged with the world at large. It followed on from that premise that they would contribute most if their talents were harnessed in a challenging and competitive economic environment.

From the day I first stepped into our offices on Abdul Aziz street – indeed, even before then – these were the guiding principles I used in building Dar Al-Handasah. It was not, therefore, surprising that I was pushing forward more quickly than some of my colleagues wished. But, as I reflected on the turning-point we had reached after the departure of my three former partners, I was more convinced than ever that the way forward rested on three pillars, which would support our distinctive approach to business.

The first of these was that we would compete with the best the world had to throw at us. It is true that, despite our growth, in 1959 we were still a small consultancy in comparison with our global competitors. But lack of size didn't imply lack of ability, just as scale doesn't, of itself, imply excellence. I was convinced that we had in our small operation people who were as good as any large Western consultancies could match against them.

Besides, I had resolved that the world would continue to be our hunting-ground for talent. We had already demonstrated in the Kuwait power-station project that it was possible for us to assemble a world-class team, even when we'd had no previous experience in that type of work. We'd hired excellent engineers from Egypt, Lebanon and elsewhere. We'd brought in Knud Hanson from Denmark, together with several first-rate British engineers and architects. A world of talent lay out there, and I was determined we would tap into it to grow the company. As the company expanded, there would be the question of how we created incentives for those who would play key roles in powering its growth. But in 1959 that was still largely a question for the future.

The second of the pillars was that we would participate actively in the development of the Arab world. We could not, as the rulers of nation states do, grab the levers of political power. But we could do something that I felt was at least as valuable – we could work on projects that made life better for the ordinary people who lived and worked in the region. As engineers, we were all in the business of development, and in the decades ahead it was to be major advances in areas such as transportation, irrigation, power supply, health and education that were to transform the lives of millions living in the Middle East more fundamentally than the speeches of any politician. We were to participate in many of those exciting developments.

Becoming involved in the economic development of the Middle East (and subsequently other parts of the world) meant we needed to find a way to engage closely with those who commissioned the projects. In the first three years of our existence, I had spearheaded that engagement by developing contacts I had already made and building on others – such as Sheikh Jaber Al-Ali who had been the principal point of contact in the lucrative Kuwait power-station deal.

Now that we were down to two partners, it was plain that I would need to redouble my efforts, but looking ahead I already had some ideas about how we would engage with potential clients as our company grew. Over the years, many consultancies have developed marketing departments. When you're selling consultancy services – which involve understanding both what your potential client wants and the sometimes wide spread of technologies you need to muster to deliver the solution – I believe that a discrete marketing section is not the answer. In development consultancy, marketing is too important to be left to marketers. Because your clients are the source of your future revenues, you need to put your best people before them – the people who will play a key role in helping to deliver the client's project to specification, on time and to budget.

Thus, as my thinking evolved in the years ahead – and as the company grew – we eschewed professional marketers and developed a specialist stream of partner-directors whose job was to develop business in particular market areas. Because these area partners covered very specific territories, they were able to build considerable grassroots knowledge of what was wanted and also develop close and trusting relationships with the key players who were in a position to award important contracts. More than that, they were also in a position to ensure that all the technical resources of the company were harnessed to deliver the client's project in the most effective way.

The third of the pillars on which we set out to build the company was a simple ambition – that we would, ultimately, play on the world stage on equal terms with the best. We had, initially, chosen to take on the finest consultancies from Europe and North America on our home turf in the Middle East. It made sense to start where we had some competitive advantages of our own – our knowledge of the culture, language and traditions of the Middle East, not to mention contacts among its business community and governing classes that we had made simply by living among them. But I was under few illusions that if we were really to prove our mettle – and honour the traditions for global excellence first articulated by the Arab polymaths of the middle ages – we would need, sooner or later, to take on the established consultancies on their home ground.

At the time, with us operating from modest offices in Beirut, that may have seemed a vain ambition. But, because I had spent so much time in America, it worried me less than it might an Arab with a more parochial view of the world – and, sadly, at that time too many Arab businesses did have a parochial view of the world. I had seen at first hand what the Americans could offer. I knew that the intelligence and skill, as well as the creativity and adaptability, that the best people in the Middle East could provide would match the best of America or Europe. (Not, as I have mentioned, that we intended to restrict ourselves to fishing exclusively in the local talent-pool.)

At the time, I was convinced we had chosen the right base in the Middle East from which both to develop our business in the region and, when we were ready, take on the world. With its French colonial legacy and its open society, Lebanon straddled both the Middle East and the West. It looked both ways and sought, at least in commerce, to understand the different cultures of business practised in both regions. Lebanon also had a fine education system. An important factor in our growth was our ability to recruit talented graduates from Lebanon's excellent universities, not least AUB.

So, with all this in mind, as I said goodbye to my former partners and looked to the future, I did so with some confidence. At the same time, I was eager to develop our business in new ways. We may have been moving fast, but I felt we could pick up even more speed.

*   *   *

It was already clear that there were opportunities all around us.

The secret was to spot the opportunity, then turn it into a profitable commission. The Kuwait power station was a case in point. The main contract was proceeding smoothly, but I realised that there might be an opportunity for us to deepen our business with the Kuwaitis in an innovative way. One day Sheikh Jaber Al-Ali mentioned to me that Kuwait had to import large amounts of chlorine for water purification. The power station was being built with a desalination plant, which was being handled by another consultancy.

The two facts – imported chlorine and the installation of the desalination plant – came together in my chemical engineer's mind, and I had an idea. 'We can make chlorine for you,' I said. He looked puzzled and I explained. The desalination plant would produce brine. By passing the brine through an electrolysis process we could create sodium chloride, which could be further refined into two other chemicals – the chlorine Kuwait needed for water purification, and sodium hydroxide, or caustic soda, useful as an ingredient in cleaning materials and other products. Sheikh Jaber was delighted with the idea, and we won another contract to manage the project building the treatment facility.

At the same time, we were also developing our business in Saudi Arabia, following the early Aramco project. We won a contract to oversee the construction of a pumping and pipeline system to bring water from underground springs adjacent to the city of Riyadh, the capital. Then we received a prestigious project to oversee the construction of a road connecting Jeddah, a city on the Red Sea with Hawiyah airport at Taif. Because the road passes through extremely difficult terrain – it zigzags for nearly 40 kilometres up into the mountains – the project proved one of the most difficult roads we have ever supervised. We progressed at just two or three kilometres a year.

While we were working on that project, Niar Al-Abidi, our resident engineer in Jeddah, who was supervising the work, had an accident and broke his leg. The building work was being carried out by Bin Laden Construction, the company founded by Mohammad Bin Laden, father of Osama, the notorious terrorist behind the 11 September 2001 atrocity in New York. (The Bin Laden family disowned Osama after he was stripped of his Saudi citizenship in 1994.) When Mohammad Bin Laden heard about the accident, he flew in his private plane to see what had happened. Al-Abidi was in a bad way, and Bin Laden placed the plane at his disposal so that he could be flown direct to hospital in Beirut. Further, he instructed his agent in Lebanon to pay Al-Abidi's hospital bills. It is, perhaps, worth recording the incident if only to place on record that members of the Bin Laden family, with numerous sons and daughters, were always capable of spontaneous acts of humanity and generosity. Osama turned out to be a stark exception.

As we moved from the 1950s to the 1960s and the number of new projects increased, I made plenty of use of the simple yet effective financial-management system I had implemented when we'd established the company. Each project was given a unique identifier that consisted of a letter for the country (for example K for Kuwait), the last two digits of the year in which the project started, and a project number. Thus the power-station project was K576. We were then able to assign both costs and revenues to each project and determine at any point in time how profitable each was. Such management accounting techniques are commonplace in these days of computerised accounting systems, but they were not so frequently used back in the 1950s. The principles behind the system have stood the test of time. It is the basis of the system Dar Al-Handasah still uses, although today it does operate on a computer.

When you're managing a fast-growing company, it's all too easy to lose track of the detail as you, rightly, follow the big picture. But in consultancy, the detail is also important, if only because you can't afford expensive mistakes that undermine client confidence. So, again at the outset, I set up a system to make sure I could keep track of everything that was happening within our growing portfolio of projects. Every letter that left the company was typed in triplicate – with the top copy going to the client, a red copy going to the partner managing the project (and ultimately into the project file) and a yellow copy coming to me for signature – and then for filing chronologically. Again, it was a simple system, but one that served us well in our early years.

By 1962, we were achieving levels of growth in our business that we could not have dreamed of in 1956 when I established the company. But then, out of the blue, came an offer that I'd not expected.

I was invited to take a ministerial post in the government in my native Jordan. It was both an honour and a challenge. It was an honour because it implied recognition in my own native land. But I was concerned about the challenge. Being a government minister would require immense commitment on my part – commitment that would take me away from Dar Al-Handasah at a crucial stage in its development.

CHAPTER 11

Developing Jordan's economy

J ordanian prime minister Wasfi At-Tal's invitation placed me on the horns of not one but two dilemmas.

The first was that I had always considered myself an activist, and here was an opportunity to exercise that activism in the front line of policy-making in my native land. Yet, while I had developed a clear point of view about the kinds of policies that Middle Eastern countries should follow – and made no secret of the fact – I had always avoided being sucked into the kind of political rivalries that active party politics encourages.

The second dilemma was no less difficult to resolve. I felt the business experience I'd gained building Dar Al-Handasah would prove useful as vice-president of the Development Board. Yet I realised the post would be time-consuming and my attention would be diverted from work at Dar Al-Handasah. This worried me, as the company's growth still relied heavily on my close personal involvement.

I turned the arguments over and over in my mind. Jordan was at a critical point in its political and economic development. I was being offered the post of vice-president of the Development Board in the government, with ministerial rank and powers, although not a formal ministerial position. I was confident that I would be able to discharge the duties involved. (After completing my engineering doctorate, I had taken some post-graduate courses in economics at Yale.) Moreover, I had enormous respect for Wasfi At-Tal, who was forming his first government – he went on to form two more.

I decided that the job I was being offered would suit me. I've never been shy of robust debate – but I didn't feel that mixing it in the political arena would be compatible with running a business which, of its very nature, had to take a non-party political position. I was averse to becoming immersed in politics as a cabinet minister, and remained so on subsequent occasions when I was invited to hold ministerial office.

But that didn't mean I couldn't make a contribution to At-Tal's government in a less overtly political way, and the vice-presidency of the Development Board fitted the bill well. After all, the Board's aim was to help in the work of regenerating Jordan's economy, and I had spent my business life working on development projects designed to improve economic performance in one way or another. The formal president of the Board was the Prime Minister himself, but as vice-president I would be its effective head. So I was confident the job would provide me with a new and exciting challenge.

Nor, when I came to think about it more, were the practicalities of doing the job insuperable. The distance between Beirut (where I was living) and Amman (where I also had a house) wasn't that great. I could commute between the two. And Laura and the children could come to Amman for some of the time, so that precious family life would remain intact.

The Development Board was partly modelled on one that had been operating with some success in Iraq. The purpose of the Iraqi board was to make certain that around 70 per cent of the country's oil revenues were channelled into long-term productive investment – the kind that would still be delivering benefits to the country even when the oil ran out. It was a wise move, as some other countries had spent their oil revenues profligately with few thoughts as to the long-term future.

But although the principle of having a development board was a good one, there were no oil reserves in Jordan. Since the country had become independent in the 1940s, it had been heavily reliant on aid, initially from Britain and later from the United States. Building an economy in a new country with few natural resources had been tough. Even so, as I took up my post in Amman, there were signs that the Jordanian economy was improving. Since the mid-1950s investment had been flowing into the potash, phosphate and cement industries. An oil refinery – the country's first – had opened at Zarka, east of Amman, in 1961. Tourism was building slowly, especially among Christian pilgrims visiting holy sites on the West Bank. More of them were coming on to visit the archaeological splendours of the East Bank, notably Petra, the 'rose-red city half as old as time'.

There were other encouraging signs. Jordan already had a good system of elementary and secondary schools. Literacy had improved by leaps and bounds since my AUB student days, when I'd taught reading and writing at a summer school in Salt. Jordan's first university was established in the year I took up my new post. The country's infrastructure of roads and railways was starting, slowly, to improve. Most encouraging, a real community of business people and professionals was beginning to grow.

When I became vice-president in February 1962 I had one overriding objective. I wanted the Board to develop an economic plan that would free Jordan's current expenditure from reliance on overseas aid. I appreciated that there would still be a need for selective overseas assistance for some capital projects, but these, I argued, should be chosen carefully so that the revenues generated by the projects could be used to repay the loans over time with appropriate interest. The central question was how we were to develop the kind of macroeconomic plan for Jordan's economy that I had in mind. I started by recruiting a group of economists, some of whom I'd known from my time in Lebanon. I assembled a team of five or six, led by the very able Edmond Asfour, who later went on to become a senior economist at the World Bank. With the team in place, we went to work.

The output of our labours was a seven-year development plan that was designed to make Jordan financially self-supporting on its current expenditure by 1969. The heart of this plan was building up Jordan's industries and infrastructure to generate economic growth. When

GDP grows, so do tax revenues – and the government needed the revenues both to invest in essential public works and to reduce the reliance on aid from outside. As I recall, in 1962 Jordan was receiving something of the order of $15m a year in US aid. The plan would have eliminated that within seven years, and by 1967 – when the Six Day War with Israel wrecked the plan and threw the economy of several Middle Eastern countries, including Jordan, into a temporary reverse – we had already reduced aid to around $3m a year.

The infrastructure and industrial investment part of the plan was supported by measures to generate adequate taxation and to improve the efficient collection of government revenues of all kinds. I also established a Budget Bureau, separate from the Ministry of Finance, in order to improve the day-to-day financial management of government programmes. I recruited technical assistance from the Ford Foundation in establishing the Bureau. The Bureau was supported by further measures to ensure that capital projects, especially those relying on overseas aid, would be subject to rigorous appraisal to ensure their viability, including the ultimate repayment of the aid.

Having put in place measures so that Jordan could run its current account without overseas aid in the long term, I also determined that we should take a fresh look at how we evaluated the loans and assistance that were needed in the short term. It was important that capital-account aid was invested in those projects that would help us stimulate economic growth. I approached the newly established Kuwait Fund for Arab Economic and Social Development to see what assistance it could provide. It was particularly fortunate that the power-station project had switched on most successfully only the previous year, and so my reputation as somebody with an ability to deliver preceded me to my first meeting with the fund's managers.

There were several immediate projects that I hoped I could persuade the Fund to support. The highest priority project was the Maqarin Dam on the Yarmouk River near the Syrian Border. But there were also other priorities. An industry I particularly wanted to see developed was phosphate mining. Phosphates had been first discovered in Jordan back in 1935, and the Jordan Phosphate Mines Company, set up in 1949, had been steadily exploiting the country's vast reserves. But in 1962 phosphate exports were still less than 300,000 tons a year. (Today they are more than 3.5 million tons.) I wanted to develop the phosphate mines at Al-Hasa, in southern Jordan, in order to increase production. Another project that needed funding was Jordan's Industrial Development Bank.

All these projects featured in my negotiations with the Kuwait Fund's managers. The negotiations went well, and the Fund agreed to provide a loan of 7.5m Kuwait dinars, equivalent to about $25m at the time, covering these and other projects: KD3m ($10m) was allocated for Al-Hasa, KD0.5m ($1.7m) for the Industrial Development Bank and KD4m ($13.3m) for the Maqarin Dam. In fact, the Maqarin project took up a considerable amount of my time at the Development Board – and it highlighted in a dramatic way the strategic importance of water in the Middle East.

*   *   *

It is easy for people in the West, where water is readily available at the turn of a tap, to dismiss the subject as unimportant. But in the Middle East, where much land is desert and water is hard to find, it is the commodity without which life simply cannot exist. It is certainly not possible to develop a modern state, with its constant demand for water for agriculture and industry, not to mention public-health uses, without an abundant and growing supply.

The Development Board, therefore, adopted the right priorities in allocating the largest single slice of the Kuwait loan to the Maqarin Dam. The aim was to construct a dam that could store as much as 400 million cubic metres of water. The Yarmouk flows into the River Jordan south of Lake Tiberias (the Sea of Galilee) from the east, close to the edge of the Golan Heights. For part of its course, the Yarmouk forms the boundary between Jordan and Syria. Both countries had signed a treaty, ratified in their parliaments, agreeing on the allocation of the Yarmouk's waters. By the time I took up my post, the project needed to move from political intent to practical implementation. I had found the matter waiting in my in-tray when I arrived at the Development Board.

I was already aware that water was one of the most politically sensitive subjects in the region, and I knew I would have to tread carefully in urging the project forward. I had first realised how divisive the subject of water could be back in 1953, when I was studying for my doctorate at Yale and working for the Organisation of Arab Students in the United States. In order to try to resolve conflicts between Israel and the Arab states over the River Jordan's water rights, President Dwight D. Eisenhower appointed an engineer, Eric Johnston, to visit the Middle East and try to negotiate an agreement. It was a matter in which our Arab student organisation had taken a keen interest.

Johnston approached his task with an open mind. He believed that the division of the water should be based upon the amount of arable land – land that was, thus, potentially capable of irrigation – in the Jordan Valley. He consulted widely with all the countries involved and with Egypt which, although it was not directly interested, wielded considerable influence throughout the Arab world. The final Johnston Plan, published in 1955, considered the irrigation needs of the Arab states first and then allocated the 'surplus' flow of water, amounting to 31 per cent, to Israel. The Israelis accepted the plan with some reservations, but the Arab side rejected it outright in a long letter to Johnston from Muhammed Amin Al-Husseiny, president of the Arab Higher Committee for Palestine. Al-Husseiny described the plan as an 'imperialistic Zionist scheme', and pointed out that Arab countries could carry out their own plans 'without having to rely for these upon American dollars'.

With the collapse of the negotiations, the Israelis went ahead with their own National Water Carrier project, which siphoned water from Lake Tiberias. The country that lost most from the failure was my native Jordan, which found vital irrigation projects delayed by the continuing uncertainty over water rights. Nevertheless, when I reached the Development Board, the Johnston Plan was still the *de facto* benchmark for water allocation in the region (and remains so today).

So, being intensely aware of the politics of water, I resolved to move carefully in seeking to take the Maqarin Dam project forward. I decided to meet with officials of other Arab governments in the region who were interested in the outcome of Maqarin. I believed we needed some expert advice on the technical aspects of water management, and appointed Salah Halwani, director-general of the Litani River Authority in Lebanon, to act as an adviser on behalf of the Jordanian government. He served us with great integrity and distinction.

On one of Halwani's visits to Jordan, I asked the army to provide me with a small military plane to fly him and myself to visit the site of the planned dam. We crossed to the Syrian side of the river and the Golan Heights. A Syrian commander received us courteously and escorted us on a tour of the Syrian military facilities. I was struck by the location of the fortifications, as well as the defended positions above the adjacent valley. I saw that the fortifications had reinforced concrete walls of between one and three metres' thickness. There were apertures in the walls from which weapons could be fired on attackers in the valley. I was impressed by the combination of fortifications and the precipitous topography. I was to remember all this amid the later catastrophe of the 1967 Six Day War. The fall of these well-defended positions was, to me, unimaginable.

But the limits of my imagination were corrected when I read General Moshe Dayan's account of the closing sequence of the war. As defence minister, Dayan was under pressure to accept a ceasefire when late in the evening the then Israeli army's chief of staff Yitzhak Rabin pleaded for permission to move forward to occupy the Golan Heights. Dayan had previously been against such an attack on two grounds. First, that it would involve Israeli defence forces fighting on two fronts − against Syria in the north and Egypt in the south. Second, that opening an attack on Syria could draw in the Soviet Union on the Syrian side. As a result, Dayan directed Rabin to retire for the evening without an attack being launched. Later that night − probably in the early hours of the following day − Dayan consulted with the army commander for the northern sector and asked if the Golan could be occupied. Informed sources seem to believe that three factors changed Dayan's mind that night. First, Nasser suddenly expressed interest in a ceasefire and urged the Syrians shelling Israeli positions to comply. Second, Dayan learnt from military intelligence that the major Syrian town on the Golan, Kuneitra, had been abandoned. Third, Dayan received information that Israeli forces had reached the Suez Canal and Red Sea, and thus an attack on the Golan would not involve Israel in a two-front war. In any event, the northern commander was confident of a swift success, and the Golan was essentially lost while Rabin slept.

Following my visit with Halwani to the Maqarin Dam site, I travelled to Syria and Lebanon and had cordial meetings with high officials. Both countries seemed positive about the aims and objectives of the scheme.

But I had underestimated the political shenanigans that the Maqarin project had unleashed. The heart of the problem was the lower River Jordan, which in 1962 flowed mostly through Jordanian territory. The Arab states were understandably concerned about Israel's unilateral water schemes, particularly those that planned to take water directly from Lake Tiberias – water which would have otherwise flowed south through the lower Jordan.

At an Arab summit that took place not long after I had left the Development Board, the Syrians proposed that the only way to combat the Israeli threat was to divert water from two headwater streams of the Jordan, the Rivers Hasbani and Banias, which had their springs in, respectively, Lebanon and Syria. In this way, water would become available for use in Jordan, Syria and Lebanon even before it reached Lake Tiberias. In contrast, the Maqarin Dam would not have stopped Israel from drawing large quantities of water from Lake Tiberias (as it now does) because the Yarmouk flows into the Jordan south of the lake. In the absence of any agreement to share water, along Johnston's lines, it was clear that the affected countries intended to grab what they could. It was a policy that I did not favour because I could see that it would only increase tension in the region. But in any event, as I had left the Development Board by this time, I was not in a position to protest.

The Syrian proposal was accepted by other Arab states, and they set up a technical committee to investigate how the objective might be achieved. The technicians concluded that local topography would prevent the Banias being diverted within Syria. There were also problems in directly harnessing the Hasbani's water, so the politicians decided to look again at the Yarmouk. The further downstream they could dam the Yarmouk, the more water they could take, because the river's capacity increased as further inflows fed it. So Maqarin was put on the back-burner and a new site was chosen, closer to the Yarmouk's confluence with the Jordan. The new project was called the Khalid Bin Al-Waleed dam. The money the Kuwaitis had pledged for Maqarin was diverted to the new dam and construction commenced.

The more militantly nationalist governments of Syria and Egypt crowed about the great victory the new project represented. But, as so often, their triumphalism was shortlived. When the Six Day War broke out, the Israelis bombed what had been built of the dam and destroyed it. But that was in the future.

*   *   *

For the present, as the months of 1962 ticked by, my work at the Development Board was progressing well. Prime minister Wasfi At-Tal was as good as his word and allowed me a free hand to direct the Board's work. At the same time, At-Tal was delighted with the progress we had made, and the seven-year plan had been approved enthusiastically by the government.

But achieving this success had been tough on me. I was still having to keep close control of progress at Dar Al-Handasah. I would spend most of a typical week in Amman, fly back to Beirut on a Thursday evening, spend Friday in Dar's office, then return to Amman on the Saturday-morning flight. Laura and the children joined me in Amman for some of the time. But although it was very gruelling, I had been used to working long hours and I'd also had a taste of a regular commute between two cities. When you're working hard, nothing buoys you more than success. And we were unquestionably delivering just what Jordan needed. I found it most gratifying to see my activism producing such positive results.

Then a train of unwelcome events led me to question whether I really could carry on.

In September 1962, there was a military coup in North Yemen. The army's commander, Abdullah Al-Sallal, who was a keen supporter of the kind of militant nationalism espoused by Nasser, seized power and declared the Arab Republic of Yemen (YAR), with himself as president. The existing ruler, Imam Al-Badr, fled from the capital Sana'a, but took up arms with his Zeidi followers in the back country. North Yemen descended into civil war between Al-Sallal's republicans and Al-Badr's royalists.

It was not surprising that Nasser declared his strong support for Al-Sallal and sent forces to help him establish a grip on the country. It was at this point that King Hussein of Jordan made what I believe to be an error. He decided to intervene in the conflict on the royalist side. King Hussein sent a squadron of Jordan's small air force to North Yemen to aid Al-Badr. But the head of the Jordanian air force and two pilots defected to Cairo with their planes. The depleted squadron was embarrassingly ordered back to Amman.

As if this was not bad enough, I discovered that the government was planning to use all of the country's limited financial reserves – just 2m dinars – to finance the military adventure supporting Al-Badr. After the months of intensive work we had done to prepare an economic plan, and having reached the position where we could see the plan starting to bear fruit, I could not possibly agree with the financial implications of the Yemeni intervention. So I resigned.

I wrote my letter of resignation and arranged for it to be delivered to At-Tal after the plane taking me back to Beirut had taken off from Amman airport. My mind was made up, and I wasn't going to have it changed. Looking back, I believe my decision was correct. As it turned out, Al-Badr's cause was doomed. He was eventually persuaded to flee the country. Al-Sallal, too, was finally overthrown by a group of his former allies and fled to Cairo. But the fighting continued, with Egyptian troops – now not wanted in the country by either side – caught in the middle and unable to withdraw without Nasser losing face.

Although I had resigned as vice-president of the Development Board, I had not turned my back on my homeland. I was to return to Jordan's public life in 1989 as a senator in the upper house of parliament. But, sadly, it was not the last time my advice was going to be ignored in the highest circles of Jordan's government.

* * *

Meanwhile, back in Beirut, I turned my attention to building up Dar Al-Handasah. I was disappointed that I hadn't been able to continue my work at the Development Board, but in 1965 a project came along that I felt would benefit many people in Jordan. Dar Al-Handasah was commissioned to carry out work on a large irrigation project that was planned by the Jordanian government for the Jordan Valley. The project was significant in the growth of Dar Al-Handasah for three reasons.

First, it was a large-scale irrigation project, and although we had undertaken water projects before they hadn't been on the scale of this. The project promised to take us into a new league as far as irrigation work was concerned.

The second significance was that it underscored a technique that I had already developed on a number of other projects, but which was becoming key to the company's expansion in this phase of its growth story – partnering with other organisations with specialist knowledge. In this case, we partnered with consultants from Nedeco, a Dutch independent non-profit foundation which promoted (and still does) consultancy know-how and skills particularly on water, environment and infrastructure projects. Considering the achievements of the Dutch in reclaiming their polders from the sea, it wasn't surprising that they should be past masters at managing water drainage and irrigation. For our part, we were becoming masters in what has since become known as 'knowledge transfer', and we learnt a lot from Nedeco that proved useful experience for future irrigation and water work.

The third point of interest was that this was one of the early large projects in which Dar Al-Handasah provided a full economic and social study of the likely impact of the proposed development on the communities that it affected. It had become clear to me in the early years of our company's growth that development projects weren't just going to be about narrow technical issues – the stresses and strains in buildings and bridges. There are stresses and strains in communities, and the purpose of development is to ease them. But that means finding out what those stresses and strains are and then working out how your proposed development project can best alleviate them. Thus we undertook a full socio-economic study of the impact of the irrigation scheme on the West and East Banks.

The Jordanian government's intention was to create more cultivated land in the Jordan Valley and to turn that land over to Palestinian refugees currently living in camps or villages mostly in the West Bank. A key objective of the socio-economic study was to discover the size of the plot of land a family would need to sustain itself, assuming the plot was provided with water for agriculture. We discovered the size was 40 dunnums (about four hectares).

We worked with Nedeco on designing the network of canals and channels to carry the water to the various plots. Around 9000 families were settled and provided with the means to earn a reasonable livelihood by growing produce for their own consumption and as cash crops. The plan was well-intentioned and we were proud of our contribution in bringing it to fruition – and in changing people's lives by taking them out of refugee camps and giving them a new start in life. But like so many plans of politicians, it fell victim to the law of unintended consequences. Over the years, many of the families sold their plots to absentee landlords who aggregated the land together into larger units for more efficient working. Now many of those units are worked by immigrant workers – Indian or Pakistani on the West Bank side (now under Israeli control) and mostly Egyptian on the Jordanian East Bank.

But the water still flows.

CHAPTER 12

The Six Day War

The Jordan flowed in 1967 too, as countries of the Middle East swept towards war. The politics of water wasn't the only cause, but it played its part.

I was living in Beirut as the storm clouds of the Six Day War gathered in the spring of 1967. I found events ominous, especially when King Hussein decided that he would join a tripartite defence alliance with Egypt and Syria. Nasser extracted a high price from the King for Jordanian admission to the alliance, including the demand that the country's forces be placed under the command of an Egyptian general, Abdul-Moneim Riad, assistant chief of the United Arab Command, in the event of the expected Israeli attack. Hussein's agreement to this demand was, in my view, a major mistake. Riad did not understand the Jordanian troops, and had no first-hand knowledge of the geography he was operating in, or of the military doctrine and tactics the Jordanian forces had practised. All three shortcomings were to prove disastrous when the attack finally came.

Although based in Beirut, I retained a deep interest in Jordan's affairs, not to mention our growing business interests there. By now, we had branch offices in both Amman and on the West Bank. In the weeks leading up to the Six Day War, I spent most weekends in Amman meeting with politicians, government officials and other influential citizens. I was alarmed that there was a growing appetite for war among most of them. There was a weary acceptance that war would come no matter what they did, among other things. I was resolutely opposed to Jordan taking part in the conflict, but I found myself in a small minority.

My friend Wasfi At-Tal had been serving his second term as prime minister since 1965. He was completely opposed both to placing Jordanian forces under Egyptian command and to attacking Israel. He told me at the time that he had argued his case with King Hussein in strong terms. 'We will lose our self-respect by placing our forces under Egyptian command and, as prime minister, I will not get into a war that I know we will lose,' he had told the King and repeated to me. The King dispensed with his services and appointed Sharif Hussein Ibn Nasser in his place. Nasser lasted only six weeks, and Saad Jumaa succeeded him. He was prime minister when the war started on 5 June with an Israeli attack on Egyptian air bases, destroying the country's air force on the ground.

Five days earlier, King Hussein had granted me an audience. He knew I was opposed to the policies he had been following, but was open-minded enough to listen to my views. He received me in a very friendly manner and I set out the views which At-Tal had already put to him in more trenchant terms. It was not difficult to understand why Hussein was allowing himself to be carried along into war. He knew of the popular clamour for war, especially among the Palestinian communities of the West Bank. He knew his own position was at threat from Jordanians who supported Nasser's approach to Arab nationalism. It may be that he felt he had no choice but to enter the war in order to appease public opinion. Possibly he believed that Jordan would have been dragged into it anyway. He was under few illusions that in a conflict with Israel Jordan would lose territory. Maybe he reasoned that if he was seen to be a willing participant in the war he would retain popular support and be in a position to negotiate the return of lost territory at a later date. Whatever his thinking, I did not change his mind and I had not expected to. In any event, any hope the King may have had of regaining lost territory proved to be elusive.

Following my audience with King Hussein, my forebodings about the likely course of events in a war with Israel proved only too accurate. I recall vividly the day hostilities began. On the morning of 5 June 1967 I was in Amman. I was listening to the Egyptian radio station Sawt Al-Arab (Voice of the Arabs) when I heard the announcement that war with Israel had started. The radio said that Egyptian forces had downed 130 Israeli planes over Egypt and that Arab forces were advancing on all fronts. If Sawt Al-Arab was to be believed – which I was sure it wasn't – Nasser's propaganda machine seemed to have victory virtually assured.

In 1967, in addition to my duties at Dar Al-Handasah, I was chairman of Jordan's Phosphate Mining Company. In those days the company mined phosphate from underground deposits at Russaifah, 20 kilometres east of Amman. The mines, I reasoned, were a key economic asset, and might be targeted by the Israeli air force. My immediate concern was to protect the lives of our miners and other staff. I telephoned the company's Amman office and ordered mining operations to be suspended. Then I set off by car for the office in order to review plans to deal with the threat in more detail with the staff.

I was astounded that Amman's streets were deserted at what was usually a busy time. On my drive, I passed buildings that housed some of the operations of the US embassy. In this area, there was more traffic, and it was heading towards the house of a businessman friend of mine, Mohamed Al-Taher. Out of curiosity I followed the traffic.

When I arrived at Al-Taher's house someone directed me to the base-ment. There I found that Al-Taher had organised an elaborate air-raid shelter. The shelter was crowded, but I spotted Al-Taher and he greeted me. He explained that he'd equipped the place as tensions had built between Israel and Egypt following Egypt's demand that UN observers in Sinai – they'd arrived in the aftermath of the 1956 war – withdraw.

I asked Al-Taher what had caused the crowd in the shelter to seek refuge. He told me they'd seen a single plane that had been circling above the city for several hours. He led me out of the basement and took me to a window on an upper storey of his house, itself built high on one of Amman's jebels (mountains). I looked up. The plane was still circling languidly.

I will never forget the contrast between the boasts of victory I'd heard on Sawt Al-Arab and the fearful reaction of the people in that basement. I felt a deep sense of sadness. The people had received the proclamation from Nasser's propaganda machine. The war for the liberation of Palestine had commenced – a war the Arab masses had demanded for so long. And yet our capital, a city of almost a million souls, awaited its fate in motionless silence as the population cowered at the sight of a single plane circling passively high in the sky.

My forebodings on the prospects for war were vindicated in the days that followed. Within two days of the war starting, Jordanian forces had fallen back deep inside their own territory on their second defence line. And, as history relates, the battle was soon over, with the West Bank and East Jerusalem, both formerly Jordanian, and other territories under Israeli control.

The tactics of General Riad, as I had suspected, proved disastrous. If only Hussein had left At-Tal in charge of affairs. At-Tal had told me his plan was to send the Jordanian army into West Jerusalem, the declared capital of Israel, and to hold it. Within the Israeli part of the city, they would be safe from aerial attack. At-Tal knew the Jordanian army would not be able to hold the West Bank. His plan, he revealed to me, would have been to negotiate West Jerusalem for the West Bank after hostilities ceased. If we had to enter a disastrous war, it seemed about the only plan that stood any chance of military success.

I spent much of the period of the hostilities in Amman, and when the war was over I returned to Beirut with a heavy heart. I was bitter that, once again, poor leadership had failed the Arabs' just cause. I was disappointed that we had lost our branch office in the West Bank – and the business that went with it – at least in the short term. But after a few days back in Beirut I realised that the setback that our leaders had just inflicted upon the Arab peoples made it all the more important that we should succeed in what we had set out to do at Dar Al-Handasah.

*   *   *

The aftermath of the Six Day War presented me with one of the most challenging tasks I have ever been asked to undertake.

The war had resulted in the loss of the West Bank (from Jordan), the Gaza Strip and Sinai (from Egypt) and the Golan Heights (from Syria) to Israeli control. Thousands of Palestinian refugees from the West Bank had flooded into Jordan. In the years following the war, the Palestine Liberation Organisation launched regular raids on Israeli positions from the refugee camps that had been established along the east bank of the Jordan.

One of these camps was in the town of Al-Karameh. On 21 March 1968, the Israelis launched a major attack on the town, claiming it was a base for the PLO. The fighting was fierce, and the Palestinian *fedayeen* were either killed or forced to flee their base. However, the decisive factor in the engagement was the Jordanian army's artillery, which destroyed Israeli tanks and forced the Israelis to withdraw.

But on the streets in Jordan, and elsewhere in the Arab world, Yasser Arafat, leader of the PLO, claimed the victory as Fatah's. It was part of the dangerous refusal to face facts and act rationally that had drawn the Arab nations into war with Israel in both 1948 and 1967. Fatah's 'victory' entered the mythology of the Palestinian movement and remains a potent symbol even today, despite the abundant evidence of respected historians that it was the Jordanian army's intervention that was decisive.

In any event, the aftermath of the battle led to my first meeting with Yasser Arafat. I was one of a group of professional engineers invited by the Jordanian government to inspect the damage at Al-Karameh. It was extensive, but we thought it would be a good idea to develop a masterplan to rebuild the town, and my company was asked if it would undertake the task. We did so, and it became the first of many reconstruction projects we undertook in battle zones around the world.

By the time I came to tour Al-Karameh with my fellow engineers, Arafat's *fedayeen* had moved out to a camp on the edge of the rift valley not far from my hometown of Salt. He invited us to visit him. What sticks in my mind even today is the theatre of the occasion. We travelled up to the camp and were invited to await our audience in a tent. We were later beckoned from the tent to meet Arafat. He was sitting on the ground, carefully cleaning a rifle. The event had been clearly staged as a symbolic scene: the great guerilla warrior engaged in the humble tasks of the camp. Mythology again. There are many Arabs who simply can't resist it.

The conversation that followed was inconsequential, and from what little I remember turned partly on the reconstruction of Al-Karameh. I left feeling manipulated, and somewhat less than impressed. It did not seem to me that the warrior on the ground – no matter how clean his rifle – was likely to lead his people to victory by force of arms.

But I had underestimated his determination to try. For two years later, in 1970, the Palestinian problem forced its way into my life again in a most worrying and unpleasant form. The influx of refugees into Jordan after the 1967 war (added to those who had been incorporated in 1948–49) had altered the balance of the country's population to the point where Palestinians outnumbered those whose first loyalty was to the Hashemite Kingdom of Jordan. Effectively, there was a state within a state. Clashes between Palestinian fighters and the Jordanian army continued sporadically. Then, on 6 September, a spectacular event occurred that brought matters to a head.

The Popular Front for the Liberation of Palestine (PFLP), a splinter group of the PLO, hijacked three airliners. Two of them, belonging to Swissair and TWA, were flown to Dawson's Field, a desert airstrip outside Amman. The third was flown ultimately to Cairo. The hijackers of all the planes demanded the release of Palestinian prisoners in Jordan and Israel in return for the liberty of the passengers. Negotiations continued, and eventually all three aircraft were blown up, after the passengers had been freed.

For King Hussein, this was an act of provocation too far. He had already endured assassination attempts and attacks on his security forces. Now he decided to hit back. He declared martial law and a full-scale civil war between the Jordanian army and Palestinian guerilla groups began. It raged for much of September until the Jordanian army began to gain the upper hand. At this point, the Arab League intervened to suggest a peace conference in Cairo. Hussein accepted, and a ceasefire agreement was signed on 27 September.

But the so-called Cairo Agreement left something of a stalemate between the two sides. And in October, King Hussein appointed for the third time as prime minister Wasfi At-Tal, in a move designed to strengthen the government and take more decisive action. He called on my services again in one of the gravest hours in Jordan's history. At-Tal had served as an officer in the British army and also in the Arab Army of Deliverance, which fought in the 1948 war. In his earlier political career, he'd had liberal sympathies and had removed the ban on political parties in Jordan during one of his former spells as prime minister. But now, he explained to me, he felt the future of the country was at stake and that the threat of the *fedayeen* had to be neutralised once and for all.

With the full support of the King, he imposed a new agreement – the Amman Agreement – on the PLO. Under its terms, they were to withdraw from the cities, taking all their weapons and ammunition with them. From his military expertise, he realised that it would be easier to control rebel forces in the countryside than in Amman. But it was essential that they could not sneak back into the city to reclaim hidden caches of weaponry in order to restart their fight. The task he wanted to lay on me was to negotiate the withdrawal of the *fedayeen* from the city and the removal of their weapons and ammunition.

It was a grave responsibility, and one quite unlike anything I had undertaken before. In the following two months, I faced determined opponents across the negotiating table, but I was also determined – and I had the full backing of the state behind me. And by April 1971, the withdrawal process was underway.

With the agreement of At-Tal, it was decided that there should be thorough searches of the city to validate that all weaponry had been removed. During the first of these searches, security forces discovered large caches of weapons. With more than a little displeasure, I called in Salah Khalef, Arafat's second-in-command, and insisted that the agreement be properly implemented. He protested that the agreement only covered the property of East Bank Jordanians, and that those who came from the West Bank could properly leave weapons on their premises. He was seeking to misrepresent the unification of the West

Bank and the East Bank in the state of Jordan that had taken place in the aftermath of the 1948 war. Those that hailed from the East Bank and the Palestinian West Bank were all Jordanian citizens – there was no distinction. Khalef's argument twisted the meaning of our original agreement beyond breaking point, and I was not prepared to entertain it. I made it clear to him that unless the original agreement was honoured to the letter, there would be serious consequences. Khalef left in a fury, but I had ensured that further large caches of arms would be removed from the urban area.

It was not the end of the matter – and there was a tragic sequel. In the months following, relations between the PLO and the Jordanian government reached an impasse. Arafat called for the overthrow of the government. By the summer, the army had resolved to counter the threat. Some PLO bases were destroyed, plotters arrested and many Palestinians expelled to other Arab countries. Finally, the Palestinian threat to the Jordanian state was neutralised.

But my friend Wasfi At-Tal paid dearly for his decisiveness. In November that year, in Cairo, Palestinian guerrillas assassinated him.

*   *   *

The fallout from the Six Day War resonates throughout the Middle East even today. The damage lies in how far it changed the mindset of many ordinary Arabs. Their response to their defeat in the 1948–49 war had been to blame incompetent Arab leaders who, at the time, were liberal Arab nationalists. As a result, liberal Arab nationalist leaders, and the democratic institutions that they had established, were generally swept aside by new leaders who promised to take a sterner view and win new wars – but who also committed millions of Arabs to illiberal nationalism within totalitarian states. The dictators, such as Egypt's Nasser, entrenched their positions by using the instruments of propaganda and the police state.

Indeed, by the outbreak of the Six Day War Nasser's propaganda machine had successfully elevated him to a position of dominance in the Arab world shared by no other individual before or since. In the eyes of the masses, he became the embodiment of their hopes and dreams. It had been Nasser, for his own political ends, who had been instrumental in ratcheting up the tension over Palestine in the run-up to the war. Nasser's rhetoric before hostilities began was precise and promised people certain victory. In an address on 29 May 1967, he told Egypt's National Assembly: 'God will surely help and urge us to restore the situation to what it was in 1948'.

But the Israelis proved more than a match for that kind of bombast. They launched a pre-emptive strike against Egypt. The Egyptian air force was knocked out in the first hour or so of combat. Then Israeli forces swiftly seized the Sinai peninsular and the Gaza Strip. Both Jordanian and Syrian artillery units went into action, but the Israelis swiftly occupied East Jerusalem and the West Bank of Jordan, and seized the Golan Heights from Syria. Far from restoring the 1948 situation, the Arabs had lost, within six days, what Palestinian territory they had retained, as well as Sinai, Gaza and the Golan Heights.

And did this debacle – as great as any military defeat can be – end Nasser's popularity and see him driven from power? Not a bit of it. When the war had been lost, Nasser made a humiliating statement to the Egyptian people in which he ridiculously attributed the defeat to the fact that Israel's initial attack came from the west rather than the east. He proceeded to declare his resignation and announce Zakaria Mohieddin as his successor. But I am convinced that his propaganda machine was still in good order and marshalling the masses. Crowds marched on the president's palace appealing for him to withdraw his resignation. It was reported that the journalist Mohamad Hassanin Haikal was in the palace with Nasser, and that security commanders feared that the crowd might panic and stampede. Haikal convinced Nasser to address the crowd and calm them with the promise to reconsider his resignation and announce his decision the following day. Nasser addressed the crowd and they dispersed. Nasser survived. He continued in office until 1970, when he fell victim to cardiac and diabetic ailments and died.

But among ordinary Arabs, more hope had died than we realised. Their dreams of regaining the Palestinian homelands were shattered. For many, the militant nationalism that Nasser and others elsewhere had espoused seemed less attractive. Quite simply, it didn't deliver what it promised. It had lost the battle for hearts and minds. Following the 1967 war, the influence of nationalist politicians dwindled. Millions in the Arab world began to look elsewhere for sources of hope and salvation for their causes. They sought refuge from the destruction of their dreams in their religion. The influence of militant Islamic organisations and parties expanded to fill the vacuum left by failed nationalist politicians such as Nasser and his like. Today, militant Islamic movements have become a major destabilising force in the Middle East, with serious repercussions for the rest of the world.

CHAPTER 13

Into Africa

Business goes on.

Despite the troubles that wars, revolutions, coups and insurrections bring, business continues to be done. And thank heavens it does. In international affairs, the fraught years of the 1960s stumbled by, but we continued to make progress at Dar Al-Handasah. And, as we did so, we expanded the breadth of experience we'd accumulated as well as the geographical spread of our company's reach. If the 1950s were about establishing the business and building its credibility, the 1960s were about moving out of the Middle East into new areas, including, for the first time, sub-Saharan Africa.

But before we moved into Africa, we were involved in what was to be one of a number of landmark projects that helped to make our name during the 1960s. The project was the American University of Beirut Medical Center – a new teaching hospital for AUB. It was a particular joy for me to win this contract partly because AUB remained – and still does – first in my affections of the universities I have attended.

But I was also delighted because the new Medical Center was to develop a reputation as the finest teaching hospital in the Middle East. The university had a long tradition of teaching medicine. The first medical students had graduated from AUB way back in 1871.

Originally, medicine was taught in Arabic, but then the medical school moved its teaching into English. By the 1960s, it was clear that if medicine was to continue to be taught at the standard demanded of modern American universities – AUB was registered in New York and obliged to observe New York state law and educational standards – new premises would be needed. Hence the decision to build the Medical Center.

The project was led by a firm of New York architects with the splendid name of Vorhees, Walker, Smith, Smith and Haines. Half way through the project Vorhees and Walker retired and the firm changed its name to Smith, Smith, Haines, Lundberg and Waehler. In those days, the American Architects' Association mandated that the partners' names should be included in the firm's title. These days, there is a more relaxed attitude and Smith, Smith, etc has become, like so many other firms an acronym, HLW, the initials of the names of the last three partners.

Our role was to act as the Lebanese consultants for the Medical Center. By now, Dar Al-Handasah had been through its first major reorganisation and we were down to two partners, with me operating as chief executive. So the task of negotiating our side of the contract with Vorhees, Walker and the rest fell heavily upon my shoulders. I suppose it was an advantage that I'd spent so much of my university career in the States. By now, flying to New York for regular meetings, taking on board the go-getting can-do culture of America, and understanding the ways people in the West liked to do business were all second nature to me.

Although the Americans were leading on the project, we probably ended up doing about three-quarters of the actual work, including most of the immense amount of detail involved in building any hospital, let alone a teaching establishment. We also acted as architects of record for legal purposes. The American partner in charge of the project, William Smith, visited Beirut about every three months, and I established a cordial and constructive working relationship with him.

For our part, we visited New York whenever we could find a reason to do so in order to learn from Smith, Smith and the others about designing and building hospitals. Although, by now, we were no strangers to large and prestigious projects – as those we'd successfully completed in Kuwait proved – the American University of Beirut Medical Center took us into areas where we'd not yet developed the world-class skills we wanted. One of these was architecture. There had obviously been architectural elements to the power station C project, but not at the level they presented themselves in the hospital.

Fishing again in the global talent-pool, we engaged an English architect called Keith Waugh to work on our side of the project. He guided us through the new disciplines we needed to learn about in order to reach the highest standards in hospital design. A hospital needs a vast range of specialist services, such as operating theatres and dispensaries, wards and waiting rooms. Even familiar building features, such as elevators, need special consideration because they have to be able to accommodate patients in wheelchairs or on trolleys. We found there were a thousand and one special factors we needed to keep in mind when planning a hospital, such as designing interiors so they can be cleaned easily and thoroughly to medical hygiene standards. Like human vacuum cleaners, we eagerly sucked up the information for future use.

In any business, knowledge is a vital asset. Sadly, in many businesses it is woefully under-exploited. Yet in consultancy, knowledge is the life-blood of the company. Which is why we have always placed such a high premium on learning new expertise and skills and keeping our existing knowledge right up to date. The American University of Beirut Medical Center was to become the first of many hospital projects we have worked on. In fact, today, one of our subsidiaries, the architects Perkins & Will, is regularly rated as number one in hospital and healthcare design in the United States.

Apart from the valuable experience and new knowledge we acquired from the Medical Center, the project also generated a steady stream of lucrative fees. We were growing and growing profitably, notwithstanding the uncertain political climate in the Middle East. Despite my hopes, there seemed little hope of resolving many of the region's underlying problems, especially those caused by the dispossessed Palestinian people.

And after the Six Day War, the economies of those Arab countries that had been involved went, temporarily at least, into reverse. That setback, I was acutely aware, wouldn't be good for our business. We were still winning new work but I felt it was time for the company to move outside our home region.

If we were serious about building a global business, the end of the 1960s wouldn't be a bad time to diversify. The difficulty was that most of the major economies outside the Middle East were already highly developed, with competitive markets. It wouldn't be easy to break into Europe or North America. Perhaps we should look elsewhere for our first venture outside our home region. The question was, in moving outwards, where should we make our first foray?

*   *   *

Some time during 1968, I fell into conversation with a friend who worked in the pharmaceuticals business. He had recently returned from Nigeria. The country was currently locked in a bitter civil war, but he'd come back bubbling with enthusiasm about the country's growth potential. Oil had recently been discovered in the eastern province, and he felt that it would bring a new wave of industrial development and prosperity to what was, at that time, a largely agricultural society. Could Nigeria, I wondered, possibly be the opportunity outside the Middle East that we were looking for? Or, in seeking to start up business in a country with an unfamiliar culture and a vicious civil war, would we just be looking for trouble?

The fact that the country had plunged into bitter strife was not a promising start. A civil war had started in July 1967 when Lieutenant-Colonel Odumegwu Ojukwu, the local military governor, declared the south-east province of the country independent as the state of Biafra. The cause of the split lay partly in the deep ethnic and tribal rivalries that dominated Nigerian politics following its independence from British colonial rule in 1960. The largely Ibo south-east of the country felt its interests were being sidelined by ethnic groups from other regions following two military coups that had taken place the previous year. There had also been a series of unpleasant killings of ethnic Ibos by different tribal groups in other parts of Nigeria. That provided Ojukwu with his immediate *casus belli*. The south-east region also just happened to be where most of the oil was located.

Nigeria's federal government launched what it called with devastating understatement a 'police action' to put down the rebellion. As many as one million were dead from fighting and famine by the time the police action concluded with Ojukwu's capitulation and flight in January 1970. But in 1968, the end of the fighting wasn't in sight. The walk-over victory that the stronger and better-equipped federal army had expected had not materialised. In fact, the previous year Biafran forces had crossed the River Niger and launched attacks close to Lagos, the Nigerian capital. Biafran commando raids behind federal lines were still taking place in 1968.

Yet despite these tragic – and, from a business perspective, unpromising – events, I felt instinctively that Nigeria was a country I ought to investigate. For a start, I'd already had more than my fair share of experience of running business in a region that was no stranger to political and military violence. I had developed an understanding of the risks and opportunities in doing business in countries with unstable regimes. I knew that most Western consultancies would take one look at Nigeria's troubles and write the country off. But, despite the fighting, Nigeria's government was still eager to develop its oil wealth – in fact more so than ever. We had built up a huge amount of experience running development projects in oil-rich economies, and I just knew that, if we could gain a foothold in the country, Nigeria would prove to be a prosperous market for us.

So Laura and I booked our air tickets, had our inoculations and flew to Lagos. Today, Lagos is a vibrant cacophonous city that assaults your senses with a bewildering variety of sights, sounds and smells. It was in more sober mood when we arrived. The war had not been going well, and this fact was reflected in the mood of some of the officials we met.

I had resolved that in order to make a proper assessment of the country's business potential from Dar Al-Handasah's perspective, I needed to visit the oil region. But that involved travelling close to the front line of the fighting. It soon became apparent that such a journey would not be easy, and that we could not undertake it without some danger to ourselves.

But my mind was made up. I hired a taxi and, along with Laura and Amin Shocair, a business friend who was in Nigeria, set off for Warri, a town in the south-east of the country, on the fringe of the River Niger's delta region. The distance was more than 300 miles. Today a network of autoroutes serves the south of Nigeria. In 1968, the roads were of very variable quality – and we were driving them in far from ideal conditions. We encountered regular road-blocks manned by units of the federal army and were required to produce our papers. When night fell, we continued our journey with doused lights so that we didn't attract the attention of Biafran forces who might have been operating behind federal lines. When the war had started, an eccentric Swede called Count Carl Gustav von Rosen had helped to set up a Biafran air force. It had, reputedly, only two planes, but that didn't mean it wouldn't use them to attack moving night-time targets. The danger was real.

Even so, as our journey slowly progressed we noticed that food was plentiful on the federal side of the lines. Roadside stalls sold fresh fruit, and I recall we bought a bunch of pineapples for a few coins. When we reached Warri, we checked into a hotel feeling relieved that we had made it. In those days, Warri was considerably smaller than the city of half a million it has become today. It was right at the beginning of the boom, and the city was yet to develop the modern oil refinery, harbour and airport that it has today. Unlike today, few oil and gas companies yet had a presence in the area. Warri was still very much a traditional provincial Nigerian town in which tribal rulers, such as the Olu of Warri, exercised significant influence.

The following day, I set about making contacts in the area. Teams had started developing the oilfield. I met officials in the government of the region and had useful talks with them. They realised the oilfields had tremendous potential. But they were also uncertain as to how much revenue the oil would generate, and they realised they lacked the expertise both to exploit the oil and to use the riches it would bring to invest in the productive long-term future of the region.

Within a few days, I had seen what I wanted, and I knew that we could have a tremendous future there. Despite the war, Nigeria was a new African frontier – a country that could use the prosperity it was about to gain to build a better future for its citizens. I had been impressed by both Lagos and Warri. There was an absence of the kind of grinding poverty so sadly seen in other parts of Africa. The streets were clean and crime levels seemed low.

Moreover, although I wasn't to meet him on this trip, as I was to do on several subsequent visits to the country, I was impressed by what I'd heard of Major-General Yakubu Gowon. He had come to power as the result of a military coup a year earlier. He hadn't taken part in the coup, but was chosen by the various factions who'd masterminded it as a compromise candidate who could manage the rivalry between different ethnic groups and prevent the whole country descending into chaos. Gowon had proved adept at that difficult task. The overarching aim of his policy was to hold the country together. He coined the slogan 'To keep Nigeria one is a task that must be done'. Not even elegant as doggerel, but it caught the mood of the people.

Our journey back to Lagos, and from there by air to Beirut, was laborious, but I spent some of the time thinking about how we could best establish ourselves in the country. There was no easy answer. We would have to open an office, and that would require investment. But, most important, we would need to find the right person to spearhead our move into this unfamiliar new market. Back in Beirut, I decided this was just the challenge a rising young engineer called Mounir Nassar should take on. I have always believed that young people should be given a chance. They have raw energy and they also have a certain kind of rough wisdom that often serves them well, especially when allied to their vigour.

Nassar had just what I look for in somebody who is going to open up new territory for us. He had excellent qualifications as an engineer, but more than that he possessed an entrepreneurial spirit. Like me, he loved winning. He had an unquenchable thirst for a challenge.

As it happened, he needed it. The business was there, but it was tough making contacts, getting to know the right people and winning those all-important early contracts that give you a name and, above all, credibility in a new market. In the first few months, Nassar experienced many sleepless nights from loneliness and the struggle to get some work for our company. I travelled to Nigeria about once a month to support him and do what I could.

By 1969, the war was clearly coming to an end as Ojukwu's forces became pinned down in their Ibo heartland. Gowon's federal government – together with the all-important state governments, which had considerable development powers – began to turn their attention to the reconstruction that would follow the war. Gowon had the vision to see that what the country needed was reconciliation rather than revenge, and that the federal government would have to make every effort to reintegrate eastern Nigeria into the country as a whole.

As the country's mood improved, the business started to flow. And soon, I have to admit, the volume of it surprised even me. We won contracts for schools, hospitals and irrigation projects. We produced as many as 70 town plans for cities, including two quadrants of Enugu. We drew up masterplans for states of the federation. We worked on transportation schemes. We were signing new contracts at such a rate that, at one stage, we had 12 offices across Nigeria and, for a few years, the country (along with Algeria, where we were also performing well) was effectively producing most of Dar Al-Handasah's profit.

But it would be wrong to give the impression that these contracts simply fell into our lap. We had to fight for them, often against other world-class consultancies. They may have had all the kudos that goes with being long-established consultancies from Europe or the United States, but we showed our potential clients that we were willing to try harder. A case in point was when we were up against one of these other consultancies for a hospital contract in Kano, a city in the strongly Muslim north of Nigeria.

It was a project we wanted passionately because the new hospital would be a beacon in the region and showcase our talents for others to see. But a British consultant was also after the work, and had devised what he thought was a clever marketing ploy. He told the client, the health minister for the region, that he already had a standard design for a hospital that, with a little adaptation, would suit Kano's needs. An existing design could be adapted more quickly and might even be cheaper than designing a whole hospital from scratch, he argued. I wasn't sure that he could produce a ready-made design that would actually meet Kano's specification. So when our team held a meeting with the health minister, I decided to call the British consultant's bluff. I suggested to the minister that an independent panel should be appointed to judge the best design. Within one month, both groups of consultants should submit their plans to the group for evaluation. The panel's decision on which consultants were selected for the contract would be final. That would be fair to both groups of consultants and help the minister make the right decision, I argued.

The British consultant was very dismissive of this suggestion. 'We don't do competitions as a matter of principle,' he sniffed. Perhaps he imagined that he was in such a strong position that the minister would cave in and accept his plan. I can't speak for the minister, but I suspect he viewed the consultant's rejection of my competition idea as arrogance. In any event, we won the business.

But the good times in Nigeria were not to last. Oil brought wealth to the country – revenues increased by 350 per cent between 1973 and 1974 alone – but it also brought corruption as well as jealousy and greed. It accelerated the urbanisation of Nigerian society, and cities became less friendly than I remembered them from my first visit, with shanty towns and rising crime. In 1975 General Gowon was overthrown in a coup and replaced by Brigadier Murtala Muhammad. He exposed what he claimed were growing levels of corruption among public officials across the country and sacked 10,000 of them without compensation. But in fact in the years ahead corruption increased, and within a few months Muhammad had been overthrown in another coup and replaced by Lieutenant-General Olusegun Obasanjo. Although Nigeria returned to uneasy civilian government in 1979, there were further military coups in the 1980s.

Dar Al-Handasah never gave up on Nigeria – and never will – but after Gowon left, our business in the country steadily declined. When Laura and I visited Nigeria together for the last time some years ago, we were shocked at the deterioration in the country – in the shabby fabric of the towns, at the poor service on offer in its hotels and shops, at the rising crime levels and endemic corruption. It is a sad reminder that wealth used unwisely can become a curse rather than a blessing. But I believe the inherent goodness of the Nigerian people will eventually enable them to win the better future they deserve.

*   *   *

As our business grew, trouble sometimes found us.

In 1969, we had a team working on a major road project in the People's Republic of South Yemen. Since the British had finally withdrawn from Aden in 1967, South Yemen had become a one-party state under the rule of President Qahtan Muhammad Al-Shaabi.

One day our resident engineer, Wahdan Oweis, was approached by a young man called Salem Ali Rubayi. We had six jeeps, which our team were using to cover the long distances and rough terrain involved in the road project. Rubayi asked politely if he might borrow the jeeps. 'Out of the question,' Oweis replied. 'We need them daily in our work.'

Rubayi was insistent. 'In a few days time, I'm going to become the president of this country. In the meantime, I need these jeeps to help my followers fight some battles.' Oweis looked at him incredulously, but Rubayi seemed deadly serious. He also had a gun. And he wasn't taking no for an answer. But he remained polite to the end: 'I shall have to insist about taking the jeeps, but I promise you we will return them in good condition.'

Oweis handed over the keys, expecting never to see the vehicles again. The coup duly took place and Muhammad Al-Shaabi was deposed. A few days later, Oweis was astonished to see a small convoy driving towards our main base. The jeeps were being returned, polished and cleaned, without a scratch on them, as promised.

The following year Rubayi, who governed jointly with Abdel Fattah Ismail in an uneasy coalition, changed the country's name to the People's Democratic Republic of Yemen. He nationalised foreign property and set up close ties with the Soviet Union. But politeness rarely pays off in politics. In 1978 Rubayi was deposed and executed.

CHAPTER 14

The sustainable enterprise

N one of us lives for ever.

But we can make it more likely that our companies will survive our retirement if we structure them in a way that makes them sustainable. From the moment I set up Dar Al-Handasah, I had it in my mind that the company should become something that would continue to prosper long after I had finished working for it – and, indeed, departed this earth. Since we cannot be immortal, leaving behind some lasting achievement is, perhaps, the next best substitute.

The reason I believe this is deep felt. For me, anything I do that is not sustained beyond my life is insignificant. If it disappears when I go, then it cannot have had much value. One of my key aims in founding a consultancy business was to establish an enterprise – a sustainable enterprise – that would go on providing jobs and creating wealth for the societies in which it operated for generations to come.

To some, that may seem a vainglorious ambition, but I certainly never conceived of it in that way. I suppose the ambition was born both of my activism and my belief in liberal nationalism. The activist in me wanted to achieve something that was lastingly worthwhile. The nationalist in me wanted to create something that would, initially, contribute constructively to the development of Arab societies throughout the Middle East. (That we have gone on to contribute to societies around the world is a source of even greater satisfaction.)

Beyond this, I think there is a simple and very practical reason for building a sustainable company. If you have established an enterprise for which thousands of people work and depend for their livelihood, then it is thoughtless, not to say irresponsible, to structure it in such a way that virtually ensures its decline when you retire or die. Not all company founders see things that way, especially in the modern world. Their aim is all too often to build a company and sell it to the highest bidder in the shortest possible time. That may be an acceptable approach if your only aim is to make money from it. But it means the unique approach you have tried to foster is subsumed, and probably lost, in a larger organisation. You have left no lasting value in the wider world.

Dar Al-Handasah has never been only about making money – although I hasten to add that we have been pretty successful at it. For me, establishing the company was about finding ways to contribute to the development of the societies we served. We have done that both by providing good jobs and career opportunities for bright young people from the Middle East and elsewhere and by using all our multiple skills in a special Dar way to leave behind us a string of projects that enrich the lives of the people who use or benefit from them.

*   *   *

By 1969, Dar Al-Handasah was growing fast. It became clear to me that if I was to turn my dream of building a sustainable enterprise into a reality, we needed to take decisive action to restructure the company. In the 13 years since our foundation, we had expanded at an ever-quickening pace. It is true that staff numbers had fluctuated depending on the particular workload we had at any one time, but the overall trend was upwards. As the end of the 1960s approached, we employed around three hundred people.

Ten years earlier, in 1959, I had parted company with three of my original partners. Now, as I contemplated how to turn Dar Al-Handasah into a sustainable enterprise for the future, I realised I would need the agreement of my remaining partner, Nazih Taleb, who held equal shares with me, if we were to make the changes I had in mind. I was by no means certain that he would agree, and my fears were soon confirmed when I approached him with my plan.

My idea, as I explained it to Taleb, was simple, although certainly unconventional. I wanted us to give away some meaningful portion of the shares of the company to a number of new partners chosen from among our senior employees. The thinking, as I presented it to him, was this. As the original two partners, we were getting older – although I still felt he and I had plenty of mileage – but the company was growing in size. If we were to create a cadre of senior managers who felt they had a real stake in the firm – and who would be committed to carrying it on after we had retired – we needed to give them a share in ownership. Moreover, the very fact of becoming shareholders as well as being executives would help the individuals concerned to grow in managerial stature. As part-owners, they would take a new view of the company and would, for the first time, have a direct personal interest in the bottom line. Most of all, we would be nurturing the next generation of Dar Al-Handasah's leaders, who would be able to sustain the company when we had moved on.

I was convinced the thinking behind the idea was sound in principle. The question was how I could effect such a shift in the ownership of the company in practice. I realised that, at this stage in the company's development, it would be unrealistic to expect the managers to buy shares in the firm, so I proposed that we should give shares to the chosen individuals over a two-year period. I was convinced that my plan would inject a real lift to the energy and commitment that the chosen managers would give to the company at a crucial period in our growth. Moreover, I was certain that the move would lay firm foundations for a sustainable enterprise in the future.

To me, the arguments were overwhelming, and I had hoped Taleb would agree with my thinking. But it was obvious the first time I mentioned the proposal to him that he was against it. There didn't seem to be any arguments I could use that would change his mind. He had his own point of view and I had to respect that. But the fact that we held opposite views on how we should manage the company in the future also meant that I had a choice to make. Did I continue with the fifty-fifty partnership I had with Taleb into what I was sure would eventually become an unsustainable future – or did I split with him and pursue my plan for the new kind of company I had in mind?

It was not a decision I agonised over for long. In fact, I didn't agonise over it at all. I knew what I wanted to do, I was certain that the plan I had in mind would work, and I was determined to turn it into reality. But it would be wrong to pretend that my decision didn't also present me with a problem. If my future didn't lie with Taleb, then we would have to split the company in the best manner we could and go our separate ways. That wasn't going to be a simple task for a company with 300 employees and a growing list of complex and continuing consultancy and engineering projects around the Middle East and elsewhere.

We decided that the only way to do this would be to divide between us the projects that were currently on the books. If we could agree on that, the staffing implications would probably flow logically. Staff working on a particular project would be offered a post with the new firm that had taken it on. In all of the projects we had on the books, either I or Taleb was the leading partner, so we used that as the benchmark for deciding who should take it over. Apart from any other consideration, it was very important that the switch-over should appear seamless from the clients' point of view. We could not allow clients to think we were more concerned with our own reorganisation than their cherished projects. Nothing upsets clients more than the thought that their consultants are putting their own interests and convenience first. We had no intention of letting that feeling develop among our clients, and it didn't.

Although the principle of splitting the projects between us was simple enough in theory, it took us some time to work out the financial implications of it all. The nub of the problem was that we both had an equal financial stake in all the projects that were running at the time we started to split the company. As a result Taleb had to pay me compensation for my share of the projects he took over and I had to pay Taleb for his share of the projects I took over. So I sat down with Taleb and, on each project, we made our estimates of what the appropriate compensation payment should be. Naturally our estimates were different, but after a few negotiating sessions we managed to reach a satisfactory compromise. Because I was taking on more of the projects than Taleb, the compensation I owed him was greater than the amount he owed me. As a result, I ended up paying him a significant sum to compensate him for loss of future profit on those projects. To me, this was a decision I knew I had to take and I was confident that my new company could generate more revenues quickly. Whatever the accuracy of the estimates at the time, to me the long-term prospects were far more important.

To be frank, by the time we had reached this stage I was more focused on the future than the past. I was keen for the negotiations to be over as soon as possible so that I could get on with the job of structuring my new company and winning more business. In any event, I have always believed that you're more likely to reach a satisfactory settlement by negotiation with any party than by rushing to the courts. When you bring in lawyers, you merely import expense and delay. That's why in a long business career stretching over nearly fifty years I have never sued anybody. And never intend to. There's an old French maxim which says something to the effect that it's better to lose a case outside a court that win one inside. I agree. That's not to imply, by the way, that I'm a pushover if anybody tries to sue me. It's happened rarely, but in those cases where I've been pushed too far I'll tenaciously fight my corner. And win.

In any event, Taleb and I each formed our own companies and I called mine Dar Al-Handasah (Shair and Partners). When I refer to Dar Al-Handasah after this date, it is this new company I am talking about.

*   *   *

After settling with Taleb, my next task was to bring my new partners on board. If my experience is anything to go by, the first reaction you provoke when you announce that you intend to give away a controlling share in your company is incredulity from the lucky recipients. The second is concern from them that the guiding hands that brought the company to its present healthy position will no longer be in control of the steering wheel. The 10 senior managers I planned to make my new partners were all thrilled by the idea of owning shares in Dar Al-Handasah – both for the opportunities it would bring them personally, and because of the improved growth it implied for the company as a whole. But at first they urged me to retain a controlling share.

It was an argument I had already run through my own mind several times. I had firmly resolved that I would not have a controlling stake in the new company. Had I done so, nothing much would have changed, responsibility would not have shifted in any meaningful way, and I would not be that much nearer to creating the sustainable enterprise I longed for – an enterprise that is not reliant on the skills and leadership of just one person. I wanted to create an environment in which the voices of the new partners would really count in the management of the company. That would never be the case if they knew that, in the final analysis, I could always out-vote them. As I told them at the time, if they could out-vote me I would always have to convince them with the strength of my argument. Which meant that new decisions would be subject to keen scrutiny and robust debate. I wanted to build a culture in which the partners vigorously and openly argued about the important issues facing the company. And that is what has happened.

There was another issue that I had also considered carefully in my mind before making my move. That was whether all of Dar Al-Handasah's employees should have the opportunity to own shares or just some of them. I decided against universal share ownership for a key reason. If all employees became shareholders, the number of shares any single employee held would not be financially significant, nor would it give any individual an extra meaningful level of influence in the management of the firm over and above what he or she already exercised. We paid good salaries (and still do) – usually above the market rate – to attract the best talent, and that fact was appreciated by those who came to work for us. And we already listened with an open mind to employees' views on the projects on which they worked and the management of those parts of the company in which they were involved. It is a poorly run company that cannot learn from the knowledge and experience of the people who work for it.

Concentrating share ownership in the hands of a few key partners was, I believed, the correct recipe to inject additional entrepreneurial flair right at the top of the company. In return for their new rewards, the partners were expected to take on considerable responsibility and be held accountable for the results they achieved. The level of responsibility they held was enhanced by the fact that we have never been a bureaucratic company – we don't debate issues to death in endless committees, and we don't clog up our corporate arteries with unnecessary paperwork. So partners were being given both the opportunity to take important decisions and the discipline of being assessed on the success or otherwise of their actions.

I had decided that, although the 10 new partners would own 60 per cent of the company between them, they would each be allocated shares according to their individual value to the organisation. Accordingly, I decided to distribute the shares over two years, with 40 per cent in the first year and the remainder in the second when the relative performance of the new partners could be assessed on the basis of their first year's work. So on 1 January 1970, I had 10 new partners, each of whom owned a stake in the company – a stake that increased the following year.

The effect of my decision was immediately noticeable on the pace of growth in the company. New business started to come in at an ever-faster rate – not only from our traditional markets in the Middle East but also from the new countries that I'd only just opened up to Dar Al-Handasah in Nigeria, Algeria and elsewhere. It seemed that, almost overnight, there was a new energy and dynamism in the company. There was a fresh vitality that encouraged all of us to attack new opportunities with unprecedented vigour.

It was soon clear that, although I now owned just 40 per cent of the company, at the rate the new Dar Al-Handasah was growing even my reduced share would soon be worth more than my larger shareholding under the previous partnership. The new partners found their shareholdings growing in value as well. I don't hold much with management jargon – preferring plain English – but this was definitely a 'win-win situation'.

*   *   *

Ten years later, in 1979, I took another long hard look at the company's structure – and whether it was continuing to achieve my objective of creating a sustainable enterprise. The 10 partners were still with us, but none of us were getting any younger – in fact, more than half were older than me – and the time would surely come in the not-too-distant future when some would retire. What would happen then? Would we appoint new partners and, if so, how? What would happen to the retiring partners' shareholding? These were important questions that needed careful consideration – especially as, by now, Dar Al-Handasah was a global operation with more than 1000 employees.

The answer seemed clear – we needed to appoint more partners. But how we were to do that in the context of the way the company was currently run needed a certain amount of careful thought. After turning the matter over in my mind for some time, I called in the company's lawyers and we drafted a new set of company bylaws that encapsulated my philosophy of sustainability. The bylaws have stood the test of time, and we continue to use them today.

In essence, we pursue our policy of sustainability by, each year, appointing new partners, who receive shares in the company. The shares new partners receive are, essentially, 'recycled' from retiring partners. The company buys back shares from existing partners who step down or who otherwise wish to reduce their shareholding. Unlike the first 10 partners, new partners have to pay for their shares at book value. We start by giving a new partner one per cent of the shares in the company. Partners can receive more shares in the future, depending on their performance. But we don't expect them to stump up the cash upfront. (Which, for them, is just as well, as in recent years the book value of their shareholding has been a substantial amount.) Instead, the cost of their shareholding is deducted from their dividend payments over a period of from five to ten years. During that period, they receive 25 per cent of their dividend in cash, with the remainder going towards paying off the original book value of their shares. If they are allotted additional shares, the same payment principle applies. When they have paid for any shares they've been allotted, they obviously receive all future dividends in cash.

There is a prohibition on partners selling their shares to outside parties. When a partner retires (or dies), his shares are surrendered to the firm and compensated for at their current book value. Those shares are then recycled to new partners. The principle applies to all, including myself as chairman.

If we are to remain a sustainable self-governing entity, we must retain control of our shareholding. So partners under the age of 50 can only sell a portion of their shares back to the company (at current book value) with the special permission of the chairman. When they've passed the age of 50, we don't normally object to partners selling up to half their remaining shareholding if they wish to use some of the money to enhance their lifestyle while their families are still young or for other reasons.

From our point of view, we want our partners to retain a significant equity holding in the company, because this underscores their commitment to it. Their shares act like golden handcuffs and ensure that our most talented partners are not tempted to move to rival consultancies. And the fact that we plough the bulk of our earnings back into the company means that when a partner does eventually come to retire and sell his shares back to the firm, the sum he receives shows a considerable premium on what he originally paid for them. We have a mandatory retirement age of 65, but this can be extended by a vote of the partners to 70 (and we may raise it to 75 because increasing life expectancies mean that more people like to work for longer).

Any existing partner can propose a new partner. It has been our practice to elect one or two new partners each year. Since our new bylaws were introduced in 1979, elections have outstripped retirements so that, as I write, there are now 30 partners – about one for every hundred employees. The election of new partners is the first item on the agenda of the annual meeting every March, and new partners take up their office with effect from the previous January. A prospective candidate needs to receive a unanimous vote of the existing partners in order to be elected. All this is done openly, and if only one existing partner objects, the new candidate is not elected. This does happen occasionally – I have had several of my own nominees rejected – but it is rare for any candidates not to be elected. This is because prospective partners have been very carefully nurtured and vetted before they have their names put before an annual meeting.

We have two types of partner – partners of operations, who run our activities in a particular country or territory, and technical partners, who specialise in a particular area of expertise, such as structural engineering and other technical subjects. Whichever category, we are looking for people who have that extra commitment and entrepreneurial flair to become partners. One factor that is not a bar to becoming a partner is age. One thing designed to have me hitting the roof is somebody suggesting that we should defer considering a likely candidate because he is not yet old enough. A sustainable enterprise needs partners of all ages, so that younger people are coming along as older partners retire. So we have partners in their thirties, forties, fifties, sixties and seventies – and if the right candidate came along, I would not object to a partner in his twenties.

I have mentioned that we expect high performance from our partners. If a partner does not perform at the level we require, we expect him to go. Our company's bylaws are quite clear on the rights a partner has in this situation. If the chairman, after informal consultation with others, decides a partner has to leave, he may retire by resigning, in which case he retires with all accrued financial rights. Although it has never happened, there is a provision for a special partners' meeting to confirm a dismissal in cases involving a breach of professional ethics or grave misconduct. If such a case were to occur, the departing partner would receive only half of his accrued financial rights. The system may seem harsh, but the partners are the key to taking Dar Al-Handasah forward, and we rightly expect all of them to make a significant contribution to our continuing progress.

*   *   *

So have I created a sustainable enterprise, as I set out to do 50 years ago?

In the long run, only time will tell. But I firmly believe that Dar Al-Handasah will continue long after I have retired from the scene. It could not have happened if I had insisted on retaining all of the shareholding for myself. I have seen too many entrepreneurs make that mistake, both in the Middle East and elsewhere. I was determined that Dar Al-Handasah should continue as an independent enterprise, and not be taken over, as so many consultancies have been, by one of the giants of the industry. To go down that route would be to lose so much that is distinctive about the way Dar does business.

But independence means ensuring that the company continues to recruit its fair share of the best young talent – and then gives those individuals opportunities they couldn't find either in smaller companies lacking the global reach we have developed or, at the other end of the scale, in the giant corporations that are all too often hidebound by bureaucracy. Bright young managers refresh a company with new energy and fresh perspectives on contemporary issues. In the end, sustainability is about giving this fresh talent its head in shaping the future of the company. Which is why we give them a share in owning the future.

And it is why I'm confident that the next 50 years of Dar Al-Handasah's history will be even more successful than the first.

CHAPTER 15

The leaving of Lebanon

B y 1976, Lebanon was descending into darkness.

A civil war had begun the previous year and had already claimed thousands of lives and devastated many parts of the country. In February, while I was in Morocco involved in discussions on a major Dar project, I received a telephone call from the office of Lebanese President Suleiman Franjieh asking me to attend a meeting to discuss reconstruction. I accepted the invitation.

Since the civil war had erupted in April 1975, Franjieh and Prime Minister Rashid Karame had been exploring different initiatives to reconcile the warring sectarian communities. One of these initiatives was a 'constitutional document' that set out proposals for equal 'confessional representation' in Lebanon's Chamber of Deputies and other reforms. The 'confessional' system had allocated particular government posts to people from different faith groups since Lebanon's original 1926 constitution. The confessional approach was maintained after independence in 1943. Among other provisions, it provided for a ratio in the chamber of deputies of six Christians to every five Muslims. Franjieh believed his proposal to equalise representation had the support of Syria's President Hafiz Al-Assad, who had considerable influence over some factions in Lebanese society. But Franjieh's proposals came with a significant caveat. They were only due to become effective when the PLO implemented a 1969 agreement that sought to regulate what weapons Palestinian militias within Lebanon were entitled to hold.

When, in 1964, Nasser had sponsored the establishment of the PLO, it was formed with a formal structure that included a military wing, the Palestinian Liberation Army (PLA). Nasser was not a man to tolerate disparate militia groups that could act contrary to centralised control. The PLA was, in essence, a regular army that operated in close unison with the regular armies of Arab states. When nascent militia units grew among the Palestinian refugee populations they were generally snubbed out, or at least tightly controlled, by the host government. This had happened in Egypt, Syria and Jordan. Only in the open society of Lebanon did the Palestinian militias find an opening.

But in a 1969 agreement, Lebanon's President Charles Helou had accepted that Palestinians should have pretty much a free hand in running the refugee camps in which most of them lived. He also agreed that they should be given wide latitude in carrying out security operations along the Israeli frontier. The Palestinian militias were also allowed to bear arms within certain limits in order to fulfil their local policing functions. In return, the PLO had agreed not to intervene in Lebanese politics. It was this policy that Franjieh was now seeking to enforce.

I think Helou originally adopted the policy with the most generous of motives. After all, Lebanon had a long and honoured history as a land that welcomed and tolerated the dispossessed. But the harsh reality is that militias never stick to agreements on arms limitations or, for that matter, anything else when it suits their purposes not to do so. And the taste of power in running refugee camps only provided them with an appetite for more. By the mid-seventies, Lebanon's Palestinians were becoming a state within a state, a fact that was resented by many native Lebanese, who felt their generous hospitality was being abused.

Although born a Jordanian, I had come to love Lebanon and everything its tolerant open society stood for. I felt deeply for the country's tragedy – as strongly as any native. I was angry at the behaviour of the Palestinian militias, and I had expressed my views forcefully.

The violence that the militias brought to bear so often intensified the harm wrought upon innocent local populations, both Palestinian and Lebanese. The just cause of the Palestinians was sabotaged by the acts of the militias. Gandhi had demonstrated in his campaign for Indian independence the power and persuasiveness of non-violent means in the pursuit of a just cause. It was to take many years – in fact until Mahmoud Abbas succeeded Yasser Arafat as leader of the Palestinians – before the Palestinian leadership acknowledged the non-violent path as the route to progress.

But it was against the 1976 background of continuing militia violence that I returned from Morocco to attend Franjieh's meeting in Beirut. Gathered there to discuss with Franjieh prospects and approaches to reconstruction were 10 individuals from the private sector – from industry, commerce, trade, tourism, services and so on. Franjieh shared with us a vision of reconciled communities as the platform for reconstruction and vigorous development in Lebanon. He then invited our views, and we began to discuss reconstruction activities.

In the course of the meeting, Victor Kasseer, head of the Association of Merchants, which had the largest membership of any business association in Lebanon, pressed Franjieh on the prospects for peace. He said that many of his members would ask him after the meeting if the war was really over. Could they, he asked Franjieh, go about repairing and developing their shops and premises with confidence? Franjieh quickly sought to reassure him. He said that Assad was committed to the constitutional document, to facilitating a political settlement, and to the return of normality to Lebanon. Kasseer nodded thoughtfully, but I wondered whether he'd been satisfied with the answer. Later in the meeting, he asked virtually the same question. Franjieh provided virtually the same reply.

We adjourned for lunch. During the meal, Kasseer again posed his question. Franjieh was now getting annoyed. He reiterated that Assad was party to the constitutional document and committed to facilitating reconciliation and progress in Lebanon. The Syrian president, Franjieh told Kasseer, was an honourable man whose commitment should not be doubted.

But Kasseer had been right to press his question. Franjieh's confidence in winning Assad's backing for his proposals was misguided. Syria never managed to muster either the capacity or the will to prevail over the PLO, essential if Lebanon was to return to stability. I was not surprised. In the cold-war climate of the time, Syria's mission in the region was predominantly to act as an agent of the Soviet camp and play the role of spoiler whenever the United States attempted to broker an Arab–Israeli peace settlement. This created the illusion of Syria as a significant regional power. But the Fatah militia faction of the PLO took exception to Syria's presumption in tying the implementation of the constitutional document's reforms to the Cairo Agreement's regulation of militia weaponry. Since its inception, Fatah had fiercely maintained its independence of any Arab government.

Within a few weeks of our meeting with Franjieh, with no signs of cessation of hostilities and amid serious fractures within the Lebanese army on confessional lines, Fatah militia units lent their support to an attempted coup led by General Abdul-Aziz Al-Ahdab, commander of the Lebanese army's Beirut barracks. Although it failed, Al-Ahdab's attempt forced Franjieh to evacuate the presidential palace for a residence in Kfour, and stirred further factional tension, making it less likely that his reforms would be adopted. Lebanon had to live through much strife before equality of representation in the chamber of deputies was implemented in 1989 as part of the Taif Agreement, which effectively ended 14 years of civil war.

*   *   *

Despite the civil war, Dar Al-Handasah continued to operate.

Our offices stayed open for business. Each morning a driver would arrive at my apartment to collect me and we would make the increasingly dangerous journey through streets, where gunmen lurked in the shadows, to our office building on rue Verdun. Except on one particular morning in March 1976, when my driver did not report for duty. I felt a sense of deep unease. I had heard gunfire in the night. But then, for months there had been gunfire most nights. I was worried about our offices – about the staff who might be working there. It had been a concern that had been on my mind for months. It had forced me to make some difficult and unwelcome decisions.

When the security situation had started to deteriorate seriously in 1975, I had telephoned the director-general of the presidential palace to ask for advice. Law and order was breaking down, and the forces of the state seemed powerless to prevent a growing wave of violence. I wanted to know how we could protect our offices and, most important of all, the people who worked in them from the armed militias that were taking control of the streets. My enquiry was helpfully received. 'You are entitled to protect yourself by any means, including using Palestinian militia if necessary,' I was told.

In a situation where gunmen rule the roost, you have few options but to work with them. So I arranged to meet Zuhair Muhsen, a Palestinian who commanded the Saiqa force in Beirut. Many Palestinian activists who had moved out of Sinai and Gaza when they were occupied after the 1967 Six Day War moved north to Lebanon and were organised into Saiqa, a special force under the control of the Syrian military. Muhsen had hundreds of armed militia in Beirut who answered personally to him.

He received me in a friendly way. I explained my problem. I was the head of an engineering consultancy that employed, in normal times, about seven hundred people. I pointed out to him that Dar Al-Handasah was completely non-sectarian in its employment policies. Both Muslims and Christians were treated equally when it came to determining salaries and promotion prospects. We had employees from the Palestinian refugee camps whose salaries went a considerable way to making the lives of their families bearable. But, I added, all this was at risk in the current dangerous climate. I needed, I explained, 24-hour protection for our offices.

Muhsen offered to send me three shifts of armed guards to protect the offices round the clock. He said I could have a dozen guards in every shift. The arrangement seemed most satisfactory. 'But how much should I pay them?' I asked Muhsen. He shrugged as though the matter hadn't really occurred to him. 'Just pay them what you'd pay your own guards,' he said. I thanked him for his help and we parted cordially.

Since that meeting, the guards had reported for duty for every shift. Until now. I telephoned the offices. The phone rang and rang. No answer. I made further calls to contacts around the city and pieced together the events that had happened during the night. It was at the time of General Abdul-Aziz Al-Ahdab's coup. The PLO Fatah militia units that lent their support to the coup had, at the same time, sought to drive the Syrian-backed Saiqa militia out of Beirut. Fatah had routed the Saiqa guards from our offices.

The offices were, as far as I could learn, still secure, but unguarded and deserted. No staff had reported for duty. (And, under the circumstances, who could blame them?) To the outside world, it might appear that Dar Al-Handasah in Beirut was closed to business.

As this picture became clearer, I became angry. I was angry that we couldn't open our offices. I was angry that our business in Beirut was being placed in peril by armed gangs fighting their own turf wars. I had not started a company and built it to a point where it was the leading consultancy of its kind in the Middle East to have it closed down by a group of bully-boy gunmen.

I was determined that the office would open.

Even if I had to do it myself.

Driving myself across Beirut that morning was not a pleasant experience. Since January, a line of checkpoints and intermittent fortifications – the 'green line' – had divided the largely Muslim west Beirut from the mainly Christian east of the city. There was always the risk of being stopped anywhere by roving militia and asked for your papers. But I made it to the offices without incident and was relieved to see that they were largely undamaged. Over the previous weeks, they had developed a few pock-marks where random bullets had hit the building during gun-fights and ricocheted away.

I unlocked the metal shutters that protected the front door, went in and took the elevator to my office on the sixth floor. There was an unfamiliar silence in the building, which was disquieting, even spooky. I sat down behind my desk and the thought suddenly struck me: I'm alone in the office – what am I now going to do? I thought about it for a moment.

Prove that we are still open for business was the answer, I decided. I picked up the telephone and rang through to the Beirut telephone exchange. I asked to be put through to our London office, then a delightful listed building in New Cavendish Street. I cannot now remember whom I spoke to on that troubled morning, but when I returned the handset to its cradle, I felt that I had proved something important.

I had demonstrated that not even armed militiamen could close Dar Al-Handasah to business.

*   *   *

Was it foresight or was it luck that had persuaded me to open new offices?

I would claim that it was merely the normal actions of business expansion. During 1974 and 1975, Dar Al-Handasah had opened offices in Cairo and London. I hadn't sensed, even then, that my beloved Lebanon would descend into such strife. But the fact we had established these bases made it easier for us to ride out the chaos that engulfed Lebanon for much of the next 16 years.

By 1974, I'd been feeling for some time that we ought to broaden our base of operations in the Middle East. We needed a 'footprint' in Europe to meet the requirements of a growing list of prestigious projects in the Middle East and Africa for talented engineers and other professionals. I set up a committee of three partners to look into these matters. They reported back that London would be by far the best base for our presence in Europe, and Cairo was a natural choice for our second main Middle Eastern office. We didn't delay in finding suitable premises in both cities.

And thank heavens that we didn't. By the late spring of 1975, Lebanon had long passed the point where words could solve its problems. The fighting was producing a series of appalling actions that inflamed bitterness among the country's different communities. Hardly a day went by without a gun-battle somewhere in Beirut or elsewhere in the country. We all risked dangers as we came to work in the morning and as we returned home in the evening.

As spring turned to summer and one international company after another quit the country, often for Cyprus or Greece, we tried to continue to run our business as normal. But it was plain that many of our employees were facing unacceptable risks by remaining. There was only one option. We had to move key staff abroad to our new Cairo or London offices. In the deteriorating conditions in Lebanon, it proved a horrendous task. Staff moved with their families, often at short notice. We helped them find accommodation and schools where they settled. We moved huge numbers of files, plans and drawings of work-in-progress. For a time, we were like an army on the march as we relocated hundreds of people to new homes and offices.

Yet, astonishingly, our business did not suffer. We still managed to complete our projects on time. Both new and existing clients continued to ask us to undertake more work. The company carried on expanding. One reason for our growth was that a steep hike in oil prices, well underway by the mid-1970s, meant that the oil economies of the Middle East were awash with money, which they could spend on infrastructure projects. The level of investment they were making was rising steeply, and as a result there was an unprecedented demand for our services. Even as we evacuated staff from war-torn Beirut, the phones were ringing with offers of new work.

As the troubles deepened, I decided that it was unsafe for Laura and our children to remain in Lebanon. Waving a sad goodbye, I packed them off to the United States. I did my best to adjust to life alone in our flat, but I missed them deeply and it was not a happy time for me. A dangerous time, too, as violence escalated.

But I was determined to try to live as normal a life as was possible under the circumstances. One day, in September 1975, I arranged a lunch at the St George's hotel in Beirut with former prime minister Takieddin As-Solh and a few other friends. The St George's was Beirut's best hotel, in normal times a magnet for politicians, businessmen, journalists and simply those who liked to enjoy the fine services it offered. As I drove myself towards the coast road, where the hotel commanded a view of the port, I could sense an extra tension in the atmosphere. Groups of gunmen lounged menacingly on street corners.

The St George's had a superb restaurant with wonderful food and, under normal circumstances, it would have been crowded. On this particular day, I recall, only two other tables were occupied – one by Prime Minister Rashid Karame with several of his ministers, the other by the parliamentarian and presidential hopeful Raymond Edde. My guests and I lingered over our lunch discussing the deteriorating situation in the country and were the last to leave. A few minutes after I'd left, a gun-battle broke out just down the road, with firing coming from the Holiday Inn. I arrived home about 15 minutes later and switched on the radio to find out what was happening. I caught the middle of a news flash: the St George's had been blown up. The explosion had occurred within minutes of our departure. I'd had a disconcertingly narrow brush with death.

As 1975 turned into 1976, the security position in Beirut became worse. Fighting between militias had been a daily event during the autumn of 1975. I didn't face the new year with much optimism that the conflict would be resolved. Life without the family had become a grim grind. After working at Dar Al-Handasah's offices during the day, I would be driven back to my apartment in the evening. It was even more dangerous to go out at night, when militias patrolled the streets and set up road-blocks with impunity. It was not unknown for them to stop cars, demand your papers and, if they didn't like what they saw, drag you from your car and slit your throat on the spot. It was safer to stay at home in the evening.

But with the family in America, and as one lonely night succeeded another, I found myself climbing the walls with boredom and frustration. In the end, I decided I could not live like this night after night. So, some evenings, I would drive myself to friends' houses, where we would talk and play cards. Sometimes, I would stay overnight to avoid the danger of driving back to my own home.

One night early in 1976, however, I was driving back from a friend's house when I was stopped at a road-block by a group of militia. They were heavily armed and looked menacing. They wanted to know who I was and demanded papers. I didn't like the look of the situation at all. I was thinking hard about how I could extricate myself from them when I saw headlights coming up the street fast. A car skidded to a halt next to mine and a group of armed men jumped out. They pointed their guns at the militia who'd stopped me, and started an argument. For a few moments there was a tense stand-off. Then the militia backed off and I was allowed to continue my journey.

Later I discovered that my friend had been concerned about my safety. He had contacts in a rival militia and had arranged for them to follow me for my own safety. It was a close call, but not my only brush with militia as I moved around Beirut trying to manage my business. And, as I have already related, my experience of militias was not limited to unwelcome encounters at road-blocks. As law and order broke down in Lebanon I faced a dilemma about how to continue to protect our premises, even though by now almost all staff had transferred temporarily to other locations. Some of the office boys we employed came to our aid. They came to work in the mornings, did their job, then went back to their homes in the evenings, where they enrolled in the ranks of local militias.

It was what Western businesses would regard as an unusual, even bizarre, situation. But it was how life was lived in Beirut in those days, and you had little choice but to accept it, even if you didn't condone it. We had, however, a strict rule: no politics in the office. What you do after work, at your own expense and your own risk, is your business, we said. That, together with the fact we were completely non-sectarian in employment policies, meant we prevented the bitterness of the streets spilling over into the company. In any event, in that dreadful spring of 1976 I was able to organise some of the office boys to act as guards for the offices, but with a strict rule: no guns. Lebanon had seen too many guns, and Dar Al-Handasah, I was determined, was not going to add to them.

With the offices secure, there was little left that I could constructively do in Beirut. Staff working on key projects had moved either to London or Cairo. I decided to join them, and flew to London. Besides, I'd had enough of running a company from a war zone.

*   *   *

But by the end of 1976, I was back in Beirut.

Hope was, once more, in the air. That October, a conference of the Arab League summit meeting in Riyadh devised a formula that, it seemed, might bring some peace to war-torn Lebanon. A pan-Arab peacekeeping force was ensconced in the country. Around 5000 troops were initially deployed from Saudi Arabia, the Gulf States, Libya and Sudan. These augmented Syrian forces, many of whom were already deployed in Lebanon. In practice, the Arab League's initiative gave some legitimacy to, and subsidised, a large Syrian force in Lebanon.

President Elias Sarkis appointed a senior officer of undoubted integrity whom I knew, General Ahmad Hajj, to command the force. Hajj discovered in a matter of weeks that the Syrian force was intent on making it difficult for other Arab forces to operate in Lebanon. He resigned, and over the coming weeks the non-Syrian forces withdrew.

As the early months of 1977 unfolded, our staff began to return to Beirut. They came back to a city that had been devastated – even the previously bustling Place des Martyrs, which dominates the centre of Beirut, had been reduced to a pile of rubble. But most of our employees seemed pleased to be back in the city they regarded as their natural home.

Incredibly, business was still booming and, as if to signal our confidence in the future, I authorised the expenditure of $400,000 on our first IBM computer. I seem to recall it had close to one megabyte of memory and needed its own air-conditioned room, raised floor and continuous power supply. We'd been advised that it could be used to automate the accountancy work. Today, it would be impossible to buy a computer which had only a megabyte of memory.

By the middle of 1977, our Beirut office was practically back at full strength. Everybody was hard at work, but I remained sceptical about the future of Lebanon because, although the peace agreement seemed to be holding, the underlying problems – especially those caused by the presence of militias – remained unresolved.

Unfortunately, my reservations proved only too well founded in the years that followed. As one catastrophe followed another, Lebanon's sovereignty as an independent state was steadily undermined. The country had become a cockpit in which other countries, notably Syria and Israel, as well as militia groups, played out their wargames. Lebanese governments found themselves increasingly in office but not in power.

Israeli-supported local militias in southern Lebanon confronted Palestinian militias with little regard for non-combatants. By the early 1980s, US President Ronald Reagan was attempting to broker a diplomatic solution, but the Israelis were determined to oust the Palestinian militias from Lebanon. The Israelis mounted an invasion of Lebanon in early June 1982 triggered by their intelligence on the build-up of Palestinian arms in the south of the country and on Palestinian involvement in an assassination attempt on the Israeli ambassador in London.

Israeli attacks on Palestinian targets deep inside Lebanon, including in West Beirut, prompted a UN Security Council resolution (508) calling on all parties to cease hostilities. The following day, Israeli forces launched a major offensive attacking Palestinian bases in Lebanon. Ground forces quickly penetrated into Lebanon towards Beirut. A further Security Council resolution (509) demanded an unconditional Israeli withdrawal to recognise international borders.

As the Israelis laid seige to Beirut, there were suggestions that US forces were to be deployed to Lebanon. US diplomatic initiatives focused on securing the departure of Arafat and Palestinian fighters from Lebanon. In mid-August, the United Nations agreed to deploy a multinational force, with contingents from the United States, France, Italy and the United Kingdom, to assist the Lebanese army in evacuating Palestinian fighters and restoring the Lebanese government's authority in the Beirut area. Arafat and the Palestinian fighters were finally evacuated from Lebanon in September and the US contingent of the multinational force redeployed to vessels offshore.

Meanwhile, in August 1982, Bashir Gemayel, leader of the Lebanese Forces Christian Militia, was elected president of Lebanon. Within days, he met with Israeli Prime Minister Menachem Begin. Begin believed that President-elect Gemayel would agree with proposals for an immediate and comprehensive peace treaty. Gemayel, however, was not willing to fall in with the Israeli's plans. He wanted time to establish his leadership, and favoured securing a later deal through the mediation of the United States. But this approach greatly angered the Israelis. As Gemayel had already offended the Syrians, who considered him a threat to their ambitions in Lebanon, he was now pinioned between two opposite camps. How he would have dealt with this dilemma we shall never know. He was assassinated nine days before his presidential inauguration.

The day following Gemayel's assassination, Israeli forces occupied West Beirut. The UN Security Council and the United States called for their withdrawal, but two days later Israeli troops stood by – some say actively assisted – while gunmen from the Christian Phalangist militia reacting to the assassination of Gemayel, their leader, entered the Palestinian Sabra and Chatila refugee camps and massacred hundreds of innocent civilians.

As I have mentioned, Dar Al-Handasah had employed people from the camps, and I shared the world's disgust at this act of barbarous savagery. The massacre also outraged many in Israel. In the months that followed, the Israeli parliament mounted a commission of inquiry that found Defence Minister Ariel Sharon responsible for the safety of non-combatants in areas occupied by Israeli forces. This eventually led to Sharon's resignation. But in the immediate aftermath of the Sabra and Chatila tragedy, the multinational peacekeeping force, which had been withdrawn only days earlier, came back to Beirut and sought desperately to keep the lid on further violence.

On the day the peacekeepers returned, Bashir Gemayel's elder brother, Amin, was elected president. His presidency started with the advantage that Arafat and the Palestinian fighters had left Lebanon. So my hopes were high that, despite the tragic circumstances of its arrival, Amin Gemayel's presidency would herald a new beginning. And it started encouragingly. In the run-up to the election of Bashir Gemayel, the Lebanese delegation to the United Nations had secured a slot for the new president to address the General Assembly on the prospect for peace. It was, however, Amin who spoke to the General Assembly as Lebanon's new president. I was delighted that his address was well received by the international community and by people in Lebanon.

Soon after he became president, he invited me to become a personal informal adviser on economic affairs and reconstruction. I welcomed the opportunity to play even a small part in the rebuilding of the country that I loved. So, as well as my long hours in Dar Al-Handasah's offices, I began a regime that included regular visits to the presidential palace. I was honoured that Gemayel treated me as a confidant whom he would consult on matters that strayed way beyond my informal brief.

One day about six months into his term, Gemayel confided in me that he was anxious to ensure he was carrying out his presidential duties well. He wanted a public airing of views on his performance. He asked Lebanese Television to broadcast the opinions of a distinguished panel. Former president Charles Helou, former prime minister Saeb Salaam, former speaker of the chamber of deputies Adel Osseirman and the distinguished political commentator Ghassan Tueni all contributed to the programme. The panel and the public were generally complimentary, and praised Gemayel's performance. He seemed to have started well. But, as I was to discover, there was already too much tension in the system for him to overcome.

The US presence in Beirut extended beyond its role as a component of the multinational force. US diplomats were negotiating an Israeli evacuation and exploring the possibility for a broader settlement. At the centre of this diplomatic whirlwind was Philip Habib, President Reagan's special envoy. He was a regular visitor to the presidential palace. (I was later to serve with Habib, a distinguished Lebanese American, on the board of trustees of AUB.)

My presence near the centre of these events brought into focus a paramount issue that troubled me greatly and lead me to decide to leave Lebanon. The issue was the continual erosion of Lebanese sovereignty. The issue came to a head one day in 1983 when I arrived at Gemayel's office. He was on the telephone. He gestured to me to read a document on his desk. I read what appeared to be the draft of a security agreement with Israel that dealt with the withdrawal of Israeli forces to the international border between Lebanon and Israel. When Gemayel came off the phone, he told me that the Americans had been active in brokering the agreement.

The draft reminded me of the 1949 armistice agreement that Lebanon had concluded with Israel. Egypt, Jordan and Syria had each also signed separate armistice agreements with Israel between February and June 1949. The Israel–Lebanon armistice differed from the agreements with these other countries in at least two key respects. First, the armistice agreements with the three were signed on the Greek island of Rhodes, where all four agreements were negotiated under the auspices of a UN mediator. But the Lebanon–Israeli agreement was signed at a ceremony held on the international border between the two countries. Second, unlike the agreement with the three, the Israel–Lebanon agreement provided for the Israelis to withdraw from territory they had occupied during the conflict and accept the pre-war international boundary as the ceasefire line.

In the new draft agreement I was now studying in Gemayel's office, Israel undertook to withdraw to the international border and pursue no territorial ambitions in Lebanon, as in the 1949 agreement. In common with the 1949 agreement, the new draft reaffirmed respect for the sovereignty and security of both countries. Nor did it prejudice a final settlement of the Palestinian issue.

In the weeks leading up to the signing of the agreement on 17 May 1983 at a ceremony on the international border, the Israelis withdrew from Beirut and were replaced by the US-led multinational force. But during those weeks – in April – a suicide attack on the US Embassy in West Beirut, leaving 63 dead, destabilised the position.

The day before, Najeeb Halaby, a distinguished Lebanese American had arrived in Beirut at the head of an official United States Task Force for Assistance to Lebanon. Halaby had had a successful career in the US aviation industry, and served as a top government official under President John F. Kennedy. He'd also been chief executive of the airline Pan Am. He was father of Queen Noor of Jordan. I met with Halaby and the Task Force shortly after the attack on the embassy. They were deeply shocked, but still wanted to discuss a plan they'd developed to secure greater Beirut. I was at pains to suggest that greater Beirut could not possibly be made safe without securing the rest of Lebanon.

Following the signing of the new Israel–Lebanon agreement on 17 May, events started to move at an ever-quickening pace. Gemayel decided to seek approval for the agreement from both the council of ministers and the chamber of deputies. Both gave their approval, but within days of its signing the Israelis rendered the agreement essentially worthless when they passed a note, via the Americans, to the Lebanese government. The note stated that Israel would not comply with the agreement until Syrian forces had withdrawn from Lebanon.

American resolve to support Lebanon and bring pressure to bear on the Syrians diminished as events spiralled out of control through the remainder of 1983 and into 1984. Gemayel was unable to overcome the obstacle of Israel's insistence on Syrian withdrawal. And as the Americans drew back, his determination to push ahead with the agreement diminished. In October 1983, there were bomb attacks on the headquarters of US and French forces which left nearly three hundred dead, including many US intelligence staff. Within four months, the United States decided to pull all of its troops out of Lebanon. The last marines departed in February 1984 in the wake of yet another atrocity – the assassination of AUB President Malcolm Kerr a month earlier. Ominously, the withdrawal of US and Israeli forces prompted Palestinian militia to seek to re-establish their armed presence.

In early February, Syrian-backed Muslim Lebanese militias attacked army units in West Beirut and effectively occupied the area. I was abroad at the time. The airport closed for several days, and my return was delayed. Virtually all our staff had to sleep in the office. It was too dangerous to go onto the streets to return home.

As the downward spiral continued into the spring, prime minister Salim Hoss travelled to Damascus and asked the Syrian army, which had withdrawn when the Israelis invaded in 1982, to return and restore order. In March, Gemayel cancelled the 17 May agreement, signalling a failure in the effort to remove all foreign troops from Lebanese soil. (Years later, I recall asking Philip Habib if Gemayel had had a window of opportunity to remove Israeli and Syrian troops, as well as the Palestinian militia groups, from Lebanon. His reply was immediate: there was no chance. Syria most definitely had the upper hand.)

With this succession of depressing events and the cancellation of the agreement, I began to lose the hope with which I had welcomed Gemayel's election. I became progressively depressed at the way Lebanon's sovereignty was being salami-sliced away, sliver by sliver, as the diplomatic process unfolded.

Nevertheless, I still continued to run Dar Al-Handasah from the Beirut office through all the difficulties. Throughout, I was determined that we would continue to meet all obligations to our clients in a timely manner, and that Dar's standards of excellence would be upheld. I am glad to say that I discovered that my determination was shared by all the firm's partners and staff. As the situation in Beirut worsened, our resolve hardened. We determined that we would not be diverted by the ugly events from the course we had set ourselves to build Dar as a sustainable institution against all the odds. But to achieve our aims, we had to use all our resourceful ways, including deploying staff to other offices.

In the middle of October 1984, I was stunned when Kamal Al-Assad failed to be re-elected as speaker of the chamber of deputies. Al-Assad had served as a capable and courageous speaker through difficult times. The chamber elects, or re-elects, its speaker every year. Al-Assad's credentials for re-election were impeccable. He had, however, presided over decisions of the chamber that were not to the liking of the Syrians – the chamber's approval of the 17 May agreement in particular. Syrian influence was brought to bear to block his re-election. This was yet another sign that the Lebanese were not the masters of Lebanon.

I came to realise that I had reached the end of the road. The vibrant open society that had first attracted me to Lebanon had been lost. The country was disfigured, and had lost its sovereignty and self-respect. I vowed to become an exile until such time as Lebanon could look fellow sovereign nations in the eye as a true equal.

Just before Christmas 1984, I called Gemayel to tell him that I planned to travel to Amman for the holiday. He invited me to have lunch with him before I left. The conversation flowed during lunch, but I did not tell him that I would not be returning from Amman. The following day, with great reluctance, I climbed aboard the plane and quit Beirut.

My leaving of Lebanon was one of the saddest days of my life.

CHAPTER 16

The secrets of winning

I knew all along that if I was to build Dar Al-Handasah into a truly global business, sooner or later we would have to take on the United States.

The United States is the mightiest market in the world. It has the biggest economy and the largest and most prosperous customers. But it is also the hardest market of all to crack – a tough no-nonsense free-enterprise system where winners take all and losers are allowed to go to the wall. Moving into America would mean taking risks, but I'd never been afraid of risks.

The real problem for me was finding a way into America. Then in early 1985, I met Hans Neumann. He was a German and had been an officer in the Wehrmacht during the Second World War. After the war, he'd emigrated to the United States and was now working as a marketing director for the Chicago-based firm of architects Perkins & Will. He, like us, had been working on a project in Saudi Arabia. He thought that we might be able to co-operate on some joint projects in the country, which was undergoing a period of rapid development.

Neumann was an intelligent and cultured man, and I liked him immediately. I decided to invite him to stay with me overnight at my London flat in Elizabeth Street while he was passing through the city on his way to Germany. We had an interesting discussion, and I asked him whether he was returning to his homeland to negotiate a new project for his company. He looked slightly rueful and admitted that wasn't the case. Instead, he was looking for further financing for Perkins & Will. In fact, he admitted that if the company failed to find more money soon, it wouldn't survive.

I was shocked to hear this news. Perkins & Will had been founded in 1935 by respected names in the American architectural profession – Lawrence B. Perkins and Philip Will. Since that time it had developed an excellent reputation as a company that designed first-class public buildings, notably schools and hospitals. It employed nearly two hundred people at its offices in Chicago. How could it be that a company with such a revered name was in such dire financial straits that it might not survive for more than a few weeks?

The answer was brutally simple. It had been poorly managed. Projects that should have turned in profits had made losses. The losses had accumulated. As the company's financial situation suffered, some of the better staff had moved on. The firm was now definitely in the corporate sick-room. Despite this unpromising scenario, I saw an opportunity. I asked Neumann what he thought Perkins & Will would be worth to a buyer. He said somewhere between half a million and a million dollars. I asked him whether Dar Al-Handasah would be an acceptable buyer. His face showed genuine enthusiasm when he said the company would welcome that.

So we turned to talking about how we could make progress if Dar Al-Handasah was to enter a bid for Perkins & Will. I was well aware that, on the face of it, buying a company even with a good professional reputation that seemed to be heading for skid row was not a course of action recommended in the management textbooks. As if to confirm the dangers, it didn't look as though American buyers were queuing at the door. But I had a broader agenda. I knew that it would be very difficult to buy into a strong American company that didn't need the money, simply because its shareholders would not accept investment from the Middle East. Some not at any price. I reasoned that the least of the difficult options if we were to move into America was to buy a failing company and turn it round. That was the course of action I resolved to pursue.

After Neumann had left my flat the following day, I put the next steps into practice swiftly. I commissioned the then accountancy firm Peat Marwick (now part of KPMG International) to carry out a full financial and legal due diligence on Perkins & Will. It took some time, and a few weeks later I received a thick report running to several hundred pages. It made for depressing reading. On practically every page, Peat Marwick's accountants had something negative to say about Perkins & Will. Their conclusion was unequivocal: don't buy this company.

Adopting standard business criteria, I'm sure their advice was correct. But I was not operating by standard criteria, and I was reluctant to accept their advice. On the basis of an analysis of the figures, I have no doubt that what Peat Marwick's analysts said about the financial health of the company was true. Perkins & Will was heading into a severe cashflow crisis. But Peat Marwick didn't have the emotional commitment I'd developed to building a global business and expanding into America. Nor did they realise how difficult it would be for a company based in the troubled city of Beirut to buy a thriving American company, no matter how generous our offer to shareholders.

Nevertheless, Peat Marwick's report had been a blunt reality check on my plans. I felt I needed a second opinion, and consulted Makram Awdeh, a Lebanese American who had much experience of business in the United States and who I'd known for some time. He read through the Peat Marwick report with furrowed brow and gave me his considered opinion: don't buy this company.

So I bought it.

Even that proved not without its difficulties. Larry Perkins, one of the founders and principal shareholders, was now an old man who played no active part in the management of the firm. Even though the company that was his life's work was facing bankruptcy, he wanted to 'approve' me before I bought his business. As it happened, I was visiting Princeton in New Jersey, where my youngest son, Talal, was at university. I invited Perkins to join me there for lunch. Whether it was the lunch, or my enthusiasm for business in America, or the imminent prospect of the receivers arriving on his company's doorstep, he approved of me. So the deal was on.

But it wasn't long before I began to wonder whether I'd bought more trouble than I'd bargained for. I'd paid $700,000 for the company, but within months it was soaking up hundreds of thousands of dollars a month of extra cash, which was coming straight out of revenues earned by Dar Al-Handasah. It was plain that turning Perkins & Will round was going to be a long haul. The starting-point had to be a strategy in which we could have confidence. So I asked the company's management to draw up a three-year rolling strategic plan. The idea was that this would be supplemented with detailed one-year operating plans that focused on bottom-line financial targets. But strategies are never enough, by themselves, to turn around a company.

It was clear that Perkins & Will also needed new leadership. Initially, I thought Neumann might be the right man for the job. But although he was an excellent marketing man, he lacked the broad understanding of the business and the entrepreneurial drive that was needed to take the tough decisions needed to turn the company round.

An early sign of the problems was a contract Perkins & Will had won in Saudi Arabia to design a new university. The fee was $30 million, and at that level the company should have been able to turn a profit of more than $5 million by the end of the project. Instead, we ended up with a loss of $5 million. The problem was that the person who'd been put in charge of the project was, like Neumann, a marketing professional, not an architect with extensive design and project-management experience. He didn't understand how to control a project of that size. There is a sequence in design, and a methodology that enables you to perform all the complex parts of a major project in a co-ordinated fashion. Without detailed experience of that, delays inevitably occur and costs rise.

Eventually, Neumann stepped down as chief executive and we made fresh appointments. Although we made some progress, I still wasn't happy that we were bringing the company into profit as fast as we should. We certainly should have been doing so because, encouragingly, we had begun to win some very prestigious contracts. We developed a good relationship with a small consultancy run by James M. Stevenson, a specialist in airport planning. With his assistance, Perkins & Will won a major contract to design a new international terminal at O'Hare International Airport, Chicago. Stevenson acted as the managing principal, with a large Perkins & Will team working on the project.

Stevenson also helped Perkins & Will negotiate the largest individual piece of business it had won to date – a $70m contract to design a new medical facility for the University of California in Los Angeles. We won praise for the design of the medical facility, and it became a significant addition to the Dar Group's growing portfolio of hospital and health buildings.

Yet despite this encouraging flow of new work, I was still not happy with the company's failure to make money. I had decided very soon after taking over Perkins & Will that we needed to expand our presence in the United States. In some respects, the American market can be parochial, and if you don't have a presence in a state it can be quite difficult to get work, especially projects financed from public funds. One company that I looked at as a possible acquisition target was Nix Mann, an architectural consultancy based in Atlanta, Georgia, which specialised in the healthcare market. I thought it would fit very neatly alongside our other interests and strengthen our growing worldwide presence in large-scale hospital and healthcare building projects.

The company had been founded by Lewis Nix and Henry Mann, who had built it up to more than a hundred people and were already thinking about how they could realise value from it ahead of their retirement in a few years' time. What I especially liked about Nix Mann was that the company had a culture of being profitable. Perkins & Will seemed to be locked into a culture of losing money. I hoped that if the two worked side by side some of Nix Mann's money-making flair might rub off on Perkins & Will.

In fact, as matters progressed, I saw a way to give Perkins & Will the kind of entrepreneurial leadership it desperately needed. The deal I structured with Lewis Nix and Henry Mann was based on us paying an upfront sum for their company and then giving them a healthy earn-out incentive based on them exceeding the profit-margin targets they'd already set for the next five years. They'd been achieving a profit margin of around 15 per cent. I suggested that if they could raise that to 20 per cent, they would take home 60 per cent of the extra profit. If they managed to increase the profit margin to 25 per cent, they'd get 70 per cent of the extra. Suffice it to say, they more than exceeded their targets over the next five years. In fact, their performance was so outstanding I became convinced that Henry Mann would make an ideal chairman for Perkins & Will when his five-year earn-out period had concluded. Mann is a person who delights in a challenge, and he was thrilled to take on the job. Since he has done so, Perkins & Will has moved into profit – but not before I had invested more than $20m in the company.

Within the United States and Canada, Perkins & Will has consolidated its position as an architectural firm by acquiring other practices across North America. In 2004, the US trade magazine *World Architecture* ranked Perkins & Will among the 10 largest architectural firms in the world. Another US publication, *Interior Design*, ranked the firm at number three in its 2004 'Top 100 Interior Design Giants'.

Since I bought the firm, Perkins & Will has carried out so many projects it is impossible to mention all of them. But there are some that I number among my personal favourites. One of these is Boeing's world headquarters at 100 North Riverside Plaza in Chicago. The building, which has been called a 'marvel of engineering' – and which won the Structural Engineers' Association of Illinois 'Most Innovative' design award – is on the west side of the Chicago River directly across from the downtown 'Loop', the elevated railway that was, itself, something of an engineering marvel when it opened in 1897. To meet the clearance requirements of the nearby commuter rail lines, the suspended south-west corner of the 36-storey building is supported by steel trusses.

Another Chicago favourite of mine is the Skybridge, a 39-storey tower with 237 residential units, a grocery store, bank, coffee shop and parking. Glass bridges span a 300-foot-wide opening and a four-storey column supports a 40-foot open roof trellis. The whole tower is 425 feet high and an American Institute of Architecture jury described it as 'a delight on the Chicago skyline'.

Not all my favourites are in Chicago! Another building that I personally admire is the Neuroscience Research Center at the University of California, Los Angeles, which won an American Institute of Architecture award. Award judges were impressed by how the lab spaces allow for interaction among researchers, while the building provides a connection to adjacent laboratory and vivarium facilities, so making it easier for scientists to collaborate on research. Also in Los Angeles, I greatly admire the United States Courthouse, which integrates modern technology, such as a solar wall – which not only makes the most of natural daylight, but also captures energy through high-tech cells embedded in the glass – with all the traditional designs associated with courthouses, such as a columned portal and a rotunda. It demonstrates that new technology doesn't have to crowd out the best of traditional design.

*   *   *

We learnt much about the need for strategy, plans and a focus on the bottom line in our acquisition of Perkins & Will, and we were to learn more when we made our second major acquisition in the United States in 1989.

T.Y. Lin International was well known for its expertise in special structures, such as long bridges, tall buildings or other constructions with unusual engineering and building difficulties. T.Y. Lin, who had given his name to the company, had been a senior professor in structural engineering at the University in California at Berkeley. He was a world authority on pre-stressed concrete structures, and had written the book that was the set text the world over for students of the subject. I felt the company's special expertise would complement what we already had in Dar Al-Handasah. But there was an added bonus in acquiring T.Y. Lin. The company already had offices in Taiwan, Singapore and Kuala Lumpur. By the end of the eighties, we were keen to expand into the Pacific Rim.

By the time I'd acquired the company, T.Y. Lin himself was no longer chairman. He had stepped down, but remained a member of the board. He had been succeeded by Y.C. Yang, who like Lin was a naturalised American citizen. The day-to-day management had been in the hands of the company's president, Eugene Zowyer. Zowyer, however, was not happy with the acquisition, and resigned. So we had to look for a replacement.

Our search proved difficult, and we went through a series of appointments that did not succeed. Finding the right president for T.Y. Lin did not prove a simple task, until we realised the answer was under our noses all the time. Eventually, we promoted John Hausman, T.Y. Lin's operations director, from within the company. Hausman turned the company round, enabled it to win profitable new contracts, and developed its global reputation for special structures.

To give an example of the technically difficult tasks T.Y. Lin undertakes, you only have to look at the Golden Gate Bridge in San Francisco. Two years after the devastating Lorna Prieta earthquake in 1989 – it measured 7.1 on the Richter scale and killed 63 people – T.Y. Lin was called in to prepare a design for a seismic retrofit for the bridge. Our team built a computer model that mimmicked an earthquake of 8.6 on the Richter scale – the strength of the notorious San Francisco earthquake of 1906 – to judge the impact on the bridge's structure. We produced a design that was retrofitted so that should the bridge suffer a major earthquake it would sustain only limited repairable damage and be open again within 24 hours.

Lorna Prieta also damaged the east span of the San Francisco–Oakland Bay bridge and, subsequently, the California Department of Transportation decided to replace the steel structure, which was sixty years old. T.Y. Lin's team provided design services for the new span, which includes two parallel five-lane roadways, a bicycle/pedestrian path and capacity for a rail link, in association with two other firms. I have long believed that good engineering can add to the beauty of our environment, and the new lighting we designed for the bridge has turned it into an after-dark landmark.

In Australia, T.Y. Lin provided design and construction engineering services for the Melbourne City Link, which includes 22 kilometres of expressways – part of which is a 5 kilometre elevated highway – two tunnels and a bridge. The whole project was designed to speed rush-hour traffic into Melbourne's central business district. This was a job where T.Y. Lin's experience of pre-cast concrete enabled it to use new techniques to speed up the construction and save money. The Melbourne City Link was the largest urban infrastructure project in Australia's history, and has saved the city's businesses around US$170m a year as well as cutting the number of accidents.

In recent years, T.Y. Lin has been evolving from its specialist structural engineering base to include projects in transport engineering and planning. As part of this expansion, the company has acquired aviation and transport-planning specialist practices in the United States.

*　　*　　*

Although much of Dar Al-Handasah's early development was driven by the boom in oil-producing economies, we had not been involved in engineering activities in the oil and gas sector. We filled this gap in our engineering portfolio in 1990 when Dar Group acquired Penspen, one of the United Kingdom's largest independent international pipeline and sub-sea engineering consultancies. From its base in the United Kingdom, the firm is active around the globe.

In 1998, we also acquired Paris-based Pierre-Yves Rochon, an interior-design practice that provides services to large companies in the hospitality industry. Pierre-Yves Rochon was the interior designer behind the refurbishment of the famous Georges V hotel in Paris, now called the Four Seasons George V. The brief was to keep the essence of the hotel, but give it cleaner lines and more elegance while avoiding ostentation and frills. When I stepped into the new lobby for the first time, with its freshly exposed Art Deco architecture on show, its restored tapestries and its custom-designed marble floor, I felt sure that many of the Four Seasons' famous guests would immediately feel as relaxed and at home as I did.

In 2004, Dar Group acquired a South African railway engineering consulting practice, R&H Railway Consultants, based in the northern suburbs of Johannesburg. R&H brings us management experience gained from developing and maintaining heavy-mineral haulage railways pioneered in several parts of southern Africa during the last fifty years. We have also established an operation in China and have developed the Dar Group in India.

As I write, Dar Group is on track to push through the landmark of achieving an annual fee income of half a billion dollars for 2005. The enterprise that I started half a century ago in Beirut now generates well over 40 per cent of its revenues from the Americas. The Middle East, our region of origin, currently contributes just over a quarter of our fee income. Europe, Africa and Asia are growing, and will continue to do so. We are consistently ranked among the top 20 international design consultants in the annual listing compiled by McGraw-Hill's *Engineering News-Record*.

In summary, this is now the global business that I have managed to lead out of the Middle East. The journey has proved an instructive one, so perhaps I should share some of the lessons about how we have done it.

*   *   *

As the Dar Group has developed we have learnt a lot about how to acquire companies and integrate them into the group. Our policy now is to acquire 51 to 60 per cent of a successful company, rather than the whole of the shareholding. That approach achieves two key objectives. First, it gives us the control that we need in order to integrate the company into the group. But it also leaves enough financial interest in the hands of management to incentivise them to grow the company and make it more profitable. It is a policy which we've found delivers rich dividends.

We have also learnt from our early acquisitions and our means of evaluating those companies that we are thinking of buying. We now adopt a much broader approach to due diligence than we did with our first acquisitions. Managers will be familiar with the concept of due diligence, which involves investigating in depth the financial and legal affairs of a business before acquiring it. We were always meticulously careful with that traditional approach to due diligence – hence, for example, the thick Peat Marwick report on Perkins & Will. However, my experiences with both the Perkins & Will and T.Y. Lin acquisitions made me realise that financial and legal due diligence are not enough by themselves. Indeed, they may not even be the most important aspects of due diligence when you're considering the long-term future of the business. Much more vital is the company's 'human capital'. In other words, what skills and experience do the senior managers have and does the company have management talent in depth?

As a result, all our due-diligence exercises now focus very heavily on the personnel in the acquisition target. What we're looking for is whether the company is structured well for succession when the leading managers retire. Indeed, often one of the reasons why major shareholders in private companies decide to sell up is so that they can retire – as was the case at Nix Mann, although Henry Mann couldn't resist the challenge I eventually offered him at Perkins & Will. (As a matter of fact, Henry Mann and Louis Nix had already identified Philip Harrison as the leader to succeed them, and now he is the president of Perkins & Will and the candidate designated to succeed Henry Mann as chairman.)

The culture of Nix Mann has so far been the closest to that of Dar, which identified my successor in 1997. Our focus on future leadership in any acquisition means that the succession pyramid within the target company has to be strong. We want to see a second tier of capable management that is ready to move up to the first tier when the time comes. And, if the company is large enough, we'll also be looking for a third tier to move up to the second. This human-resources due diligence has now become a major part of any acquisition programme that we embark upon.

Any business that wants to achieve success in markets as diverse as North America, Europe, the Middle East and Asia must focus consistently on choosing and developing its people. Choosing the right staff at all levels is important for a successful business, but making the right choices for senior appointments is particularly vital.

When I first started making appointments all those years ago, I would do so on the basis of a simple judgement after interviewing the individual in a relatively informal way. Since then, I have refined the system I use for interviewing and assessing candidates for senior-management posts.

It is based on awarding each candidate a maximum of 12 points and requiring a minimum of 10 to qualify for appointment. I award up to five of those points for the individual's buy-in and enthusiasm for our company mission. All companies in the Dar Group set out to achieve the highest standards of technical excellence in their chosen fields. Further, we are deeply committed to working closely – I might almost say intimately – with our clients in the process of developing and bringing their projects to fruition. Finally, we strive for the highest standards of professional integrity. So when I interview, I am looking for a candidate who is committed heart and soul to that whole package rather than one who may mouth the words but not feel them in his or her heart of hearts.

I award a maximum of a further four points for the individual's commitment and capacity for hard work and, vitally, for hitting deadlines. No doubt many companies say they look for these qualities in senior management applicants and, undoubtedly, some do. But I sense that there are other companies for which testing candidates against such criteria is little more than a *pro forma* exercise. If you want to recruit the very best people, you have to conduct a searching examination of the individual's true commitment.

For us, hard work and hitting deadlines is something of an obsession. We have this thing we call the 'Dar bug'. It's about mobilising ourselves in the service of a client so that we exceed their expectations and achieve their objectives in a timescale that other consultancies would consider simply impossible. It's what we believe makes us different and gives us an unbeatable competitive edge. (Perhaps it's just as well for our competitive advantage that the Dar bug doesn't seem to be infectious among other development consultancies!)

With potential management candidates now awarded a maximum of nine points, I now apply the final test, for which I award up to three points. This is an assessment of the candidate's intelligence. It is fair to say that the individual won't even be sitting in front of me if he or she hasn't made a favourable first impression with intelligence. But I use the intelligence points either as a final confirmation that we have the right candidate or, occasionally, as a tie-breaker if I've seen two or more candidates who've scored the same number of points on the first two tests. Needless to say, I'm not looking for an abstract thinker whose head is in the clouds, but an individual who knows how to apply good practical intelligence to the multiplicity of problems they will face in the varied and ever-changing world of development consultancy.

I have found the Dar points system to be an excellent way to recruit the best candidates for the toughest jobs. But in the modern world, where all companies face ever-increasing demands to perform better, it's not enough just to recruit good people. You have to develop them once you have them. One reason for doing this is that if you don't, they'll leave for a competitor where they can enhance their qualifications. So building successful teams long term is heavily about staff retention. (And that's becoming even more important when the competition for engineering graduates from the best universities worldwide is more intense than ever – both from other consultancies and investment banks.)

But successful team-building is also about giving good people the opportunity to grow, so that they enhance their own prospects even as they contribute more to the company's advance. For example, every year we take promising young engineers, many from our offices in the Middle East, and send them to the United States to study for a master's in engineering. Sometimes they'll study for it part time over two years while still working, sometimes full time over one year. Either way, we continue to pay their salary while they study, and when they tack those extra letters MA or MSc after their name, they also find a raise in their monthly salary cheque.

I firmly believe that engineering and development consultancy is a knowledge business. And both the depth and breadth of knowledge that our engineers, planners, architects and professionals in economics and finance need is expanding all the time. So we encourage them to attend relevant international conferences or seminars on both technical and management topics. Being a global company, we also encourage staff to go on working visits to other offices in the group. This is an excellent way not only for them to gain knowledge of new working methods but to acquire a feel for new and different cultures. It provides valuable experience they can put to work in delivering an even better service to clients as they work in a global company.

Turning Dar Al-Handasah into a global company despite the odds stacked against us has been one of the driving forces in my life. I realised early on that if we were to stand comparison with the best in the world in engineering and development consultancy – to compete with them and beat them – we would have to do so on their home turf as well as in our own region. I also knew that in acquiring and maintaining world-class knowledge and skills we would need to go to those places where such standards often emerge first – in North America and Europe. Being a player in those markets means that we are active, alongside other leaders, in helping to develop and define world-class standards.

Being a player in the developed world also adds to the contribution we are able to make in the developing world. It means that we are able to be a first-hand player when it comes to transferring technological knowledge and skills from the developed to the developing world. Besides that, we acquire tremendous insights into the kinds of world-class skills that are needed in the developing world and the ways in which they may be most effectively applied.

In a sense, I feel that we at Dar Al-Handasah have played a small part in reversing a pernicious feature of history. From the seventeenth to the twentieth centuries, colonisers from Europe exploited their overseas possessions for the value they could extract from them – whether that value flowed in gold, groundnuts or, most evil of all, slaves. Building a company that acts as a kind of technology bridge from the developed to the developing world reverses the flow of value. We are now bringing new technologies to the developing world – helping to build up their industries and infrastructure and improve the quality of life for their people. I do not want to give the impression we are philanthropists. We do this because it is our business and we do it for a profit.

But, as I look back on the 50 years since the company started, I can't help feeling that it's been a deeply satisfying way to earn a living.

CHAPTER 17

For King and countries

In November 1989, I was in the United States attending to some
business matters when I received a telephone call from a friend in
Jordan. He was excited and calling to tell me that he'd just seen
on television that I'd been appointed a member of Jordan's Majlis
Al-A'yan, or house of notables, the upper house of the Jordanian parliament. In plain terms I was a member of the senate.

It was news to me. Nobody had asked me whether I'd like to serve
in the senate. Nobody had even hinted that my name was under
consideration. I was at once immensely surprised and deeply flattered.
I should, perhaps, explain that under Jordan's constitution, members
of the Majlis Al-Nuwwab, the house of deputies – the lower house –
are elected, but members of the senate are appointed by the reigning
monarch. At the time, this was King Hussein.

Of course there was no question of me declining such an appointment. Nor did I wish to. I was delighted that I was being given the
opportunity to play a part in the legislature of my native country. Both
the nationalist and the activist in me were fired with enthusiasm. The
40-member senate, I already knew, played a significant role in the
public affairs of Jordan. Together with the 80-member lower house it
constituted the legislative branch of government.

I was appointed, like all senators, for a term of four years. I arrived at Jordan's parliament building for my first session of the senate with some apprehension. I need have had none. I was warmly received by my fellow senators. In the days ahead, I was appointed to serve on two of the permanent committees – the finance and economic affairs committee and the education committee. Both of these were subjects in which I had a keen interest, and where I believed I would have something positive to contribute.

The one concern at the back of my mind was whether I would be able to give the amount of time required to my duties as a senator alongside my considerable responsibilities at Dar Al-Handasah. Jordan's parliament meets for about a hundred and twenty working days a year, both houses meeting at the same time. A third of a year is a significant extra burden to add to an already heavy workload. But I tackled the problem as I usually do when faced with extra work – I extended my working hours.

*   *   *

The Jordanian constitution lays down certain criteria to be fulfilled by members of the legislature. Members of the lower house must, of course, be elected by their constituents, and must be at least 30 years old. Members of the senate are appointed by the King and must be at least 40 years old. But criteria for senators are more extensive. Members of the upper house must qualify in one of the following categories: former prime ministers; former speakers of the lower house; former ministers; former deputies who have served at least two terms; former presidents and members of the supreme court; former ambassadors; former military officers with the rank of major-general or higher; and those who have significantly distinguished themselves in the service of the nation.

The wise authors of the constitution recognised the requirement for the popularly elected lower house to be counter-balanced by the upper house. While the lower house represents the people, and is accountable to them through the ballot box, the upper house is able to bring into the legislature experienced individuals irrespective of their immediate popular appeal. In bicameral systems an unelected upper house plays a key role in scrutinising and revising legislation passed from a lower house more directly subject to immediate constituency interests and political expediency. The upper house includes those with the experience, expertise and capability to provide wise counsel and consider proposed legislation in the context of the long-term interests of the nation and its constituent communities. The role of the upper house is to counsel the elected chamber when further thought and revision is warranted. The will of the elected house should, of course, prevail after due consideration of the senate's views.

The role of the upper house as a wise counsel is, I believe, particularly important in a young democracy, like Jordan's, especially in the turbulent environment that has characterised the Middle East over the past half century. As volatile popular opinion reacts to immediate events in the region, the upper house serves as a stabilising influence bringing to bear its reservoir of experience and capacity to counsel the lower house on the broad long-term implications and impacts of proposed legislation.

The chief of the royal court and the King's other advisers have a great responsibility for ensuring that appointments to the upper house mobilise individuals qualified to provide both the wisdom and the stability vital to long-term development and progress. I believe that the authors of Jordan's constitution served the nation extremely well in detailing the criteria that qualify individuals who constitute the senate. I deeply regret the failure to appoint to the senate distinguished individuals who meet the constitution's criteria, and whose experience, wisdom and capability are beyond doubt. For example, former prime ministers who have served as empowered heads of the executive have, in my view, a critical role to play in the upper house. The criteria for appointments laid out in the constitution should be faithfully followed to ensure that the capabilities and quality of the upper house befits the role it has to play in Jordan's future.

My own appointment in 1989 came at a time when Jordan was emerging from a 23-year period in which there had been no elections to the lower house. The previous election had been in 1966, just prior to the disastrous 1967 war with Israel and the turmoil in which the region was engulfed. The 1966 house of deputies was composed predominantly of members who could be categorised as either conservative nationalists or from the political centre. As I remember, there was one deputy with leftist leanings and one Islamist.

The 1967 war completely changed the political backcloth. As a result, the parliament elected in 1966 remained in office. But in 1988 Jordan renounced its administrative responsibility for the West Bank. This meant it was possible to reconstitute the parliament to exclude West Bank representation. To take account of this, the electoral law was amended so that 80 deputies would be elected to the lower house from new electoral districts. The 1989 election was held on these new districts.

In 1989, the only organised political group in Jordan of any substance was the Islamic Action Front, the political wing of the Muslim Brotherhood, originally established in Egypt in the 1930s. The Brotherhood had been active in Jordan for decades providing social services and support to the poor and needy. The social agenda of the Brotherhood, together with the weakening of the nationalist cause in the wake of the 1967 war, gave the Front an edge in the 1989 election. In all democracies such charitable social activities would, of course, be deemed to pose a conflict of interest for a political group. The Front's edge was also strengthened by features of the electoral law in force at the time. These features favoured a well-organised minority party's ability to maximise its representation in multi-member electoral districts in which each elector had multiple votes.

The 1989 elections took place amid economic crisis. In the decade before the election, Jordan had run large fiscal deficits of 10–18 per cent of GDP. Fiscal imbalance was coupled with chronic balance-of-payments current-account deficits. Twin internal and external imbalances depleted foreign-currency reserves and produced a substantial foreign-debt burden (that peaked at just over 200 per cent of GDP). Inflation and currency depreciation were severe. The crisis came to a violent head just before the election, when the government raised fuel prices without accommodating revisions of regulated transport tariffs for freight haulage and public transport. There were mass demonstrations in Ma'an in southern Jordan protesting against the negligence of the government. The protests spread to other towns in the south. The police confronted demonstrators. In the ensuing violence there were fatalities among the casualties. At the time the prime minister, with a delegation of other ministers, was visiting the United States. The King recalled the delegation, and the prime minister and his cabinet stepped down. Such was the difficult backdrop to the 1989 elections.

The elections were characterised by extensive negative campaigning. The Islamic Action Front won nearly one third of the 80 seats in the lower house. The result was greeted by King Hussein with the caustic remark that we need to advance to Islam.

So when I first became a senator the legislature was emerging from a vacuum that had lasted more than two decades, since the 1967 war, and the Jordanian economy was in poor shape. Jordan's substantial budget deficits were offset by large inflows of official aid. The economy was also buoyed by substantial inflows of workers' remittances from Jordanians working in the oil-boom economies of the Arabian Peninsula.

Despite large fiscal deficits, the economy often showed signs of vigour. The worrying issue was the ever-deepening dependence of the economy on continuing inflows of aid and of workers' remittances. Jordan's economic development was not driven by the robustness of the Jordanian economy. It was driven by the propensity of friendly governments to provide aid, and by the willingness of other Arab nations to host expatriate Jordanian workers. Jordan's ability to sustain economic advance was fragile in the face of fickle official aid flows vulnerable to political circumstances. It also depended on the continued willingness and capacity of expatriate Jordanians to continue remittance flows from neighbouring economies.

Jordan had never enjoyed, since the days when it gained its independence, the opportunity to develop the kind of robust economic growth taken as the norm by the oil states of the Middle East. For a start, Jordan had no oilfields of its own as the platform of a domestic economy. The destabilising wars of 1948 and 1967 had drained the country's treasury and disrupted its economy. Half of the population had been lost when the West Bank was occupied by Israel. And the large influx of Palestinian refugees through the period had posed a significant burden on the government.

On the other hand, I was convinced that Jordan had the potential to become a robust and thriving economy if only it would take the right steps. This would involve some harsh measures. Even so, as I turned up at the parliament building in Amman for my first meeting as a senator, it was against a background of economic crisis. The government had abandoned the Jordanian dinar's peg to the International Monetary Fund's Special Drawing Rights (SDR), a basket of solid hard currencies. The IMF was riding to Jordan's assistance with a programme designed to stabilise the economy and introduce structural reforms that would stimulate future growth.

I had some clear ideas in my own mind about the steps the government needed to take. Although I was a first-time senator – a new boy, if you like – I decided there was nothing to be lost in speaking out. I believe my opinions may have gained weight among fellow senators from my track-record in building Dar Al-Handasah into an international company. But having your views listened to with interest, and changing policy for the better are two different things, and it wasn't until I became chairman of the influential finance and economic affairs committee at the start of my second term as a senator, in 1993, that I began to exert some influence on the shape of economic policy in Jordan.

*　　*　　*

By far the greatest crisis during my first term as a senator came on 2 August 1990, when Iraq invaded Kuwait. As it happens, I was in San Francisco visiting our subsidiary company T.Y. Lin when Saddam Hussein marched his troops across the border. I received a telephone call from Ossama Omar, Dar Al-Handasah's director of operations in the Gulf, asking me if I'd heard the news. 'What news?' was my immediate reaction. An agitated Omar urged me to turn on CNN. I did so and watched horrified the events of the invasion being broadcast live.

Omar had every reason to be agitated. Dar Al-Handasah had recently been bidding for a major contract in Kuwait. We'd been fortunate enough to win it, and Omar had travelled to Kuwait City for

204 OUT OF THE MIDDLE EAST

the contract signing. For one reason or another, the signing session was delayed by a day or two. After it was completed, Omar had flown out of Kuwait only hours before Saddam's troops moved in.

My immediate reaction to the news was to cancel further engagements in the United States and return to Jordan. Apart from the fact that the invasion could have a serious impact on Dar Al-Handasah's business interests in the region, I was also aware that I could be called on to give my views as a Jordanian senator. When I arrived back in Amman, I was horrified to find that a substantial portion of the city's population was jubilant at Saddam's move. In the early days, the invasion had seemed to wrong-foot the Americans, and it brought to the surface those latent anti-Western feelings that exist among some Arabs.

It also played on Arab nationalist feelings, but, as I have mentioned before, there are two kinds of nationalism – the chauvinistic kind that is ultimately destructive, and the liberal humane nationalism that celebrates the best in a culture and seeks to share it with the world. Saddam, like Egypt's Nasser before him, used nationalism as a cover for tyranny.

I was pleased to find that, despite the pro-Saddam feeling in the country, King Hussein was adding his weight to international voices seeking a diplomatic solution to the crisis. I didn't delay in making my own views known in government and parliamentary circles. I also spoke out publicly against the invasion. My views were reported by the *Washington Post*'s Nora Boustany. On 28 August 1990, the *Post* published her piece on growing concerns in Jordan over the pro-Saddam view. Boustany quoted my remarks:

> I feel strongly that the invasion and annexation of Kuwait were wrong and in violation of the United Nations and Arab League charters. Taking over territories, let alone countries, by the use of force is totally inadmissible as a matter of principle. I believe that the UN Resolution 661 [which imposed a trade embargo on Iraq and occupied Kuwait] should be implemented unconditionally, and that includes the withdrawal of Iraqi forces from Kuwait, as well as the restoration of the Kuwaiti government.

Resolution 661 had more practical implications for Jordan than most other countries. Jordan shared a land border with Iraq, and if the embargo were to be broken it could be expected that many of the proscribed goods entering Iraq would pass through Jordanian territory. If this were to happen on any significant scale with the complicity of the Jordanian government, it could provoke sanctions against the country from the international community.

My public stand made me extremely unpopular in most sections of the community. Hardly anybody agreed with what I had to say. Out of a population of around four million people in Jordan at the time, I doubt whether those who held views similar to mine numbered more that a few hundred. Friends urged me to be more circumspect in expressing my opinions. They told me they'd heard that there were pro-Saddam extremist elements that would take pleasure in silencing me. In the context of violent Middle Eastern politics, I had no illusions about what 'silence' meant. But I refused to use weasel words, and continued to speak out bluntly about what I believed to be a thoroughly evil act of invasion.

Throughout the crisis, I kept in touch with friends from Kuwait. Abdul Rahman Al-Atiqi, a former Kuwaiti oil and finance minister, and currently an adviser to the Emir, had fled to Saudi Arabia at the start of the invasion. He was maintaining clandestine contacts with loyalists inside the country, and told me about the horrors being perpetrated by Saddam's so-called 'liberators'. On a visit to Washington DC, I met Hassan Al-Ibrahim, a former Kuwaiti minister of education. He told me about the terrible ravages he'd heard were being visited on Kuwait and its people by Saddam's troops.

The events following the invasion have been exhaustively recorded. Diplomatic efforts to reverse the invasion failed. A coalition military force was assembled, and it launched an attack that drove Saddam's army in disarray from Kuwait – but only after Iraqi troops had pillaged the country and murdered many of its finest people. Since those terrible events, the Kuwaiti people have shown great resilience and enterprise in rebuilding their homeland. In view of what happened, I believe the strong stand I took prior to the military action was completely vindicated. It is totally unacceptable to allow force to rule, and it would have been an outrage against international justice had the United Nations allowed one of its member countries to be wiped from the map as an independent state.

I hope that Iraq may be able to put the troubled history of the past – including its occupation in 2003 by coalition forces led by the United States – behind it and rebuild a better future. It is a country with enormous economic potential endowed, as it is, with huge oil reserves, two great rivers and an educated population.

On 20 October 2003, at the time of the Madrid Donor Conference for Iraq, I contributed an article that was published in the *Financial Times*' comment section. In the article, I emphasised that addressing the damage and disruption of the war was only a part of the challenge. It was necessary to undo the damage caused by neglect of economic assets, to eliminate the distortions of central planning and to shift Iraq from a state of isolation to engagement in the global economy. I urged that 'donors' attention must focus on helping build an Iraq that will adopt an open, liberal market economy'.

As a neighbour and major trade partner, it is strongly in Jordan's interest that Iraq should realise both its democratic and economic potential. And, given the international trouble Iraq has caused for a generation or more, in the world's interest too.

*   *   *

Another foreign-affairs issue in which I played a part as a senator was Jordan's reaction to the 1993 Oslo Agreement, which set out a 'road map' for resolving peacefully the issues relating to the territories illegally occupied by Israel.

Some time before the Oslo Agreement was signed in August of that year, I met with a friend who was a confidant of Mahmoud Abbas, now president of the Palestinian Authority. Abbas was then (as now) seen as a moderate advocate of the Palestinian cause, and was closely involved in the secret Oslo negotiations. Abbas's confidant had received a call tipping him off about the nature of the deal that was about to be struck. He told me the details, and I passed them on to Abdel-Salam

Majali, who was then prime minister of Jordan. Majali knew of the negotiations, but not of the shape of the agreement that was likely to emerge. He used the information I'd given him to brief King Hussein. When the agreement finally became public, I spoke again to Majali and impressed on him my view that it was a step in the right direction towards a permanent peace.

Later the same year, I was able to gauge the impact the Oslo Agreement had made on public perceptions of the Palestinian issue around the world when I went, as a senator, to a meeting of the International Parliamentary Union in Canberra, capital of Australia. Practically everybody at the meeting, I was pleased to find, felt the agreement was a significant step towards a resolution of the issue. I had been selected to address the meeting on Jordan's behalf, and I used my time to outline the progress that we were making in negotiating a Jordan–Israel peace agreement. (It was, in fact, later signed by Majali.) The strength of support from delegates at the conference for the peace process encouraged me to feel that we were, at long last, making real progress.

In the wake of the Oslo Agreement, much work started to establish Palestinian institutions. In 1994, I went to a meeting in Amman called to bring together business leaders to discuss investment initiatives in Palestine. I was surprised when one of the leading Palestinians at the meeting invited me to come into a side room for private discussions. He told me that the group intended to set up a Palestinian investment company, and he wanted to know whether I would become its founder chairman. I must admit I was surprised to be asked, as I wasn't a native Palestinian, but I was strongly pressed to take the post, and agreed.

The Palestinian Development and Investment Company (Padico) was founded in 1994, and I served as chairman for the first four years of its life. In the first year alone, we managed to raise $150 million for investment. During my period of office, we established a stock exchange (at Nablus) and let a concession to operate fixed and mobile telephone services through the Palestinian territories. We also established a large portfolio of investment projects covering industry, tourism, real estate and transportation. During the four years I led Padico, its portfolio of investments grew to around $1 billion.

Despite some progress, the Palestinian question remains unresolved today. But I remain convinced that the solution lies through rational debate and, where necessary, peaceful protest.

I once met Jehan Sadat, the widow of Anwar Sadat, the Egyptian president assassinated in 1981 by rebel army officers angered that he was stretching out the hand of reconciliation to Israel. Sadat (along with the Israeli prime minister Menachem Begin) won the Nobel Peace Prize for his work in negotiating the 1978 Camp David Accords, brokered by US president Jimmy Carter, which brought peace between Egypt and Israel.

Mrs Sadat told me that during the secret negotiations on the agreement, her husband had telephoned Yasser Arafat and begged him to fly to Washington. Sadat had believed it might be possible to reach a final resolution on the Palestinian question with Begin. Arafat had seemed reluctant, but Sadat had urged him at least to come to see what offer might be on the table – he could, after all, always refuse it. But Arafat refused to move. Later, in 1994, Arafat won the Nobel Peace Prize too.

But there is still no peace between Palestine and Israel. I do not believe violence – the rocket attacks and suicide bombers – will achieve Palestinian aims, because it will not engage the sympathy of world opinion. At root, the Palestinians have a just cause, and they must use just means to win support for it. Non-violent civil disobedience is the way forward. It would engage the support of activists of all religions and none who believe there is a long-standing injustice that ought to be righted. It worked for Mahatma Gandhi in India – and he was fighting a British empire that was, at the time, far more mighty than Israel. Gandhi, when asked what he thought about Western civilisation once famously remarked: 'I think it would be a good idea'. I feel sure he would take the same view of peace in the Middle East.

*   *   *

The lower house of the Jordanian parliament elected in 1989 entered the final year of its term in 1993. Serious questions were being raised concerning the constitutional validity of the election law. It was reported that King Hussein shared these concerns, particularly in the light of the prospects for a peace settlement following the Madrid Conference held in October 1991. The King chose to initiate debate on the matter among members of the senate and summoned them to a meeting on 5 July 1993.

He opened the meeting with a statement on the state of the nation and the regional and international situation, and then invited remarks from the senators. I'd anticipated that the King would want to start a discussion about the broad challenges facing the country, and had collected my thoughts before the meeting. I was the first to contribute to the discussion, and focused on three challenges.

The first was to ensure that the general election, expected in the following autumn, should be conducted with the full respect to equality for all guaranteed by the constitution. This, I stressed, could only be achieved by amending the electoral law to provide for the one-person-one-vote principle. The second was the continued implementation of economic, fiscal and monetary reforms agreed by government with the IMF. The third was the government's continued commitment to the success of the peace process initiated at the Madrid Conference.

The King thoughtfully commented on my remarks, concentrating mainly on the electoral law. He then invited the views of each senator. A good number opposed the one-person-one-vote principle, but a majority endorsed it. On 17 August 1993, the King delivered a speech announcing that, after broad consultations, he had directed the government to implement it.

*   *   *

Later in 1993, I was invited to serve a second term as a senator and, in 1997, a third. By the second term, I had found my feet in managing parliamentary business, and I was elected as chairman of the finance and economic affairs committee. This was one of the most important committees, and gave me a position of influence – although not executive power – over the management of the country's fiscal affairs and economic policy. I was also made a member of the influential judicial affairs committee. Most of the members of the committee were lawyers, so it was something of an education for me to learn from their perspective on the issues that came before the committee. But, as a non-lawyer, I think I was also able to make a useful contribution to debates. As something like 95 per cent of parliamentary business came before one or other of these two committees, I was kept exceedingly busy.

In fact, if anything I made extra work for myself. I took my responsibilities as chairman of the finance and economic affairs committee very seriously, and usually attended meetings of the comparable committee in the house of deputies as well as chairing the senate committee meetings. I acquired a reputation as a senator who spent more time working on legislation than most of my contemporaries or predecessors. But then I believed I was being given a privileged opportunity to guide the government of the country of my birth, and I intended to apply every available ounce of my energy to the task.

One of the toughest parts of the job as chairman of the finance and economic affairs committee was reviewing the annual budget. The budget was drawn up by the government and submitted to both houses of parliament for debate. It was something that I believed we had to review very carefully, not least because, for most of my period as a senator, underlying fiscal and economic policies were central to Jordan's progress through a difficult period of economic adjustment and reform. I won't pretend that I didn't clash with some finance ministers over their proposals – or their inaction on other reforms I believed should be undertaken.

The climax of the annual debate on the budget in the senate came when I made a speech reviewing, and not infrequently criticising, the government's proposals. My approach was one based on the tenet that serious proposals warrant serious review and a constructive critique, even if I disagreed with the proposals.

For my part the annual budget debate's requirement to engage in complex arguments with knowledgeable opponents, whose views were often contrary to mine, was at once exhilarating and exhausting. The budget debate was widely reported outside parliament, and it was gratifying that each year I would receive hundreds of telephone messages or letters following it. I was pleased that many seemed to agree with what I'd had to say. But did I make any impact on government policy?

When you're trying to influence government policy – which, itself, is being pulled this way and that by both the views of ministers and the vested interests seeking to influence them – two things are important. First, you must have a very clear idea about your own ideas – what they are and why you hold them. Second, you must focus on those areas where you think you can have some real influence and an ability to make an impact. That was my approach.

During my 12 years in the senate – and especially during my eight as chairman of the finance and economic affairs committee – I pursued a number of consistent themes. The first was the need to control the budget deficit, which seriously destabilised the economy. When a government spends more than it receives from taxes and other revenues, a number of highly undesirable consequences flow. First, the country's debt, and thus the cost of servicing the accumulated borrowing, increases. Second, interest rates rise to take account of the extra risk premium investors seek when they agree to buy Jordanian government bonds (to fund the deficit) rather than those of countries which don't have persistent structural deficits. Third, these factors add to the pressure on inflation.

Despite running persistent deficits, Jordan had partly countered these problems by linking its currency to the SDR. The breaking of that link shortly before I became a senator imported new risks into Jordan's economy. The largest was that the currency would depreciate, which would have been helpful to exporters but would have made imports more expensive, thus tending to fuel inflation. In fact, the worst dangers were averted. The restructuring programme that the IMF promoted enabled the economy to make sufficient progress so that by 1995 it was possible to peg the Jordanian dinar to the US dollar. The dollar peg enabled Jordan to regain the benefits of a trade-friendly stable currency.

I strongly supported further measures to promote foreign trade, such as the creation of Jordan's 'qualified industrial zone' programme, introduced in the mid-1990s, which allowed manufactured goods that had 7–10 per cent Israeli content to be exported duty-free to the United States from especially defined zones within Jordan. In 2000, shortly before I finally stepped down as a senator, Jordan signed a free-trade agreement with the United States. I backed this, along with other government moves to reduce trade tariffs and quotas, to join the World Trade Organisation and to sign up to a partnership agreement with the European Union.

I was also pleased that in 1999, midway through my last term as a senator, the minister of finance brought in an international team of experts to advise on budgetary reform. The team proposed that the government should shift from the traditional method of budgeting, which focused heavily on the 'inputs', of how much money was being spent, to a 'performance budgeting' approach that emphasised more the 'outputs' that the expenditure was supposed to deliver. Performance budgeting could, I believe, encourage governments to ensure that public spending was focused on achieving strategic objectives. It also introduced a much higher level of accountability in public spending by making the officials who spent the money responsible for delivering the outputs that the expenditure should achieve.

Throughout my period as chairman of the finance and economic affairs committee, Jordan faced a constant struggle to ensure that public expenditure in the country did not exceed what could be raised from tax revenues and other receipts. One issue I hammered away at time and time again was the amount of government intervention in private industry. Such intervention could be costly in two main ways. It encouraged the government to provide subsidies when the industries found it difficult to compete in the open market. Further, the industries concerned had little incentive to become more competitive, because they knew they could rely on the government to bail them out of trouble.

I was impressed with the impact of privatisations in other parts of the world, and I was determined to push for them in Jordan. One of the country's main primary industries since the 1930s had been phosphate mining. The government had held a majority stake in some of the companies involved in this industry. I pressed for them to be privatised, and eventually some government shareholdings were sold.

Similarly, there was a measure of privatisation in Jordan's telecommunications industry. At the end of the day, privatisation was a matter for ministers, but I do believe that my speeches and committee discussions about the subject helped to push the subject higher up the government's agenda. I received many calls from people who thanked me for pressing the issue.

But privatisation was only one way in which Jordan's economy needed to be brought into the modern world. The economy remained hostage to an earlier era in which it was considered that an omnipotent state was well placed to plan economic advance, and that the initiative of the individual was best harnessed to a grand central plan orchestrated by the state. Development experience around the world provides clear evidence that the state is usually far from omnipotent, and that it is individuals' initiative that is the engine of development. That initiative is best marshalled within a market-friendly environment in which the state has the major responsibilities for ensuring a stable macroeconomic environment that supports the operation of market mechanisms, and for regulating and facilitating the provision of a wide range of public services and infrastructure.

Jordan's economy had much baggage from the previous era that served to distort the economy and the incentives driving the application of individuals' effort. The corporate-tax regime, for example, was simply illogical. It applied different rates of tax to different industries. Agriculture paid no tax, in manufacturing industry tax was 15 per cent, in trade and services 25 per cent, and in banking 35 per cent. The impact of this was to inhibit the development of activities in higher-taxed industries. But it was the higher-taxed industries that, in economic terms, provided more 'added value' to Jordan's economy and had more potential to contribute to growth. Not surprisingly, there were strong vested interests keen on preserving the current system. I made myself pretty unpopular in some quarters by pressing my case for reform in an uncompromising way. But I regret that, on this occasion, the vested interests were too strong for me. Jordan retains its multiple tax rates to this day.

Another subject I was very concerned about was what I regarded as the unsustainable level of social-security payments, particularly pensions, in the state sector. In the last 10 years that I was senator (up until 2001), pension payments to former government employees, including the military, had tripled, accounting for 16 per cent of central government spending – more than the interest paid on the government's domestic and foreign debt combined. Government pensions accounted for 4.7 per cent of GDP in 2001, getting on for double the figure 10 years earlier.

The problem was the way state pensions were funded. Unlike private pensions, contributions were not paid into a pension fund that was, ultimately, used to pay the benefits. Instead, government pension liabilities were paid, as they arose, out of general taxation. It was, I felt, literally a recipe for ruin, as actuarial studies showed that the system would become unsustainable within about twenty years. Moreover, it had malign effects on the country's labour mobility, as talented people who worked in the civil service would not move to wealth-producing work in the private sector for fear of losing their generous pension entitlement. Once again, I made myself unpopular by confronting authorities with the facts but, also again, the vested interests proved too strong to dislodge.

I guess that in public affairs – as in life – you sometimes have to settle for something rather than nothing. And although I failed to make as much headway on some of the policies that I believed passionately in, on others I did make heartening progress. Education was one such issue. In one respect, it was an economic issue. For building the stock and capability of Jordan's human capital was one of the most pressing questions the country faced when I first became a senator.

It was true that education had come a long way since those far-off days when I trekked up the steep roads to the British school in Salt. Now every child had access to elementary and secondary education, and the country had opened its own universities. But I wasn't convinced that the quantity of spending was producing the quality of education that the country needed. Our schools and universities weren't turning out young people with the skills and aptitudes necessary to grasp opportunities for advancement in an open and competitive economy. More than that, we needed to produce a new generation of confident

Jordanians who could engage productively with the modern world around them.

Once again, it was time for me to start speaking, writing and lobbying for the policies that I believed Jordan urgently needed. When you operate within a parliamentary system, I have discovered, you have to learn to be patient. But you also need the determination to be persistent. I pressed for improved education policies throughout my 12 years as a senator. On this occasion, I am pleased to say that progress was made both during my terms of office and subsequently. Both the Ministry of Education and Ministry of Higher Education adopted more focus on the quality of education. There was investment in information technology in schools and colleges, improved English-language teaching from the first grade, and a raising of standards in science teaching and examinations. The Jordanian government also engaged the United Kingdom's Quality Assurance Agency for Higher Education to help in reviewing the performance of its universities' departments.

*   *   *

I found the 12 years I served as a senator among the most fruitful and satisfying of my life. But everything has to come to an end – and 12 years is a long time to carry a heavy burden of parliamentary work, especially as the chairman of an important committee, as well as running an international business.

Sadly, King Hussein died in 1999. He had served the country and the region, and championed the causes of peace and the legitimate rights of the Palestinian people so well since his accession to the throne. Testimony to the affection and regard in which the King was held was provided by the historic funeral procession in which I participated along with more than seventy heads of state and international leaders as well as thousands of other mourners. The funeral took place after the King had lain in state for two days, during which mourners were able to pay their final respects.

King Hussein was succeeded by King Abdullah II. The period of transition from one monarch to the next is always a difficult time, and Jordanians were naturally anxious. As chairman of the upper house's finance and economic affairs committee, I played a role in discussions that took place on financial and economic policy. Shortly after his accession, the new King convened a three-day workshop to discuss development policy. It was held at the Mövenpick Hotel on the banks of the Dead Sea, and I was invited. I was given the task of chairing the group dealing with the development of human resources in Jordan. The accession of a new king – and the high hopes he brought with him – seemed a fitting moment to be thinking about how we could create a country in which all the population contributed their fullest to its prosperity and peace.

I was not appointed by the new King to serve a fourth term as senator. I cannot say that I was surprised – it is unusual to serve even three terms. I had found my work as a senator very satisfying, but over a period of 12 years it had placed a considerable extra burden on my working life. So I was not disappointed that I was not being required to continue with my duties. Besides, a few years earlier, I had taken on another appointment to which I had become deeply committed.

*   *   *

In 1990, AUB appointed me as a member of its board of trustees. The post is both an honour and a job. A real job, too. The board meets in New York three times a year. In addition, I serve on the executive committee, several other committees, and chair one committee and co-chair another. Between formal meetings, we hold teleconferences to discuss matters such as key appointments or budgetary matters that need to be approved before the next meeting.

For me, it is an intensely worthwhile job. AUB is actually registered in New York state, rather than Lebanon. This means that it is subject to the laws of New York in the same way that Columbia University or any other college with a physical presence in the state is. The board of trustees is responsible for ensuring that the university complies with the laws and files all the necessary reports and documents that the regulatory authorities of New York state require.

Above all, as a board of trustees we have to maintain the standards of education laid down by the state of New York. We achieve well above the minimum required standards, and it is generally recognised that the quality of education at AUB is on a par with America's Ivy League. In particular, our medical school has developed a worldwide reputation for its teaching.

But sadly AUB is still a rare beacon of excellence among educational establishments in the Middle East. It is a matter of profound sadness to me – and ought to be a matter of acute concern to politicians and policy-makers in the region – that the standard of scholarship and learning too often does not live up to that which we know from a study of the medieval thinkers and educators the Arab world can produce. In this case, perhaps the Arab world ought to be advancing to the past.

In 2003, AUB invited me to make the commencement address – at the occasion when students graduate. It was an opportunity to set out my views on education as the essential cornerstone of any civilised and progressive society to a thoughtful and, as it turned out, receptive audience. 'The core cause of its decline from a position of leadership in progress and advance of the civilised world has been the progressive erosion of the value Arab society has placed on the role of the mind and its faculties of rational and critical analysis,' I told my audience.

I laid my views uncompromisingly on the line:

> A propensity for authoritarian regimes in the Arab world has imposed political and social frameworks that have suppressed freedom of the mind and expression and inhibited the spirit of curiosity and critical enquiry that fires individuals' creative endeavour. Development progress is not merely a matter of enhancements in levels of material wellbeing. Sustainable progress has dimensions that feature aspects of freedom of choice, including: freedom from fear and persecution; the ability and freedom to choose and hold accountable those exercising the powers of governance; and the ability and freedom to choose in what way to satisfy one's wants and aspirations. While ideas drive knowledge-intensive progress in the advanced world, authoritarian regimes in the Arab world seek to control ideas and, thereby, shackle progress.

'We are,' I told my audience, 'at a nadir in the esteem in which the Arab world is held by international public opinion.'

Hard, but true, words. Yet as I looked down on the sea of faces on that hot June day, I couldn't help feeling hope, despite all the problems the Arab world faced. Before me were hundreds of young graduates who had been taught the importance of scrupulous scholarship and freedom of expression during their time at AUB. They were well equipped to go out into the modern world, to engage their contemporaries in the international community in constructive dialogue and to lead the assault on those in the Middle East and elsewhere who were enemies of the open society.

We live in a time when there is an urgent need for more constructive engagement between the Western world and the Middle East. The students I saw that commencement day seemed to me well equipped to start the hard work of building sturdier bridges of understanding between those two worlds. Whether they will do so, only time will tell, but I sensed there were many among them who were determined to begin that great work.

CHAPTER 18

Rebuilding broken communities

E arly in 1991, I was awakened one morning at two o'clock by
the insistent ringing of the telephone beside my bed.

It was my cook, with an urgent message: 'Mr Hariri is
on the line and wants to speak with you now'. Rafik Hariri was a
dynamic individual who was widely expected to take office as
Lebanon's prime minister as the country prepared for the challenge of
post-war reconstruction.

He came from Sidon in the south of Lebanon, and after graduating
from AUB in 1965 moved to Saudi Arabia in search of a better life.
His search ended with considerable success. After spells as a teacher
and an accountant, he established his own business. It flourished and
became one of the major conglomerates in Saudi Arabia. He maintained close contact with Lebanon, and utilised both his influence and
personal wealth to support the country of his birth. As that influence
extended into the political and diplomatic arenas, he became
influential in moves to reconcile the communities in Lebanon and to
secure peace.

It was Hariri's energy and initiative that drove the reconciliation
process and negotiations that resulted in the Lebanese National
Assembly meeting in Taif in Saudi Arabia in October 1989 to approve

the agreement that took its name from the town and brought an end to the civil war in Lebanon. (Regrettably, the war continued to claim victims after the Taif Agreement had been signed, notably when René Mouawad was brutally assassinated two weeks after being installed as Lebanon's first post-Taif president. The two weeks that Mouawad managed to devote to forming a government of reconciliation had showed very positive signs of progress.)

The Taif Agreement had left Hariri with many political challenges, including a continuing Syrian presence in Lebanon. According to the agreement, the Syrians were due to leave within two years – although they took 15. Then there were the tasks of marshalling and guiding a war-weary nation through reconstruction and recovery. Immediately the agreement was signed, Hariri applied his energy to post-war relief operations and to preparations for reconstruction. Increasingly, most Lebanese looked to Hariri as the man to take up the reins. As expected, he was appointed prime minister in October 1992.

It was this man whose voice I heard as I hastily sat up in bed trying to shake off my tiredness. He got straight down to business. He had decided it was time to begin on the serious reconstruction of Lebanon, and he needed my help to do it, he told me. The small hours of the morning may, to Western readers, seem an unusual time to begin a serious talk about such an important matter of business. But in parts of the Arab world, it is by no means unusual for people at the tops of their organisations to use the witching hours to make contact with one another while lesser mortals slumber. It was time to show confidence about the future by rebuilding the country, Hariri told me.

Although I had exiled myself as a permanent resident of Lebanon, and now lived mostly in Jordan, I maintained a house in Beirut. Dar Al-Handasah still had its head office in the city. So I wasn't surprised that Hariri had called me about this. I was pleased, too, because it would enable me to pick up work that had been tragically interrupted. Back in 1983, shortly after the Israelis had withdrawn from Beirut after causing so much physical damage to the city, I had been asked by the then president Amin Gemayel to reorganise Lebanon's Council for Reconstruction and Development, the CDR. It was a time of what proved to be false optimism, but a lot of thought was being given to reconstruction planning.

I had found that the CDR operated rather like a government department with one director. I believed it lacked the necessary dynamism to tackle what was, by any standards, a massive reconstruction task. The body needed a new structure, which, I felt, would achieve two important objectives. First, it should have the necessary creativity to conceive of the major projects that would be needed to rebuild a nation as advanced and diverse as Lebanon. Second, it would need the dynamism as well as the managerial skills to realise complex plans on time and within whatever budgets were agreed.

We certainly didn't need a large and bureaucratic body. So, after thinking it over, I decided that a small group of people with specific responsibilities would work better than the rather unfocused structure that had operated until now. As a result, I suggested that the CDR should have a president supported by two vice-presidents and four other members, who would each hold a specific portfolio. The four portfolios I'd decided on back in 1983 were planning, project implementation, co-ordination and finance. The vice-presidents didn't hold portfolios but were, like the president, free to take a broader view of the council's work. Gemayel accepted my reform proposals, and they are still in place as I write.

Nevertheless, although the structure for administering reconstruction was in place by the end of 1983, the political circumstances for doing any extensive reconstruction work had to wait until the next decade came along. Which is why Hariri was now making this early morning call and asking for my thoughts on how we could rebuild Beirut. I had some direct experience to draw on. Beirut would not be the first city I'd seen revived after a period of civil unrest. In 1970, I'd been in Amman when prime minister Wasfi At-Tal had instructed minister of public works Munib Masri to clean up the city after the armed insurrection that led to the disarming of the PLO in Jordan. Masri had completed his work well, and I'd been impressed. But, now, Hariri was asking me to take on a job that far exceeded the challenge Masri had faced.

To give an example of the scale of the task, one only had to look at the Place des Martyrs, once the vibrant centre of the city, now a mess of rubble and ruined buildings amidst which the indomitable traders of Lebanon tried to carry on their business. With the twisted logic that fuelled their hatred, the militias had known what they were doing when they'd destroyed the Place des Martyrs. It was the kernel of the unity of the capital and the country. The Place des Martyrs, a memorial to the heroes who, in 1915, had stood up against Ottoman rule and helped to hasten its end, was the joining point in the city where mainly Muslim West Beirut met the mainly Christian east of the city. It was no accident that the green line dividing Beirut for years ran through the square. The militias may have disagreed on almost everything, but on one point they were at one – they wanted to disable the unity of Beirut and of Lebanon in order to realise their own factional ambitions. And they had very nearly succeeded.

When I came to walk round the Place des Martyrs and look more closely at the damage, I saw how malicious the militias had been in their evil intent. It is by no means unusual for buildings to sustain superficial damage during a war or civil insurrection. Such damage is often not too difficult to put right. But the destruction in the Place des Martyrs went far beyond that. The militias had reduced some buildings to their foundations. In others, they had wreaked such extensive internal damage that it was impossible to save the structure. Nevertheless, no matter how difficult reconstruction would be, we had to start.

Hariri was in no doubt about what the priorities should be. We had to focus on those parts of the reconstruction plan that would regenerate the economy. I agreed with him completely about this. During the early years of trouble, the Lebanese economy had proved remarkably resilient. But in the fifteen years leading up to 1990, when the violence finally came to an end, it was estimated that as many as 150,000 Lebanese had been killed, a fifth of the population had been displaced, and a quarter of million had fled overseas. And that wasn't counting the extensive physical damage. No country can take that kind of punishment without finding its business life undermined – and by 1990 the country's economy had imploded. It had to be rebuilt fast.

I realised right at the outset that rebuilding the country would involve more than reconstructing its economic sinews – we also needed to rebuild its heart. And nowhere represented the heart of Lebanon, especially Beirut, more than the Place des Martyrs. In the pre-war era Beirut Central District had been a meeting place for all elements of society. It was host to the interaction among confessional groups that was so characteristic of the Lebanese spirit. I believed reconstructing the Central District would be a symbol of reconciliation, and reawaken the spirit of Lebanon.

Hariri asked me who would lead the planning effort for the Central District. I suggested Henri Edde, one of Dar's senior architect planners. Hariri contemplated my choice for a moment, then agreed. I asked Edde to start work immediately. Inevitably, the work went through several stages before we finally provided a plan that was approved and, eventually, implemented by Solidere, the company set up to develop and reconstruct Beirut city centre.

Our engineers and planners had drawn up a masterplan for regenerating the whole city-centre area. It mapped out land use, and we decided that the area should be recreated as a vibrant place with a 24-hour lifestyle. So we designed a mixed commercial and residential development. There would be apartment buildings where people could live, but there would also be shops, offices and places of entertainment, such as cafés and restaurants, where people could mingle and enjoy one another's company. The centre of Beirut had to become, once again, a place of happiness and enjoyment, rather than of hatred and misery. We made a bold decision to remove all the buildings on one side of the square, so that it was possible, for the first time, to see the port and the Mediterranean beyond. It made the Place des Martyrs a less enclosed area, not so much a crucible in which passions fomented but a space open to the wider world, where people could go about their work and leisure in a relaxed environment. It has given me intense pleasure to see how successful the plan has been now that the Place des Martyrs – and indeed the whole of Beirut city centre – is, once again, a living, vibrant place that people enjoy.

But putting the heart back into the city wasn't our only task. The rest of the country also needed serious reconstruction work. My earlier close ties with the CDR provided a point of contact for Dar Al-Handasah to play a part in developing the organisation's national reconstruction programme and for planning and implementing specific projects.

Our first step was to carry out a survey of the extent of the damage across the country and prioritise issues for action. Because the damage was so extensive, that took some time. It was clear even from our preliminary survey that there would be years of reconstruction work ahead. So we drew up plans to reconstruct infrastructure services – transport links, power, communications, water and drainage were all high priorities.

We designed and managed the construction of new roads to enable people to travel more easily. Back in 1983, there had been plans for a road linking West and East Beirut – another symbol for a reunited Lebanon. Now we took those plans down from the shelf and dusted them off, as well as drawing up further schemes to enhance the country's road network in order to speed its economic recovery.

We also drew up plans for a new international airport at Beirut. The original had been damaged in the conflict, but it was also out of date and didn't have the capacity needed in a country that was determined to power forward its economic growth. Our plan included a terminal that could handle six million passengers a year and a large duty-free area with an option to expand the airport's capacity by a further six million in the future.

When it came to the reconstruction of Lebanon's telecommunications network, I hit a problem that I tackled in what I believe was a typical Dar way. We had pitched for the contract, which was being awarded by competitive tender. The committee that had been set up to evaluate tenders duly awarded us the contract. That was the good news. The bad news came a few days later. Hariri had decided that the job was of such importance it should be awarded to a European contractor that had completed a similar project successfully in Saudi Arabia. My team had worked hard putting our pitch together, and they were spitting blood at this rebuff, which they believed was unfair. They wanted me to intervene personally with Hariri and try to get the decision reversed.

I calmed them down and told them I didn't think we should regard the project as lost yet. I didn't think the European company had taken on board the peculiar difficulties that would exist in carrying out a major telecommunications project in a country still in the early stages of reconstruction and not yet completely stable. 'Let's play the long game,' I told them. 'I have a feeling this project will come back to us.'

And come back it did. A few months later, I received a telephone call from Fadal Chalak, the president of the CDR. Chalak said he was fed up with the performance of the European company. They were too slow, he told me, and they'd failed to supervise some developments in the new mobile-phone network also being built in the country. He said he'd written a letter firing them, but before sending it he wanted to check with me that Dar Al-Handasah would take over the contract.

Don't fire them, I advised him. It would be much better to negotiate with them and restructure the contract. We will work with them, take on some of their staff and give them a portion of the work, I suggested. Chalak wanted to know why I was willing to offer an olive branch to a company that had been handed a contract we had technically won. It was a question of continuity and confidence, I explained. Keeping them involved would mean that we would be able to pick up where they had left off. But, equally important, at this delicate moment in Lebanon's reconstruction, it would not look good if a European company was shown the door unceremoniously. The word would get around. Other European firms would be wary about doing business in Lebanon. That would hamper the country's economic development.

Chalak took my advice, and we picked up the contract. I remember the first phase was to recover five hundred thousand telephone lines, but it soon grew to a point which eventually involved more than one-and-a-half million. At the project's peak, we had more than four hundred people working on it.

It has been a source of personal satisfaction to me to see how Lebanon has been able to reconstruct its infrastructure during the past decade. Indeed, it has gone further and made advances that benefit many of its citizens. In the early years of the new millennium, we were asked by the government to draw up a physical masterplan for the whole country. Our masterplan shows the projected land use and main infrastructure networks for transport, power, water and drainage. But for me the technical details are less important than the fact that it points to a brighter future for a country that has suffered grievously in the past.

*   *   *

Lebanon is not the only part of the world in which Dar Al-Handasah has been called upon to apply itself to the business of reconstruction after civil strife.

As I have related, Dar started its Nigeria operation in 1970. The south-eastern region of the country had suffered a heavy toll during the 1967–70 civil war. In the aftermath, oil revenues provided the wherewithal for reconstruction and development programmes. Dar was active in rehabilitating infrastructure facilities, and in upgrading and planning extensions of the principal towns in war-torn areas.

A chance meeting between our resident partner in Nigeria and officials who were visiting oil facilities led to our initial entry into Angola. We had identified the recently independent Angola as a target for Dar. The country had enormous potential, and since the abrupt departure of the colonial Portuguese there was a virtual vacuum of engineering and planning capability. So the chance contact proved opportune.

One piece of luck followed another. While our team was visiting the Luanda offices of the Angolan oil company Sonangol, they met representatives of Texaco. In partnership with Sonangol, Texaco was developing a significant field off the north coast of Angola, and had identified the need for a substantial service base and wharf facilities at Soyo. The Texaco team faced the challenge of developing the service base rapidly in what they considered a remote location. They were concerned at how fast the work could be done using their usual European engineering and planning consultants.

This was an opportunity too good to miss. It was risky operating in a country that had recently been so unstable as Angola. But reward comes with managing and overcoming risk. So we decided to undertake the engineering design of the Soyo wharf and oil service base, which we completed on schedule. The project was important for Angola, since it was to play a significant role in developing oil-export revenues. So it wasn't surprising that it got us noticed in high places and established Dar as a serious player in the country.

There was much to be done. Civil war had raged in Angola for much of the period since the country had been declared independent from Portugal in 1975. Thousands had died in the fighting, and many of the five hundred thousand Portuguese and other Europeans who'd lived in the country under colonial rule had fled, often adopting a scorched earth policy of destroying their businesses, factories and warehouses in their wake. There had been huge damage to the country's infrastructure.

Dar arrived in Angola at the end of the 1970s. The Popular Movement for the Liberation of Angola (MPLA), backed by Soviet influence and Cuban forces, controlled most of the country and had established the People's Republic of Angola with Luanda as its capital. The MPLA was bitterly opposed by the US-supported National Front for the Liberation of Angola (FLNA) and the National Union for the Total Independence of Angola (Unita), also initially supported by the United States as well as South Africa. The FLNA and Unita had proclaimed their own People's Democratic Republic of Angola in the south of the country, centred on the town of Huambo.

In the early 1980s, Unita's control over southern Angola became a problem for South West Africa, then controlled by South Africa, but now independent as Namibia. The South Africans became increasingly concerned about fighters from the South West Africa People's Organisation (Swapo) operating from bases in southern Angola. So, in 1983, South Africa proposed to withdraw its forces from Angola if the Luanda government would guarantee that areas it vacated were not occupied by Cuban forces or Swapo units. The proposal was finally crystallised in the 1984 Lusaka agreement. These events provided a backdrop for international support for reconstruction in Angola. For Dar, they provided the start of another planning and engineering challenge.

In 1985, the United Nations Development Programme commissioned us to undertake reconstruction planning for the southern provinces of Angola. They had been devastated by the war. We also undertook a series of projects to rehabilitate and develop the national building-materials industry, critical to any reconstruction effort.

The following year I travelled with Laura to Angola, where we were invited to meet with the Angolan president, José Eduardo dos Santos, leader of the MPLA. He was being urged to hold democratic elections. But he recognised that the restoration of peaceful civil society in Angola depended on rebuilding the shattered country's infrastructure, and thus its economy and prosperity.

He received Laura and me in his office, and I sensed that, although he greeted us graciously, he was sceptical about our motives. No doubt he'd held many meetings with businesspeople, drawn to the country by Angola's oil and diamond riches, and with their eyes on the main chance. So it was not surprising that he should have displayed some reserve as he greeted us.

I wanted him to feel that I was different from other businesspeople he'd met – that my interests were broader than just making money from the country, that I genuinely empathised with him and the aspirations of Angolans. So I told him: 'Consider me an Angolan.' He smiled and asked me what I meant. I explained:

> I come from a region of the world that has also had its troubles. We understand the fear and bitterness that civil war sows. We understand the pain and suffering your country has been through in its fight to rid itself of colonial rulers. We sympathise with you. Of course, we want to help you in planning, designing and supervising your development projects, but we will be doing that professional work with a passion that comes from the solidarity we feel for you and your aims.

He nodded and I felt that I'd touched something inside him that other foreign businesspeople had never reached, and probably didn't understand.

In the years that followed my meeting with dos Santos, Dar's work on reconstruction planning continued, despite the fact that Angola's southern provinces were still troubled by Unita action. In a sense, the battle for Angola had been the story of the global cold war in microcosm – with the West and the Communists supporting rival sides. When the cold war expired, hopes for peace in Angola rose. The fact that we were on the ground meant that we were able to move fast when opportunities to push forward reconstruction projects presented themselves.

The MPLA government and Unita signed a peace settlement in 1991. Even though the United States recognised dos Santos's government from 1993, Jonas Savimbi, Unita's leader, refused to accept the results of presidential elections or the MPLA government's legitimacy. Not until Savimbi's death in 2002, during a raid by government forces on Unita units, did the civil war begin to draw to a close.

Although we had continued to do work throughout these troubles, I was naturally concerned for the safety of our engineers and their families, given the fragile security situation in the country. To make them as safe as possible, we constructed a special compound near Luanda in which about forty of them lived. As I write, the situation in Angola continues to improve. At Dar, we've taken a positive view of the country's future. We are constructing a new Dar compound to house eighty people.

*   *   *

Dar Al-Handasah has completed reconstruction projects in a growing list of countries. Nigeria, Lebanon, Angola, Algeria and South Yemen are only some of them. We live in a world in which, sadly, there is still conflict, and I have little doubt that our expertise in reconstruction will be called on for years to come. Our focus on this kind of work doesn't only rest on our technical expertise. Many of us have first-hand experience of the human tragedy caused by civil strife. We understand that reconstruction isn't just about putting up buildings or re-laying roads. It's more about putting the heart back into communities. You can't do that unless you have a real and deep empathy for the hopes and fears of the communities in which you are working.

Over the years, we've developed our skills in a way that enables us to overcome the special difficulties you often find in reconstruction projects. For example, in wars or civil strife it's not just that existing infrastructure is damaged. Often the maps, drawings and records of that infrastructure vanish as well. You don't have the kind of background information you would expect to have on a normal project in a stable and developed country. You have to find ways to research that basic information quickly in order to plan the project.

And you have to be able to move fast. Because civil wars destroy facilities the population needs in order to lead a normal life – hospitals, schools, water and drainage systems, for example – you cannot afford to take years over rebuilding them. Often the provision of such basic facilities is central to making ordinary people's lives more bearable, and thus reducing discontent and the potential for more strife. So reconstruction is not just about bricks and mortar. It's also about rebuilding confidence among people – about convincing them that life can get better and that there are other ways of settling disputes than killing one another.

Yet, for all this, one of the biggest impediments to reconstruction is often the low capacity of the very governments who ought to be driving it forward. It is easy to see the reasons for this. Often those in government are, themselves, exhausted by years of violence. They are trying to hold together uneasy coalitions that are the source of their power and that, if they fall apart, may lead to further fighting. They may differ over priorities. They lack sophisticated technical skills in planning, budgeting and project management that are the key to reconstruction. And a key reason for all this is that when civil war hits a country many of the most talented people emigrate, as was the case in both Lebanon and Angola. Too often, those left running the bureaucracies that support government are power-hungry and second-rate officials.

The low capacity of governments shows itself in poor decision-making. For example, I recall a time when we were called in to look at a drainage project in Lagos, Nigeria. The authorities had been renewing the city's inadequate drainage system in a piecemeal fashion. As a result, there were isolated drainage installations that merely moved the water from one part of the city to another. We had to explain to the officials in charge that they would be wasting their money unless they planned an integrated drainage system, designed to remove the water right away from the city.

One of the ways in which we try to overcome the problems of low government capacity is to persuade the authorities to let us draw up a masterplan that provides the foundation for future action. The masterplan is usually supported by an economic assessment of the impact of the proposed projects contained within it. This enables decisions to be taken on a sounder basis with a better knowledge of their likely outcome. Where this approach is applied, I have found that it reaps considerable benefits.

For me, reconstructing shattered communities has always been more than a business. In fact, I don't believe anybody who didn't empathise with the feelings of the people in cities, towns and villages that have experienced the trauma of civil unrest could do the job effectively. In reconstruction, understanding people's hopes and fears for the future and then factoring those into your reconstruction plans is the key to success. But I won't deny that Dar Al-Handasah has also benefited from a business spin-off from its reconstruction work. When the rebuilding is complete, then it is time to move on to development – and a trusted consultant that has helped a society through the difficult years is often the first choice when brighter times return.

*   *   *

I shall never take another telephone call from Rafiq Hariri – at two in the morning or any other time. He was assassinated in a terrorist attack on 14 February 2005. His killing sparked a wave of peaceful protest such as Lebanon, the region and possibly the world had never seen before. On 14 March, one month after the terrorist attack, one-and-a-half million people from all regions of Lebanon marched to the Place des Martyrs. They were from all walks of life and all sects. They accounted for around 40 per cent of Lebanon's population, providing an unprecedented expression of popular opinion. The people in unison united in peace to demand an end to the killing and violence that had consumed Lebanon for a generation.

In the summer of 2005, Lebanon held parliamentary elections that now offer the promise of the country advancing, at last, from under the shadow of Syrian dominance. Lebanon is a nation endowed with a diversity of faiths. In order to create a sense of justice among all groups, political institutions should provide balanced responsive representation of the different constituent communities. Further, in a country with more than eighteen sects, it is imperative that a secular state accords equal treatment to all citizens. The French and Turkish models, which have traditionally influenced constitutional arrangements across the Arab world, provide guidance on how this can be achieved. Unless Lebanon adheres to the principles of a secular state – in which marriage, family affairs and inheritance are dealt with through the legislative process and mediated by a competent impartial judiciary – the country risks repeating the worst horrors of its recent blood-stained history.

CHAPTER 19

Friends and mentors

I little imagined the long journey I was embarking upon when I first set out from my home for the American University of Beirut in 1945. Nor could I have imagined that I would meet many of the men who have shaped the Middle East (and it has, sadly, not yet been shaped by many women). Some of those men became my friends and confidants, others I regard as mentors. At times, when life has become difficult – and many of us who live in the Middle East have known difficult times – they have provided me with both moral and intellectual strength and stimulation.

I suppose the first great man I ever met was Dr Charles Malek. I knew of Malek even before I arrived at AUB. He had already established a formidable reputation as a noted philosopher. At least half of my teachers at high school in Salt between 1942 and 1945 were AUB graduates and had studied under Malek. Elder brother Jamal, who went to AUB in 1944, and other Jordanian students also studied under Malek. It was difficult for any student not to be influenced by him. The question was only the degree of influence. As I was preparing to go to AUB during the summer of 1945, I learnt a lot from my teachers, my brother and his friends about AUB. Malek always figured large in any conversation. I learnt that the required courses in the freshman and sophomore classes were common for all students, irrespective of their chosen major, and that philosophy was one of the courses required in the sophomore class. So many students had an opportunity to attend Malek's lectures.

When I reached AUB, I was thrilled, as I've already mentioned, to discover that Malek was the resident professor in charge of the dormitory to which I'd been allocated. At that time, the thought that he might eventually become one of my closer friends never entered my mind. To a freshman like me, Malek might as well have been a god on Mount Olympus.

My opportunity to get to know him came a few years later in the United States, in the autumn of 1951, when I was trying to set up the Organisation of Arab Students in the United States. Dr Fayez Sayegh, an AUB graduate who had majored in philosophy studying under Malek and who was now one of his senior aides in the Lebanese Embassy in Washington, effected the introduction. Malek was the first of the Arab ambassadors to Washington I was to meet, and he was keen to support our enterprise. I met him on several occasions.

If I had come far since I first attended AUB, Malek had travelled further. He was ambassador both to the United States and to the United Nations, and had been a member of the small committee that (in 1948) drafted the Universal Declaration of Human Rights. Even today, it is impossible for me to read words from the ringing preamble to the Declaration – 'whereas recognition of the inherent dignity and of the equal and inalienable rights of all members of the human family is the foundation of freedom, justice and peace in the world...' – without hearing his voice. When Lebanon became a member of the UN Security Council in 1953 – the first Arab state on the Council – Malek, as ambassador, was the chosen representative. He went on to become the president of the UN General Assembly in 1958–59. Few have held the position with greater distinction.

I have a particular personal memory of Malek's distinguished contribution to the UN Security Council. In 1953, the Israelis were provoked by a minor incident in the village of Qibya in Jordan's West Bank, near the armistice line between the two countries. The Israeli government ordered Ariel Sharon, then a middle-ranking officer in the Israeli army, to respond to the incident. Sharon raided the small Jordanian military unit in that area, killing a number of soldiers, and then attacked the village so viciously that scores of civilians were killed. Jordan lodged a complaint in the Security Council. Malek asked me to attend the session, and arranged a pass for me to enter the Council chamber. With his powerful way of speaking, Malek stunned the Council with his trenchant criticism of the harsh penalty that was exacted from the village's innocent civilians. He called it barbaric and a highly disproportionate response that resulted in the death and injury of a large number of people, including women and children.

In June 1953, I invited Malek to be one of the speakers at the Second Arab Students Convention, held in Earlham, Indiana. Malek delivered a courageous and comprehensive speech that dealt with the political, economic and social problems and challenges that the Arab peoples were facing, especially in the wake of the military coup that had taken place in Egypt the previous year. He urged Arab governments to adopt rational, well-thought-out policies to tackle the Middle East's problems, and to stand against the prevailing demagogy that threatened to darken the region. A minority in the audience admired the speech, but unfortunately the majority were angered by Malek's logic and reasoning. I was sitting next to the podium from which Malek was speaking. I could see his hands held behind his back twisting with passion – even painful passion – as he reacted to the anger in the eyes of the students. He was only asking them to use their minds, with their powers of rational analysis.

Malek married late and did not have a child until 10 years later. I was one of the few who received a handwritten message that Habib, his son, was born. Habib went on to follow in the footsteps of his father and also received his PhD in philosophy from Harvard University. Like his father, he pursued a successful career as both an academic and politician.

To me, Malek was like a personal teacher. Although I was an engineer and a scientist, I had always been fascinated by the subtleties of philosophy. Malek opened my eyes to many of the wonders of human thought – and especially to the power of rationalism as a means of advancing argument. He held several important posts in Lebanon's government, including the ministries of foreign affairs, education and arts between 1956–58, when I was establishing Dar Al-Handasah in Beirut.

I have always admired men, like Malek, who seem to gain what power and influence they have from an inner moral force. Another such man was Musa Al-Alami. I first met him in 1962 when I was vice-president of Jordan's Development Board. Al-Alami was the son of a Palestinian landowner and had gained a law degree from Cambridge University in the United Kingdom. He'd spent much of the 1930s working in various posts for the British administration in Palestine. After the Second World War, he set up a special fund to help Palestinian farmers defend their land from the growing wave of Jewish immigration.

The fund received financial support from the American overseas-aid budget. The money was channelled through the Development Board. I remember Al-Alami coming to my office at the Development Board to discuss some issues concerning his fund. It was a privilege to meet him, especially as I had long admired his work. Like me, he was a born activist. When he saw a problem that needed to be solved, he couldn't just stand by. He had to do something. His life had been filled with constructive work in aid of the Palestinian cause. He'd set up information offices in Jerusalem, Beirut, London and Washington, and he'd founded an Arab Development Society, based in Jericho.

But what I most admired about him was the clarity of his thinking. Al-Alami realised that, after the Balfour Declaration (in 1917), momentum for a Jewish state in Palestine would grow inexorably. He also realised that it would not be possible to resist this momentum by force of arms. His answer was to encourage the native Palestinians to love their land, to bind themselves to their landscapes in such a close way that they would be immovably tied to their farms and small-holdings despite the expected wave of Jewish immigration.

He saw the creation of the state of Israel, which inevitably meant the taking of some Palestinian land, as a struggle between civilisations. He realised that the Jews who were coming from many parts of the world would be better educated and organised than many native Palestinians, and he saw the need to raise the education and commitment of the Palestinian people accordingly.

I will always remember Al-Alami as a charismatic man and a profound thinker. I recall at our meeting at the Development Board offering any assistance I could provide for his projects. I was not at the Development Board for long, so I cannot say how much use he made of its services after I'd left, but I did watch his continuing work with admiration. We met occasionally until his death at the age of 87 in 1984.

Al-Alami personified a truth about the Middle East that is not always appreciated by observers from outside the region – the key battle of the past century has been a battle of ideas rather than a clash of arms. It has been the battle between dictatorship and totalitarianism on the one hand and freedom and democracy on the other. Al-Alami, like Ahmad Baheaddin, who became a good friend, was on the side of the angels. Baheaddin was the editor-in-chief of *Al-Ahram*, the most influential daily newspaper in Cairo.

I first met Baheaddin in the late 1950s, when I started to travel to Egypt regularly on business, sometimes with Laura. One evening I went with some friends to a café called Day and Night, at the Semiramis Hotel, a well-known haunt of writers, artists and intellectuals. Baheaddin was there at the centre of a lively circle that, I noted, included several attractive young women. We hit it off straight away, partly because, like me, he was an avowed believer in a liberal version of Arab nationalism and partly because, also like me, he had a huge love of life.

Baheaddin wrote a daily column in *Al-Ahram* that was a model of what a newspaper opinion piece should be – relevant, sharp and engaging. He had a way of dealing with a complex subject that went right to the heart of the matter. Even more, he wrote in a way that brought the subject to life and engaged his readers' intellect and emotions in the argument he was making. He wrote at a time when the Egyptian press was still subject to censorship, but he was sinuously cunning, and found ways to circumvent the censor's red pencil so that he could say what he wanted. For example, he frequently wrote about Egypt's role in the Arab world, a subject that did not attract so much red pencil treatment as other topics. Again, he would write about domestic Egyptian issues such as the environment, agriculture or municipal management. His constant aim was to raise Egyptians' awareness about the need to create a free and open civil society.

It was not surprising that his columns used to attract a huge response from readers, and he received dozens of letters a day. This presented him with a practical problem. He was exceedingly short-sighted, and had difficulty reading, even though he wore very thick glasses. To overcome this disability, he employed a small team of assistants to read letters to him, and he would dictate replies. It was a mark of the man that, despite his fame as Egypt's leading newspaper columnist of the day, he would take time out to listen to his readers' views and provide a considered response.

I remember him particularly as one of the first people to advance the argument that the Palestinian issue could never be solved with the gun. He was adamant that Palestinians would only win their just struggle by elevating their civilisation and demanding their rightful place as people of peace. He was one of those thinkers who have deeply held serious beliefs yet is capable of setting aside worries about the world to enjoy life to the full. I still miss his rumbustious company.

A man who practised the philosophy so eloquently expressed in Baheaddin's columns was Rohi El-Khatib, mayor of the Arab sector of Jerusalem until 1967, when the Israelis deported him to Jordan for refusing to accept their dissolution of his democratic local authority. I first met El-Khatib in the early 1960s when Dar Al-Handasah was awarded some projects in Jerusalem. He came to visit me in my office in Beirut, and we soon became friends. Laura and I would often fly to Jerusalem to visit him over a Saturday or Sunday. We would invite El-Khatib and his wife to join us whenever they came to Beirut.

What I especially admired about him was that he worked tirelessly to improve the lives of the ordinary citizens of Jerusalem in a completely unshowy and unpretentious way. He encouraged the economic development of the Arab part of the city using novel ideas. For example, he set up a scheme to provide micro-loans to traders who wanted to start or develop small businesses such as a hotel, restaurant or shop. He set out to attract tourism to the city as a way of generating economic growth. He protected the holy places of all religions within his part of the city. He was deeply committed to and loved living in Jerusalem, and it was a tragedy for him when the Israelis sent him packing.

I particularly admire people who are prepared to take a stand on issues they believe to be important, and who work to advance those views. Sometimes, as in the case of Abdel-Aziz Al-Saqr, those views appear out of step with conventional wisdom, and it is not until years later that their profundity is fully appreciated. I first met Al-Saqr as a result of the business we developed in Kuwait in the wake of our successful power-station project. Al-Saqr became the first speaker of the Kuwaiti national assembly, elected in 1963 following the ending of the British protectorate two years earlier.

He was a powerful figure in Kuwaiti public affairs. He was influential on economic policy and, in my view, had impeccable democratic credentials as a defender of the independence of the legislature against the executive. But his most controversial views were reserved for the role of oil in the Kuwaiti economy. Contrary to almost universal belief in the 1960s, he held that oil could prove to be as much a curse to Kuwait as a blessing. In one sense, that perhaps he did not expect, he was right. Saddam Hussein invaded Kuwait in 1990 to seize its rich oilfields.

But Al-Saqr's argument was founded not so much on external threats as on the impact that oil would have on Kuwaiti society. He could see the huge oil revenues being ploughed back into a wealth of public services, such as education. The problem was that because oil dominated the economy, there were too few job opportunities for Kuwait's growing ranks of highly educated students when they graduated. Al-Saqr realised that an economy dominated by one commodity would lack diversity and could, in the long run, stifle the creativity of the national spirit. But people who advance such unfashionable views in the face of apparent economic success are not always popular.

In my view, being right is more important than being popular. Another whom I regard as one of my most important mentors, Wasfi At-Tal, paid the ultimate price for being right, but not popular – at least, not popular in all quarters. As I have related (in chapter 11), I first came to know At-Tal well in 1962 when he invited me to become vice-president of the Development Board in Jordan. At the time, he was serving his first term as prime minister. He went on to serve two more terms, including, fatefully, the term in which he was assassinated. For me, he is a person who grows larger rather than smaller in the memory as time passes – one test, I suppose, of true greatness.

He possessed great wisdom, and demonstrated a commitment to political liberalism in his first-term premiership when he lifted a ban on political parties in Jordan. But he was also firmly committed to the maintenance of the Hashemite Kingdom of Jordan, and when, as he saw it, the country's independence was threatened in 1970 by the military activities of Palestinian *fedayeen*, he did not hesitate to take strong action to curb them. In taking his courageous stand, he knew he would be making enemies.

In November 1971, he left Amman for Cairo to attend a meeting of the Arab League at a time when relations between Jordan and Egypt were in a fragile condition. He had had some forewarning that he might be the target of a political assassination, but he told me: 'I cannot afford not to go. I have been misunderstood, and I must clarify my position.' He was referring to the strong position he had taken over the Palestinians in Jordan, which had not been popular in other parts of the Arab world.

It was to be his last trip. Four gunmen from the terrorist group Black September approached him as he was returning to the Cairo Sheraton after a session of routine defence talks with the Egyptian government. They shot him in the head and, according to newspaper reports, one of the gunmen knelt and lapped Tal's blood from the steps. Tal's last reported words were: 'They've killed me. Murderers, they believe only in fire and destruction.'

*   *   *

As I have spent many years both living and running a business in Lebanon, it is not surprising that I came to know many of the country's leading politicians. In 1972, I received a telephone call from the office of Suleiman Franjieh, who had become president of Lebanon two years earlier. I was invited to meet Franjieh at the presidential palace. I was intrigued, and wondered what he wanted to see me about. It turned out that he was having a problem with some of his ministers who held different opinions over a number of development schemes. He wasn't sure whose opinion to back, and he wanted to sound out my views on the subject. I was flattered to be asked, and duly gave him my considered opinion on the projects, which concerned irrigation, drainage and roads.

What impressed me about Franjieh was his complete lack of show. He worked from an office that was considerably more modest than my own. He did not surround himself with secretaries and advisers. He took his own notes. I came away with the impression of a simple and sincere man who wanted to do the best for his country. That first meeting was followed by others, and we developed a friendship.

He called for my advice on a number of occasions, including some of the important turning-points in Lebanon's troubled history. I have already recalled (in chapter 15) the occasion in 1976 when Franjieh invited me to join a group to discuss reconstruction plans following the first round of the Lebanese civil war. For me, that meeting marked the start of my association with a number of attempts at reconciliation and reconstruction in the country.

Like many who rise high in Lebanese politics, Franjieh had deep reserves of personal courage, and he needed to plumb these to the very depths in June 1978 when his son Tony, together with his daughter-in-law and grand-daughter, were murdered by a gang alleged to have connections with the Phalangists. I went to give him my condolences, and he asked me to sit with him during the three days he received visitors. He was an emotional man, and for much of the time he was in tears, bewailing the viciousness of the thugs who'd not only gunned down his son and daughter-in-law but had mercilessly slaughtered his baby grand-daughter as well as the family's pet dog.

Sadly, in those troubled years, violence was never very far away in Middle Eastern politics. Eventually, it caught up with another of my friends, Salah Al-Din Bitar. As I have mentioned earlier (in chapter 9)

I first met him in 1958, when he was serving his first term as foreign minister of Syria.

His reason for contacting me in 1958 was to seek my assistance in arranging meetings with leading figures in the Lebanese Christian community. His visit came shortly after Lebanon had drifted close to an all-out civil war between the Muslim and the Christian communities, following a coup in Iraq and the union of Syria and Egypt into the United Arab Republic.

I found it significant that Bitar wanted to meet only three influential Christians. They were Pierre Gemayel, the founder and leader of the Christian Phalange Party, George Nakkache, the chief editor of *Orient-Le Jour*, Lebanon's leading French newspaper, and Ghassan Tueni, the chief editor of the influential *An-Nahar* newspaper. He knew it was the Christian community that was most troubled by the developments in Syria and elsewhere, and he wanted to provide a voice of reassurance. But then I already knew that Bitar was a statesman who could see the broader picture.

I duly arranged a meeting with Tueni, a close friend of mine, but left it to Bitar to make direct contacts with Gemayel and Nakkache. Bitar's decision to hold these meetings underscored, for me, the courage of his convictions, and our friendship developed from that point. But his political career ended when he was deposed as prime minister of Syria in a military coup in February 1966. He came to Lebanon for a short period, then left for France.

By now, he had fallen out with many of his former colleagues in the Ba'ath party. He was bitterly disappointed that the original ideals of the party had been lost when it had accepted a series of military coups in Syria and Iraq. Although he was an exile, he wanted a mouthpiece for his views, and he approached me as well as a handful of other friends to see if we would help him with finance to set up a weekly paper. It was called *Al-Arabi*, and he ensured it was circulated to opinion-formers throughout Syria.

Bitar was an active member of the Syrian expatriate community in Paris. This, together with his trenchant views expressed regularly in his paper, made him a thorn in the flesh of Syria's president, Hafez

Al-Assad. In July 1980, he was returning to the one-room office where he produced his paper when a gunmen shot him as he was getting into the elevator. Needless to say, the Syrian government denied press speculation that it had been behind the killing.

Ghassan Tueni was well on his way to establishing a reputation as an influential journalist, statesman and man of letters by the time I got to introduce him to Bitar. Tueni had already graduated from AUB when I arrived as a student. He had moved on to Harvard, where he received a MA in political science. But he ended his studies and returned to Lebanon when his father, Gibran, died in 1947. Gibran Tueni had founded *An-Nahar* in 1933. It had developed as a vigorous liberal-nationalist standard-bearer that had criticised the French colonial administration and the Republic of Lebanon's independent government that followed it. After Gibran's death, Ghassan continued his father's tradition and developed *An-Nahar* into one of the Arab world's most respected and outspoken newspapers.

By the time Tueni had return from Harvard, I'd departed for my own studies in the United States, so I didn't meet him until I returned to Beirut and became an assistant professor at AUB in 1956. By then, Tueni had already made his mark as a political campaigner. Aged only 26, and alongside the more senior Camille Chamoun and Kamal Jumblat, he had successfully campaigned against the unconstitutional second presidential term of Bishara Al-Khoury (which I've described in chapter 7).

Tueni was elected to the Chamber of Deputies in 1951, and was to serve two terms. He held a series of ministerial appointments until 1977, when he was appointed Lebanon's ambassador and permanent representative to the United Nations, where he served with distinction until 1982.

He was, above all, a friend whom I admired as a man of principle. His dedication was such that on two occasions he was a prisoner of conscience, held in confinement by the authorities because his outspoken views were too uncomfortable for them. Tueni's trenchant opinions were based on the logic he applied to the philosophical and historical contexts in which he placed the injustices or inconsistencies he campaigned against. I served alongside Tueni on the board of trustees of AUB. He brought to bear his considerable knowledge and experience of the philosophy and history of education in the debates of the Board's academic committee.

Another of my good friends, Raymond Edde, also ended life, like Bitar, as an exile in Paris, although mercifully he escaped a violent death. But not by much. Edde, who had played a prominent role in Lebanese politics since the country had gained its independence, fell out with many other Christian politicians during the 1975–76 civil war. He was particularly angry that the Christian parties seemed content to accept a plan by US Secretary of State Henry Kissinger to divide Lebanon into statelets along religious lines in return for the opportunity to rule those parts of the country they found themselves controlling. Edde realised that this was a recipe for the dismemberment of Lebanon, even though Kissinger's scheme might have met the factional ambitions of lesser men. Edde survived one assassination attempt on him in May 1976. Then in November and December of that year, there were two further attempts outside his home in Beirut's Sanayeh quarter. Mercifully, both failed.

Shortly after, Edde left for a visit to Egypt. Before his departure, the late Kamal Jumblat, a close friend and lifetime political ally, showed him a list of names of those targeted for political assassinations. According to Edde, the first name on the list was Jumblat's, and his was the second. When he arrived in Cairo, he was received ceremonially with all due protocol, and taken immediately to meet President Anwar Sadat. With Sadat, he discussed conditions in Lebanon and the way in which Egypt could help. During the next few days, Sadat assigned Edde a car, together with an aide and guards. When Edde decided that it was time to return to Lebanon, he paid a final visit to Sadat. The president was adamant that Edde should not return to Lebanon. When Edde objected, Sadat opened a drawer in his desk and showed him a list of targeted political assassinations in Lebanon. It was the same list Jumblat had shown Edde – with one exception. Edde's name now appeared at the top of the list. Faced with overwhelming evidence that his life was in mortal danger, Edde took a flight to exile in Paris.

(Sadly, Kamal Jumblat, a cultured and capable politician who was the second name on Sadat's list, was assassinated in mid-March 1977, only a few weeks after he'd shown his own assassination list to Edde. Jumblat was highly respected internationally, and many groups voiced revulsion at his killing. Unfortunately, his murder, like many others during this period of strife in Lebanon's history, was not investigated by the authorities.)

In exile, Edde worked tirelessly in the cause of a sovereign Lebanon. He regretted the lack of American resolve to apply its influence to rid Lebanon of external interference in its affairs. His regret deepened with the Israeli incursions into southern Lebanon in the late 1970s and the invasion in 1982. From France, he sought to mobilise European opinion. He wanted Europe's political leaders to persuade the United States to use its influence to secure an Israeli withdrawal.

I became friendly with Edde during his 24 years in Paris. He continued to take a lively interest in Lebanese politics. I thought of him as 'Mr Democracy'. He had strong principles, which he wasn't prepared to compromise. That made him an uneasy ally for other Lebanese politicians, for whom shifting alliances were the stuff of power-broking. Not that Edde wasn't a sinuously clever political thinker when the occasion demanded.

Such an occasion arose in the wake of a geopolitical shift of power in the Middle East during the cold war. In 1958, a leftish nationalist coup in Iraq led to the collapse of the pro-Western Baghdad Pact. In the tense political climate that followed, Lebanon's pro-Western President Chamoun faced opposition from groups of Lebanese supporters of Egypt's President Nasser. As Chamoun's presidential term approached its close, it seemed probable that his likely successor would be General Fouad Shehab, to whom Nasser did not object. Edde wanted to emphasise the principle that a Lebanese election was for the Lebanese, and not a power-broking opportunity for a major world power (the Soviet Union), conducted with the consent of a regional power (Egypt). So he ran against Shehab. As a result, Shehab failed to get the two-thirds majority required in a presidential election's first round. Shehab scraped home in the second round by a single vote, and Edde had made his point in a subtle but very public way.

But Edde was a Lebanese patriot first and foremost. When he realised that the new president's initial attempt to form a cabinet was hesitant and stumbling, he went to the palace and informed a surprised Shehab that he'd be willing to assist in forming a small inner cabinet of four individuals as a transitional arrangement. Shehab accepted Edde's proposal. Edde persuaded Rashid Karame to serve as prime minister and got Pierre Gemayel (with whom he'd never allied himself) and Hussein Queini, several times a future prime minister, to join him in the cabinet. Portfolios were divided among the four, with Edde taking the Interior Ministry among others assigned to him. His highest priority was to stop revenge killings, then rife at the time. He sent an urgent, but commendably brief, bill to parliament. It stated simply that the penalty for murder was death. I remember viewing this as a good start.

Edde also helped to stage a meeting between President Shehab and Nasser in 1958 in a manner that protected the dignity of Lebanese sovereignty. He was opposed to Shehab's original plan to meet Nasser in Damascus. Edde felt it would look as though Shehab had been ordered out of Lebanon for the meeting, and he believed that would demean the office of the presidency. Instead, he arranged for the two to meet in a tent skilfully pitched to straddle the Lebanon-Syria border. Inside, the leaders faced each other across a table – Shehab on the Lebanese side, Nasser on the Syrian.

It is worth mentioning, in passing, that Shehab had had no political experience prior to becoming president. He was, however, a man of integrity, and commanded national respect. After his election, he adopted a solid socio-economic agenda. He vowed that during his six-year term he would provide every town and village in Lebanon with a road link, electricity, running water, a school and a clinic. By and large, he delivered.

I recall the last time I met with Edde. It was in March 2000. I was in London on a stop-over on my way to New York to attend an AUB board of trustees meeting. I travelled to Paris for the day, and had an enjoyable lunch with Edde, which was accompanied by our usual intense discussion of 'events'. As I left, I agreed I would contact him when I returned from New York.

When I returned to London I called the Paris hotel where Edde was living. He was not in, and no-one knew when he might be back. I called back daily and received the same response. I became worried, but could get no news of him. Some days later, I was having lunch at the Dorchester Hotel in London with Khairallah Khairallah, a journalist acquaintance. During the meal he took a telephone call. He looked grim. He broke the news to me that Raymond Edde was dead. I virtually broke down and Khairallah had to help me to return home.

Although, like Edde, I had exiled myself from Lebanon, his funeral in the country of his birth was an occasion to suspend my absence. I briefly returned to Lebanon to attend Edde's funeral in mid-April 2000. The following month, Israeli forces withdrew from Lebanon. As their military forces rumbled south, the thought in my mind was that my friend was not with us to witness an event that he'd laboured tirelessly to secure.

Another who had a deep love for the country was Saeb Salaam. He was prime minister of Lebanon on no fewer than four occasions between 1952 and 1973. I first met him at a dinner given by a mutual friend. He was much older than me and more distinguished, but I think he took to me, and occasionally he invited me to visit him. Salaam's story was the story of Lebanese independence. He was one of the first people to sign the Lebanese independence flag, and he coined the slogan 'one united Lebanon' as a way of trying to emphasise what brought the country's people together rather than what drove them apart.

What I particularly admired about him was his tolerance – a trait I like to feel I possess myself. But the problem with tolerance in politicians is that it can sometimes be portrayed as weakness. This is especially the case in a febrile political climate such as Lebanon has known for much of its history. Yet, with Salaam, the tolerance shone through as strength. He was larger than life, which, for a start, helped because it made him the centre of attention wherever he went. He wasn't afraid to stick his neck out to defend what he perceived to be the reasonable point of view that challenged established ideas.

Another great Lebanese patriot I knew well was Takieddin As-Solh. He was prime minister twice. Like Salaam, he was a symbol of the unity of Lebanon. For a number of years, when I was living in Beirut, I would hold a regular lunch for politicians. When he attended, he was always the focal point of these gatherings, partly because his views were widely respected across the spectrum of different communities, and partly because he was a veritable fount of knowledge on Lebanese history. He was able to inform a discussion on almost any topic with minute detail from the country's past. I think his deep knowledge of what Lebanon had gone through helped him get to the heart of contemporary problems. He saw the present through the lens of history.

I was closer to As-Solh than Franjieh, Edde or Salaam. As-Solh would discuss with me any political subject that happened to be bothering him at the time without any reserve. He held nothing back, and I admired this frankness.

Sometimes, it is only looking back that you realise how much friends and mentors have enriched your life. They do so in many ways. In the case of the people I have mentioned here, they have provided examples of the values by which I have tried to live my own life.

Many of my friends and mentors have now died. But for me they will always be alive in my memory. I guess that is the true measure of the enriching role they have played in my life.

CHAPTER 20

High privilege

There is the satisfaction of watching a figment of the imagination emerge through the aid of science to a plan on paper. Then it moves to realisation in stone or metal or energy. Then it brings jobs and homes to men. Then it elevates the standards of living and adds to the comforts of life. That is the engineer's high privilege.

So wrote engineer and US president (1929–33) Herbert Hoover. I was so impressed with this quotation when I first read it that I incorporated it into one of our company's brochures. For me, it sums up the deep personal satisfaction I feel when I see one of our important projects anywhere in the world come to fruition.

I also think it's something of a rallying cry for engineers and architects at a time when the world is in danger of writing us off as mere technicians. Nothing could be further from the truth. For engineers are the new magicians who are helping to invent the twenty-first century. They make waters gush when none trickled before, span impossible distances with bridges that seem to float on air, reclaim land from the sea upon which stand elegant buildings that reach towards the clouds.

As Hoover sensed, there is something much deeper in engineering than mere mechanics. Other talented engineers have had similar thoughts. Back in 1981, Tracy Kidder won a Pulitzer Prize with a book called *The Soul of a New Machine*. It told the story of a team of engineers designing and building a new computer. At Dar Al-Handasah we design and build structures of many different kinds, from bridges to drainage systems, but I like to think that all of our teams develop the kind of 'soul' in their projects that Kidder discovered among those designing the Data General computer. Certainly (to change the metaphor) many of our projects are designed to put new heart back into communities, perhaps to reinvigorate their economy by improving infrastructure, as with our design of an earthquake-proof bridge on the transeuropean highway in Turkey, or simply to make life more bearable by removing inconveniences, as with our rehabilitation and upgrading of water supplies in south-east Luanda, the capital of Angola.

I suppose what I am saying here is that the very best of engineering and architecture goes way beyond satisfying a functional need. It adds more, perhaps by creating a beautiful structure that can be admired as well as used – or that, maybe, can even inspire – in the manner of the great cathedral-builders of the middle ages. Even in this utilitarian modern age, an engineer or architect who uses his mind can create miracles.

Which is why I believe more young people should consider making a career in engineering, both for the challenge it offers and the immense satisfaction that doing it well brings. Every year at Dar Al-Handasah we recruit around a hundred and forty newly qualified engineers around the world, mostly from the best universities. Yet, in recent years, we have had to compete for the services of the best new engineers with investment banks and other employers. Healthy competition in any market – including the labour market – is good. But I hope more of the best engineers won't turn their backs on careers in engineering. For the coming century offers some of the most exciting challenges engineering has ever faced, not least in reconciling the growth of population with the conservation of resources.

Every age offers new opportunities to the young. Back in 1956, when I started Dar Al-Handasah, it was the opportunity to create a truly Arab development consultancy in the Middle East. But new windows of opportunity are always opening, and those young engineers and architects who succeed will be those with the courage and determination to pass through them. The future belongs to the young, and they must find their own ways to shape it. But for those who are set upon establishing their own enterprises, I believe there are important lessons from Dar Al-Handasah's experience.

*   *   *

The first lesson is to be the best. It ought to be a simple rule, but many do not take enough notice of it. Clients don't want to do business with the second best, so success depends on achieving world-class standards. Yet I know from my own experience how daunting that aim can be to a young engineer or architect setting out on his or her career.

When I first set up Dar Al-Handasah, I determined that we would match and beat the best of the American and European consultancies that currently won the pick of contracts in the Middle East. It seemed obvious to me that we could only beat them by being better. Our problem in the Arab world, at that time, was not a lack of intelligence or ability, or even qualifications. There were plenty of people in the Middle East who had all three. It was a lack of ambition that held the Arab world's engineers back. There were plenty of people with excellent technical skills, but they practised as individuals or in teams too small to be able to offer the broad range of experience – including major project management – necessary on the largest contracts. So Dar Al-Handasah represented a quantum leap in what the Arab world had to offer in the field of development consultancy.

Which brings me to my second point. I was determined that Dar Al-Handasah would set exemplary standards in fully respecting professional ethics. Of course, ethics are important in every profession, but too often they're acquiesced to rather than actively promoted. I believed we had to adhere faithfully to the best ethics of our profession, and be seen to do so. That was important in the early days of our company because it was a factor that gave clients confidence in us. We were dealing mostly with government bodies and large commercial organisations, all many multiples bigger than we were. Our total commitment to professional ethics was a visible signal that, despite our size, we were important players and we wanted them to take us seriously and judge us by the highest standards.

As we have grown, high professional ethics have continued to be vitally important, not least because of the safety dimension. The kind of projects we work on – major air terminals, leisure complexes, ports and roads, to name only a few – are used by thousands and, sometimes, millions of people. We have to ensure they are constructed to the highest possible standards to safeguard the wellbeing of those who use them. But more than that, our commitment to professional ethics acts like a beacon in our profession. It is a signal to those engineers and architects anywhere – especially the most talented – that Dar Al-Handasah is a company where their skills and creativity will be both valued and nurtured.

Which is why we've attracted some of the best people across a wide range of specialisms in engineering, architecture and development consultancy. This is the key to what I believe is one of the most critical of our success factors – our ability to act as a multi-disciplinary consultancy. It's not just that the largest projects inevitably require a wide mix of different technologies and skills – or that as technology advances, the range of specialisms grows – although both those factors are important. It's more that finding solutions to development problems, which is one of the things that Dar Al-Handasah is best at, means taking a look at complex environments in which a range of issues is intimately interwoven. We never lose sight of the fact that when you change the physical environment – by building a bridge or developing an irrigation scheme, for example – you also change the way in which people live in that environment. Perhaps that bridge makes it easier for some people to get their goods to market, but perhaps as a result it increases the competition on traders who'd had the market to themselves. Or maybe customers as well as traders will be crossing that bridge and there will not now be enough room in the market to accommodate them all. Issues such as these come writ large and small in development projects, and we focus heavily on dealing with them in the solutions we propose.

Successful development means taking into account the human impact of the physical changes you are making. Which is why, in a typical large development project run by Dar Al-Handasah, the project team will not only include engineers, architects and technicians, but economists and even sociologists, who assess what the impact of proposed changes might be. In the development consultancy world, people sometimes speak of 'prestige' projects – often to mean those that excel in some technical or aesthetic way or were, simply, very large. To me, the greatest level of prestige in any development project comes from improving the lives of the people it was meant to serve. 'You made my life better,' is the highest praise we can receive.

And that is something we seek to do wherever in the world we operate. For it was always my belief, from Dar Al-Handasah's earliest days, that we would move out of the Middle East and compete on the global stage. Indeed, as the company developed, it became clear that if we were to win and retain the kind of leading position among global development consultancies that we were seeking, it would be imperative that we should become a global player. One reason for this was that, quite simply, you can't claim to be one of the world's leading development consultancies unless you actually provide your services around the globe.

But there is also a deeper reason. Politicians and pundits talk about 'globalisation' in abstract terms. But real globalisation – the development of an integrated and, increasingly, unified global market – is never more important than in development consultancy. One reason is that a world-leading consultancy needs to learn about the latest trends and developments all around the world. No one continent or country has a monopoly on good ideas. More than that, Dar Al-Handasah has to be among the first to learn about cutting-edge ideas and technologies, because our ability to apply the latest best practice is a key to retaining competitive advantage. In particular, the fact that we have North American and European companies acknowledged by independent observers as leaders in their respective fields – such as Perkins & Will, T.Y. Lin and Penspen – means we are able to access the latest thinking from the world's most advanced markets and apply it in the developing world, where we do much of our work. It's just this kind of knowledge transfer that is the key to helping the developing world build its own skills and expertise so that it can, in time, compete on equal terms with companies from more advanced markets.

As I hold this view, it is not surprising that within Dar Al-Handasah and our subsidiary companies we take a truly international view of our activities. One consequence of this approach is that we seek to attract the very best talent from around the world to work for us. Moreover, when we have recruited talented people, we seek to grow them into true citizens of the world. We promote the international exchange of ideas by encouraging staff to visit our offices in other countries to learn about new technologies and ways of working. In this way, many of our leading engineers, architects and consultants develop a true world view, while at the same time retaining deep experience and knowledge of their home markets. It is a combination that we have found world-beating in the past.

And I expect it to power our growth in the future.

*   *   *

I spend much time myself travelling the world.

You can't run a truly global company from one place. No matter how comprehensive management reports are, they can't compensate for actually seeing what is happening on the ground – and meeting the people who are making it happen. So I continue the long journey, which started in 1956, from continent to continent. But my own travels will not be the end of Dar's journey. I believe that Dar is now the sustainable enterprise that I always hoped it would be. Those who take the company on will, I hope, develop the vision and fulfil their own personal and professional aspirations by improving the lives of communities around the world.

But my own journeying is not yet over.

Sometimes I travel back to Salt, the town where I was born. It is bigger now, perhaps 80,000 people instead of the 30,000 of my child-hood days. But streets in the older parts of town still wind up the steep sides of the rift valley. On a clear day, you can still see the Dome of the Rock in Jerusalem.

Nearly thirty years ago, we conducted a *pro bono* project for the local Salt government administration. We produced a masterplan for the development of the town. It was a project that was close to my heart because there is much about old Salt that deserves to be preserved, such as the Italianate houses built by the town's notables in the nineteenth century and the school where I was educated. But there was also much that needed changing. A town that doesn't move forward atrophies, and the best of its people drift away. So our plan was designed to preserve the richness of its heritage but also provide a sensitive approach for future development that would cherish the diversity of Salt's many communities.

Soon, it will be time to update that plan. Salt, like other thriving towns, must be allowed to grow.

Perhaps I shall return to see what progress is being made and what plans the town has for the future.

Revisiting Salt is always a pleasure. It provides an opportunity to contemplate the crowded life that started for me in the town's much-loved streets.

Much has changed in the Middle East – and in the world – since those days. Not all the changes have been for the better, but I remain optimistic that the values of liberal nationalism, freedom and democracy as the basis of truly open societies in which all people can fulfil their true potential will win through in the Middle East in the end.

Index

KAS = Kamal A. Shair. Personal names beginning Al- are entered under the next part of the name, e.g. Al-Zaim under Zaim. Sub-headings are in chronological order.